Studies in Rhetorics and Feminisms

Series Editors, Cheryl Glenn and Shirley Wilson Logan

PRAISING
GIRLS

The Rhetoric of Young Women
1895–1930

HENRIETTA RIX WOOD

Southern Illinois University Press
Carbondale

Copyright © 2016 by the Board of Trustees,
Southern Illinois University
All rights reserved
Printed in the United States of America

19 18 17 16   4 3 2 1

Cover illustration: "Staff of *The Weather-cock,*" *The Weather-cock,* 1901. *Courtesy of the State Historical Society of Missouri Research Center–Kansas City.*

Library of Congress Cataloging-in-Publication Data
Wood, Henrietta Rix.
Praising girls : the rhetoric of young women, 1895–1930 /
    Henrietta Rix Wood.
    pages cm. — (Studies in rhetorics and feminisms)
Includes bibliographical references and index.
ISBN 978-0-8093-3442-1 (pbk. : alk. paper) — ISBN 978-0-
    8093-3443-8 (ebook) 1. Rhetoric—Social aspects—United
    States. 2. School prose—Social aspects. 3. Young women—
    United States. 4. Praise. 5. High school students' writings.
    6. School orations. 7. Feminism—United States—History.
    I. Title.
P301.3.U6W66 2016
808'.0420820973—dc23   2015024126

Printed on recycled paper. ♻

The paper used in this publication meets the minimum
    requirements of American National Standard for
    Information Sciences—Permanence of Paper for Printed
    Library Materials, ANSI Z39.48-1992. ∞

For my family, Alan, Adrienne, and Tessa Wood

CONTENTS

List of Illustrations ix

Preface xi

Acknowledgments xxiii

1. Girls and Rhetoric: Contexts 1

2. Amplifying Identity: Barstow "New Girls" 22

3. Persuading Diverse Audiences: Haskell Girls 56

4. Glossing (over) Historical Realities: Lincoln Girls 88

5. Creating Consubstantiality: Central Girls 115

Conclusion: Rhetorical Ramifications 145

Notes 151

Works Cited 161

Index 177

ILLUSTRATIONS

Illustration by Ruth Harris 2

"Staff of *The Weather-cock*" 30

Editorials illustration 43

Illustration by Janet Glover 44

Illustration by Louise Haas 45

Illustration by Hortense Meade 46

Illustration by Ruth Munger 47

Cover of *Indian Legends* 79

"History Club" 109

Helen J. Tann and the "Worms of the Dust" 125

Central High School 131

PREFACE

PRAISING GIRLS: THE RHETORIC of Young Women, 1895–1930, is about ordinary girls who engaged in extraordinary rhetorical activities during the late nineteenth and early twentieth centuries in the United States. Part of the generation that includes Eleanor Roosevelt, Zora Neale Hurston, and Zitka-la-Ša, these young women challenged conventional wisdom of the day that girls were paragons or problems, the angels of the house or the delinquents of the street. Using print as a podium, they defined their identities and created community during an important period in the history of women and rhetoric and the history of the country. In the process, they productively complicate rhetorical theory and historical narratives.

A rhetorical and historical case study, *Praising Girls* analyzes the published writing of diverse young women in a representative midwestern city as epideictic discourse. Drawing on archival sources, rhetorical and historical theories, and feminist rhetorical methodology, this book reconceptualizes epideictic rhetoric as a tool used by young women rather than a prerogative of powerful men giving speeches of praise or blame. I assess the texts of girls from four schools in the Kansas City, Missouri, area within their historical and cultural context, offering insight on constructions and ideologies of gender, race, and class of the period, as well as rhetorical instruction and practice, education, local history, and print culture.

Praising Girls is significant to feminist rhetorical studies for two reasons. First, scholars of the history of women and rhetoric, including Nan Johnson, Shirley Wilson Logan, and Carol Mattingly, have mapped the persuasive performances of adult white and African American women in the United States, but limited and scattered attention has been given to young women and girls of different races and classes. Lindal Buchanan addresses the rhetorical education of white antebellum girls in *Regendering Delivery: The Fifth Canon and Antebellum Women Rhetors* (2005), and Jessica Enoch, Amy Goodburn, Jane Greer, and Lauren Petrillo discuss the persuasive pursuits of girls in articles and book chapters. To date, however, there is not a monograph that assesses the rhetorical acts of young women; therefore, my study begins to fill a gap in the scholarship. Secondly, to fully comprehend the rhetorical aims and achievements of women in the twentieth century, we need to understand their training and experiences as girls. For example, Lucile Bluford, a well-known

xi

xii

Preface

African American activist in Kansas City and longtime editor of an influential African American newspaper, began to acquire her rhetorical skills as a high school student journalist writing editorials about the importance of racial solidarity, as I discuss in chapter 4. While most of the girls in this study did not attain the public stature of Bluford, who attracted national attention in the late 1930s for challenging racial segregation at the University of Missouri, they contributed to and influenced their communities as professionals, volunteers, and mothers who were empowered by their early epideictic endeavors.

This project also is relevant to rhetorical studies. *Praising Girls* reinforces the value of interdisciplinary archival research to the field, demonstrating how new voices and alternative perspectives extend understanding of rhetorical theory. The primary sources of this study, culled from local archives, challenge assumptions that epideictic rhetoric is the exclusive province of elite male orators. While the best-known examples of this rhetorical category include the eulogy of Pericles in ancient Greece and the Gettysburg Address of President Abraham Lincoln during the Civil War, my study establishes that epideictic rhetoric can be delivered in print by ordinary rhetors. Focusing on the published texts of young women as occasions for epideictic discourse broadens the scope of this branch beyond its traditional association with ceremony and crisis. Epideictic rhetoric continues to be the means by which groups, whether they are local constituencies or nations, forge unity; therefore, my analysis enhances knowledge of community building in the present as well as the past.

Methods and Methodology

Distinguishing between the methods, or how I gathered information, and the methodology, or how I analyzed it, of this project is not as simple as it sounds. As the project evolved, my methods affected my methodology, and vice versa. That said, this project began in an archive. I had studied the private writing of girls in the early twentieth century and was interested in their published writing, so I went looking to see what could be found. I started by locating the yearbooks of Miss Barstow's School through the State Historical Society of Missouri Research Center–Kansas City. Wading through boxes of carefully preserved annuals of the first college preparatory school for girls in the city, I studied the editorials, articles, columns, creative writing, and art work of the privileged white girls who attended Barstow in the early 1900s. I proceeded xiii

Preface

inductively, looking for patterns and thinking about what questions these primary sources could answer. Lest this sound a tidy, linear process—it was not. As David Gold observes:

> The process of doing archival research is largely organic. Though we may apply a critical lens or favor a particular theoretical approach, the basic methodology of archival research remains the same: read absolutely everything and try to make sense of what happened. (18)

The process also is recursive, as I moved from the Barstow yearbooks to secondary scholarship to school records and histories and back again to the yearbooks, trying to make sense of what happened at Barstow.

In the course of reading these primary sources and discussing them with colleagues, I realized that Barstow girls were using writing to forge and celebrate their collective identity, which is the goal of the epideictic rhetor. Furthermore, they studied epideictic rhetoric in school, and they were praising themselves during an epideictic era, as scholars, such as Frederick Jackson Turner, articulated the "American character"; as activists promoted women, workers, and African Americans as worthy of equal rights and recognition; and as politicians tried to foster national unity by blaming industrialists, immigrants, and labor union members as threats to national unity. The recent renewed scholarly interest in epideictic rhetoric, inspired by events such as the oratory of President George W. Bush following terrorist attacks on the United States in September 2001, also encouraged me to use this category as a lens for viewing the rhetorical performances of girls.

Initially, I envisioned a national or regional study and devoted a summer to surveying online databases, searching for primary sources from secondary schools that enrolled girls of different races and classes. I learned that a public high school in Indianapolis, Indiana, was racially integrated in the early 1900s, so I spent a week at the Indiana Historical Society, reading microfilm of the school newspaper. To my dismay, I discovered that most of the stories in the newspaper did not have bylines, so I could not tell who wrote what and thus could not assess the writing of white and African American girls at a coed school.

Lesson learned. I returned to Kansas City and resolved to conduct a local study, as I knew that area archives held the student publications of the Haskell Institute, an off-reservation boarding school for Native Americans in nearby Lawrence, Kansas; Lincoln High School, the first public high school

xiv
Preface

for African Americans in Kansas City, Missouri; and Central High School, the first public high school for whites in Kansas City, Missouri. The fact that I could find archival sources for affluent white girls, Native American girls, African American girls, and working- and middle-class white girls in a forty-mile radius created useful and necessary boundaries for my analysis. It made sense to set parameters on this project, which delves deeply into issues of gender, race, and class. By limiting my inquiry to a single geographic setting and a thirty-five-year period, I was able to discern more fully the similarities and differences in the rhetorical responses of diverse young women to the assumptions that they faced and the agendas that they pursued.

Moreover, historians and popular commentators long have recognized Kansas City as a crossroads of the country, a site where the North, South, and West met, a location where different classes and different ethnic and social groups gathered and negotiated their differences. The major historical trends that influenced the nation after the Civil War are evident in Kansas City: urbanization, Jim Crow codes, the rise of the public high school, and the domination of girls in these new public institutions that trained many more citizens than did the colleges and universities of the period—to name only a few of these forces.

In addition to reading the contributions of girls to their school newspapers, literary magazines, and yearbooks, I read secondary scholarship on epideictic rhetoric, gender ideology, the history of women, the history of education, and the history of Kansas City. When I began analyzing the texts of girls, I turned to new sources to help me contextualize their writing. I pored over the U.S. Census and Kansas City directories to determine where girls lived in the city and the names and occupations of their parents. I found a sociological study of African Americans in Kansas City in the early 1900s and consulted the records of the Kansas City public schools for programs of study and assigned textbooks. I tracked down the obituaries of girls and called upon archivists, authors, and librarians for clues about where to find more information. My research took the shape of an ever-widening spiral, as primary sources provoked new questions that required searching for new sources to answer them.

To discern the epideictic dimensions of the written rhetoric of girls, I rely on the methodologies of feminist scholars of the history of women and rhetoric including Buchanan, *Regendering Delivery*; Jessica Enoch, *Refiguring Rhetorical Education: Women Teaching African American, Native American, and Chicano/a Students, 1865–1911* (2008); Cheryl Glenn, *Rhetoric Retold:*

xv
Preface

Regendering the Tradition from Antiquity through the Renaissance (1997); Jane Greer, *Girls and Literacy in America: Historical Perspectives to the Present* (2003); Nan Johnson, *Gender and Rhetorical Space in American Life, 1866–1910* (2002); Shirley Wilson Logan, *"We Are Coming": The Persuasive Discourse of Nineteenth-Century Black Women* (1999); Andrea Lunsford, editor, *Reclaiming Rhetorica: Women in the Rhetorical Tradition* (1995); Carol Mattingly, *Well-Tempered Women: Nineteenth-Century Temperance Rhetoric* (1997); and Jacqueline Jones Royster, *Traces of a Stream: Literacy and Social Change among African American Women* (2000). In the last twenty years, these scholars have adapted traditional methodologies and developed new ones to expand a historiography that, as Gesa E. Kirsch and Royster note, long had focused solely on men as rhetorical subjects, privileged Western-world speakers, and directed attention to political, judicial, religious, and academic realms that men traditionally have dominated (30).

Delineating feminist rhetorical inquiry, Kirsch and Royster suggest that at its best, it is marked by "four critical terms of engagement": critical imagination, strategic contemplation, social circulation, and globalization (19). Critical imagination requires feminist scholars of rhetoric to strive to represent faithfully and in historical context the work and lives of seldom-heard women, using the strategy of "listening deeply, reflexively, and multisensibly" to avoid anachronistic impositions of their own assumptions and values on historical figures (20). Strategic contemplation is a deliberative process that enables researchers to

> go beyond a critical examination of how archives can—and often do— reinscribe imperialist, patriarchal, Western rhetorical traditions and beyond the fact that the personal location of any individual researcher may be complicated by race, ethnicity, class, sexuality, disability, or any number of specific personal identities. (89)

Employing the strategy that earlier scholars called meditation, Kirsch and Royster explain that "strategic contemplation makes room for the researcher to acknowledge her or his own embodied experiences while engaging in inquiries that permit the researcher to gain perspective from both close and distant views of a particular rhetorical situation or event" (89). In other words, the researcher must constantly acknowledge his or her own multiple identities while contemplating the circumstances that shaped the identities of his or her subjects.

xvi

Preface

Social circulation entails acknowledging the myriad networks "in which women connect and interact with others and use language with intention" (Kirsch and Royster 101). It also means disrupting binary divisions (i.e., public/private) of the social circles in which women have moved in order to see how they acted rhetorically within settings not traditionally regarded as rhetorical sites, such as local garden clubs (101). The fourth critical term of engagement that Kirsch and Royster identify is globalization, which means more than "highlighting and magnifying connections and disconnections between the classical traditions of Greece and Rome and our own contemporary national scene in the United States or across disciplines, genres, and arenas" (24–25). Globalization also requires acknowledging "the varieties of work that is happening here and varieties occurring around the globe—across both time and space" (25).

Praising Girls relies on the first three terms of engagement to amplify the voices of young women rarely heard in narratives of either rhetorical or social history. Exercising creative imagination, I situate their rhetorical texts within the historical contexts that shaped these young rhetors and their persuasive performances. As part of my strategic contemplation, I acknowledge that my study privileges the published persuasive texts of a minority of girls, given that in 1900 only 10.4 percent of adolescent girls attended high school in the United States (Rury 63).

I also am mindful of how the nature of archives shaped my study. Archives are constructed by people who collect, donate, and preserve texts and artifacts. Consequently, archives inherently are subjective and exclusive rather than objective and inclusive. Influenced by their assumptions, agendas, and in some cases, their budgets—or lack thereof—archivists decide what to preserve and what to discard, what to put in protected public storage and what to store in vulnerable private spaces, whether to conserve texts on microfilm or in digital files, or allow access to fragile paper copies. All of these decisions have an impact on the sources available to researchers—and to their subsequent analyses. For example, I could not locate copies of the Lincoln High School yearbook prior to 1915, even though there is evidence that the annual of this African American institution was launched in 1900. In contrast, copies of the all-white Central High School yearbook from its inception in 1899 are readily available. As a result, I could not compare the rhetorical productions of African American and white girls at these two

xvii
Preface

public high schools in Kansas City for the first fifteen years of the twentieth century, a comparison that might have been fruitful.

What is as troubling as this gap in my analysis are the reasons for it: Was it an accident or a lack of historical foresight that prevented the preservation of these early Lincoln yearbooks? Was it a judgment on the part of white school officials about the value of the publications of African American students during the Jim Crow era in Kansas City? As Kirsch and Royster point out, archives can reinscribe imperialist, patriarchal, and Western biases that include racial bias. Given that possibility, the advice of Robert J. Connors resonates: "The Archive must be explored, analyzed, cross-checked, deconstructed, reconstructed, made meaning of, be stripped, checked, and polished" ("Dreams and Play" 17). To make meaning of an archive, researchers must figuratively interrogate the collection as a cultural construction that may reveal as much through omission as inclusion.

My strategic contemplation also acknowledges my own identities as a white, middle-class, heterosexual feminist scholar of the early twenty-first century who is attempting to analyze the rhetorical enterprises of girls of my grandmother's generation. The concept of social circulation informs my argument that school-sponsored publications are a valid site for investigating the rhetorical activities of young women. Last, this study is local rather than global, yet it charts "connections and disconnections between the classical traditions of Greece and Rome" in a historical period of the United States, and as an interdisciplinary undertaking, it crosses "disciplines, genres, and arenas."

I concur with Gold's conclusion that archival research "is a bottom-up process and messy as hell—and, more to the point, scary, requiring faith that something will be found, even if it's not what you first went looking for" (18). Gold's adjective "bottom-up" evokes the methodologies of social historians and girls' studies scholars whose work has influenced my analysis, including Joan Jacobs Brumberg, *The Body Project: An Intimate History of American Girls* (1998); Jane H. Hunter, *How Young Ladies Became Girls: The Victorian Origins of American Girlhood* (2002); and Catherine Driscoll, who urges feminist scholars to add girls to genealogies of women in *Girls: Feminine Adolescence in Popular Culture and Cultural Theory* (2002). History from the bottom up means re-viewing a place and time from the perspective of marginalized observers, such as girls. The girls in this study include those xviii

Preface

whose lives were shaped and, in some cases, limited by race and class, as well as gender and age. While I focus primarily on how these girls defined themselves, I also consider how they viewed the place and time in which they lived: their schools, the Kansas City community, and an era marked by sexism, racism, immigration, nativism, industrialization, cultural nostalgia, imperialism, and war. Clearly, there is an intersection between the methodologies of feminist scholars of history and rhetoric and those of social historians and girls' studies scholars who practice history from the bottom up; both groups try to recover the voices of disenfranchised citizens to theorize and retheorize rhetoric and history.

Relying on classical traditions of epideictic rhetoric and recent studies that expand understanding of its functions and forms, I register girls as epideictic rhetors in narratives of the history of women and rhetoric, contribute to current conversations about this rhetorical branch, and recognize young women as historical agents whose experiences illuminate broader narratives of the late nineteenth and early twentieth centuries.

To summarize my interdisciplinary approach in *Praising Girls*, I use the interpretive paradigm of the case study to analyze the public texts of young women, in and near a city that was a microcosm for the nation, as a rhetorical and historical phenomenon. Surveying primary sources from a variety of archives in the Kansas City area, I deduce that the contributions of diverse girls to school-sponsored publications during the late nineteenth and early twentieth centuries constitute epideictic rhetoric. I then use rhetorical and historical theories and feminist rhetorical methodology to explicate these texts. I argue that the girls in this study adapted theories and models of epideictic rhetoric, which they studied in school and encountered in public discourse, to define themselves and their communities. I also maintain that their rhetorical performances illuminate contemporary conceptions of epideictic rhetoric, such as George A. Kennedy's contention that epideictic rhetoric glosses over historical realities and Kenneth Burke's theory of consubstantiality. To avoid anachronistic impositions of contemporary rhetorical theories, I position the rhetorical performances of girls in historical context, explaining how these performances both reveal and are informed by the cultural constructions and social forces of the day. The following chapter previews briefly describe how I adapt and employ interpretations of epideictic rhetoric as the means for concluding that the girls in this study regender this persuasive category.

xix
Preface

Chapter Previews

Chapter 1, "Girls and Rhetoric: Contexts," offers rhetorical, historical, and cultural contextualization for understanding the persuasive discourse of the young women in this study. It reviews classical and contemporary perspectives on epideictic rhetoric, considers the new rhetorical opportunities and challenges that girls of the late nineteenth and early twentieth centuries confronted, surveys gender ideology of this period, and discusses Kansas City as a location for young female rhetors.

Chapter 2, "Amplifying Identity: Barstow 'New Girls,'" addresses white girls, who set the cultural standard for all girls of the late nineteenth and early twentieth centuries in the United States. It charts the collaborative efforts of upper-class girls at Miss Barstow's School to position themselves as part of a cohort of young women known as "new girls" that began to emerge during the late nineteenth century. Barstow girls used epideictic rhetoric to construct a community of young female scholars who prized academic, athletic, and public performance. Declaring who they were in the pages of their school yearbook, they also made clear who they were not through commentary and fiction that reflected the racism and classism of the period. Barstow girls repeated and restated this definition for nearly twenty years, thus expanding understanding of the epideictic strategy of amplification and its impact on a relatively homogeneous audience.

My discussion of amplification depends on Aristotle's vague definition of this rhetorical device, as developed by Richard A. Lanham and Nevin Laib. Lanham notes that rhetoricians complicated the conception of amplification, which he simplifies as the "dividing and particularizing" of an assertion (9). Laib identifies five forms of amplification—magnification, proof, emphasis, restatement, and enlargement—that I use to categorize and analyze the epideictic rhetoric of Barstow girls.

Offering an alternative perspective, chapter 3, "Persuading Diverse Audiences: Haskell Girls," considers the epideictic rhetoric of Native American girls who contributed to a newspaper and folklore anthology the Haskell Institute published that were distributed to indigenous and white readers nationwide. Demonstrating the multiple purposes of epideictic rhetoric, these young women educated readers about Native Americans, preserved Indian culture, and celebrated their status as "progressive Indians." By speaking

xx

Preface

to both sympathetic and resistant auditors, Haskell girls show that astute epideictic rhetors can reach heterogeneous audiences.

Dale L. Sullivan's articulation of epideictic rhetoric as a "constellation of purposes" that includes education, preservation, and celebration is the theoretical foundation of this chapter. It enables me to assess how Native American girls at Haskell used each facet of this constellation to form and praise their identity in the rhetorical genres of two print venues. I also depend upon the scholarship of Gideon O. Burton, Jeffrey Walker, and Kennedy, all of whom expand Aristotle's brief treatment of audience. Burton emphasizes that rhetorical analysis must consider how an audience shapes a text; Walker contends that epideictic discourse influences the opinions and beliefs of audiences; and Kennedy notes that epideictic rhetors should attend to the expectations of audiences. Last, I use Mikhail M. Bakhtin's conception of dialogism or double-voicing to argue that Haskell girls employed this technique to deal with competing discourses about Native Americans.

Chapter 4, "Glossing (over) Historical Realities: Lincoln Girls," evaluates the two epideictic tactics that African American girls used to praise young people of color during the Jim Crow era in Kansas City. Through epideictic rhetoric published in their school yearbook and newspaper, Lincoln High School girls alternately obscured and emphasized the factors that affected their lives. Participating in the epideictic campaign of African American professional print culture, these young women through their poetry and prose promoted the "New Negro" principles of race pride, self-help, racial solidarity, and the development of an African American middle class. To forge unity, Lincoln girls countered the racism of whites and blurred differences of class and ideology within their school and wider community.

The key rhetorical concept of this chapter comes from the work of Kennedy, who maintains that epideictic rhetoric "glosses over historical realities" (*New History* 22). Although Kennedy does not go into detail about the negative connotations of this phrase, it propels my exploration of the historical realities that African American girls encountered and how they alternately gloss and gloss over those realities to achieve their epideictic goals.

Chapter 5, "Creating Consubstantiality: Central Girls," explores the epideictic efforts of working-class and middle-class white girls who confronted factionalism at the largest public secondary school in Kansas City—a harbinger of the modern high school. By the 1890s, the Central High School student body was splintered into factions based on gender, academic class,

Preface

literary societies, and athletic organizations. Central girls responded by encouraging inclusivity, school spirit, and collaboration in epideictic rhetoric that they created for the school literary magazine, yearbook, and newspaper. Putting Burke's epideictic theory of consubstantiality into practice, these young women encouraged members of their audience to recognize the ideas and ideals that united them—or could unite them—rather than focusing on differences that did or could divide them.

"Conclusion: Rhetorical Ramifications" suggests how my approach and findings might guide new lines of inquiry into the epideictic projects of other marginalized groups of the past and present. Like the young women in this study, immigrants, ethnic and religious minorities, and members of the lesbian, gay, bisexual, transgender, queer, intersex, asexual, and ally (LGBTQIA) community—to name only a few groups—have used print to represent their collective identities and forge solidarity. These sources are stored in myriad archives that remain to be investigated and can offer important rhetorical and historical insights when they are assessed according to the model of *Praising Girls*.

ACKNOWLEDGMENTS

MANY PEOPLE MADE THIS project possible. Jane Greer helped me envision and develop this study, and I appreciate her expert guidance and generous support. Diane Mutti Burke, Jennifer Phegley, Dennis Merrill, and John Barton shared their knowledge and counsel, asking hard questions and helping me find answers. Cheryl Glenn and Shirley Wilson Logan, editors of the Studies in Rhetorics and Feminisms series of Southern Illinois University Press, offered astute revision advice. I am grateful to Southern Illinois University Press reader Catherine Hobbs for her thoughtful suggestions. The SIU Press staff helped me make this a better book, and for their diligence and expertise I thank acquisitions editor Kristine Priddy, project editor Wayne Larsen, and editorial assistant Amy Alsip. And many thanks to copy editor Mary Lou Kowaleski. The English Department, the College of Arts and Sciences, the School of Graduate Studies, and the Women's Council of the University of Missouri–Kansas City provided financial assistance.

I thank archivists and librarians who aided my work, including Stuart Hinds, Teresa Gipson, Kelly McEniry, and Scott Gipson of the University of Missouri–Kansas City Libraries, Dr. Kenneth J. LaBudde Special Collections; the late David Bauer of the Miller Nichols Library at UMKC; David Boutros of the State Historical Society of Missouri Research Center–Kansas City; Bobbi Rahder of the Haskell Cultural Center and Museum; Barbara Larsen of the National Archives–Kansas City; Jeremy Drouin of the Missouri Valley Special Collections, Kansas City Public Library; and Christopher Leitch of the Black Archives of Mid-America, Kansas City, Missouri.

Through the years, colleagues and friends have encouraged and sustained me. I thank Linda Voigts, Joan Dean, Virginia Blanton, Jennifer Frangos, John Herron, Jeffrey Rydberg-Cox, Sherry Neuerburg, Nancy Hoover, Lindal Buchanan, Nan Johnson, Deborah Maltby, Madaline Walter, Margot Stafford, Deirdre Devine, Liz Seaton, Alex Ledgerwood, Annie Riggs, Ann Sundeen, Kate Stuart, and Don Ipock.

I owe my greatest gratitude to my family. My parents, the late Charles and Mary Ann Rix; my siblings, Char Crane, Tammy Gaumer, Chris Rix, and the late John Rix; and my in-laws, Madeleine Wood, the late Peter Wood, Barbara Wood, and Don and Elaine Wood, always have supported my scholarly pursuits. My daughters, Adrienne Rix Wood and Tessa Rix Wood, grew up

xxiv
Acknowledgments

with this project. These accomplished young women have inspired me by their own achievements. Most of all, I thank my husband, Alan Wood, for his patience, good humor, and unwavering faith.

Parts of chapter 4 were previously published in my article "Transforming Student Periodicals into Persuasive Podiums: African American Girls at Lincoln High School, 1915–1930," in *American Periodicals* 22.2 (2012): 199–215 (copyright 2013 by the Ohio State University Press; reprinted with permission). The writing of girls at the Haskell Institute is addressed in my article cowritten with Lori Ostergaard and Amy Mecklenburg-Faenger, "Making Space for Writing: School Girls' Newspapers, Writing Clubs, and Literary Magazines, 1897–1930," in *Feminist Challenges or Feminist Rhetoric? Locations, Scholarship, Discourse*. I discuss Central High School in a chapter of *In the Archives of Composition: Writing and Rhetoric in High Schools and Normal Schools*, which I coedited with Ostergaard.

PRAISING GIRLS

CHAPTER 1

Girls and Rhetoric: Contexts

IN 1911 RUTH HARRIS drew a schoolgirl to illustrate the editorial section of the yearbook of Miss Barstow's School (fig. 1.1). Like Harris and her peers at the first female college preparatory school in Kansas City, Missouri, the figure in the drawing was white. Unlike many popular depictions of young women of the period, she is not reading silently or striking the ethereal Gibson Girl stance; she is energetically blowing a herald's trumpet that emits the word "Editorials." Representing Barstow girls as active, vocal, and opinionated, Harris challenges assumptions that these young women were the passive, reticent, and disinterested daughters of the Kansas City upper class.

The sketch signals the tenor of the persuasive discourse of two classmates who wrote commentaries for this section of *The Weather-cock*. In the first column, Madeline Haff asserts that the school's dramatic club is essential to the training of Barstow girls. She notes that education in "the time of our grandmothers" was limited to lessons in reading, writing, and arithmetic but that girls of her generation needed to develop speaking skills to prepare for their future public roles (Editorials 22). Amplifying the Barstow ethic in the second column, Rebecca Gray confounds conventional wisdom that these privileged girls were more devoted to leisure than labor. Urging her classmates to sustain school spirit through their efforts and achievements, Gray advises: "Go at your work with a vim that will make your successors wish to follow in your footsteps; and in your sports win for your class and school such honours as will inspire others to keener competition" (Editorials 23). Read rhetorically and in historical context, these visual and written texts function as epideictic rhetoric, a persuasive category the ancient Greek rhetorician Aristotle named that delineates and commends group identity.

1

2
Girls and Rhetoric

Figure 1.1. Illustration by Ruth Harris, *The Weather-cock*, 1911. *Courtesy of the State Historical Society of Missouri Research Center–Kansas City.*

At the same time that Barstow girls transformed their yearbook into a podium to deliver epideictic rhetoric, young women throughout the United States used school-sponsored publications to engage in a form of persuasion historically associated with prominent male orators. In public secondary schools that opened after the Civil War, increasing numbers of young women found unprecedented opportunities for rhetorical training and expressions and many more girls attended high school than college during this period. Comprising the majority of high school students by 1900, girls took advantage of amateur periodicals to define their collective identities and construct community. The art, editorials, essays, and creative writing that the young white, Native American, and African American women of different socioeconomic classes in this study produced for school publications can be interpreted as epideictic rhetoric that productively complicates both classical and contemporary conceptions of a category that allegedly long has excluded women.

This volume demonstrates that female students at four secondary schools in the Kansas City, Missouri, area used epideictic rhetoric to define themselves in an era that alternately infantilized, idealized, and demonized young women. While elite white girls at Miss Barstow's School represented themselves as scholars, athletes, and public performers, Native American girls at the nearby

3
Girls and Rhetoric

Haskell Institute, the second largest off-reservation boarding school for Indians in the United States, praised indigenous peoples and forged pan-Indian unity. African American girls at Lincoln High School, the first public secondary school for students of color in the city, advocated racial unity and "New Negro" principles. White working-class and middle-class girls at Central High School, the first public secondary school for whites in Kansas City, used epideictic rhetoric to respond to factionalism at their school, one of the largest high schools in the country. As they fostered group identity and solidarity, these girls also intervened in public discourses on gender, race, class, racism, education, imperialism, and World War I; thus their rhetorical activities are of interest to scholars of social history, girls' studies, and print culture.[1]

Reconceptualizing Epideictic Rhetoric

Representing their collective identities, these young women encourage the reconceptualization of epideictic rhetoric. Although Aristotle describes epideictic rhetoric as persuasive speech in which "there is either praise [*epainos*] or blame [*psogos*]" (*On Rhetoric* 48), George A. Kennedy is among scholars who contend that epideictic discourse "needs to be looked at in a variety of ways not recognized by Aristotle" (*New History* 4). Defining what became the preeminent model of epideictic rhetoric in the Western world, Aristotle characterizes this category as a performance by a male orator seeking to honor or censure an individual man or group of men on a ceremonial occasion, such as the funeral oration of Athenian statesman Pericles in 431 B.C.E. Aristotle's definition reflects the patriarchal attitudes and practices of ancient Athens, which prohibited women from public speaking and generally rendered them unworthy of mention. Identifying the key components of epideictic rhetoric as speaker, speech, and audience, Aristotle regards the appropriate subjects as masculine and the key figure as amplification. His epideictic formula posits the binary of praise or blame, excluding the possibility that there can be both, as well as other elements, in epideictic discourse.

Another tradition of classical rhetoric allows for the interpretation of epideictic discourse as the means by which women who were discouraged from speaking in public—in either ancient Greece or during the late nineteenth and early twentieth centuries in the United States—could form female group identity. Named for the most prominent rhetorician of Aristotle's day, the Isocratean tradition relied on written rather than oral rhetoric.[2] One of

4
Girls and Rhetoric

Isocrates's rhetorical goals was to promote Panhellenism, the movement to unify the often contentious city states of Greece. To that end, he published in pamphlet form the epideictic speeches that he wrote to encourage Athenians, Spartans, Thebans, and other factions to think of themselves as Greeks and to act as a group (Kennedy, *New History* 44). Isocrates established an antecedent for written epideictic rhetoric that fostered communal identification through the *Panathenaicus* (339 B.C.E.), in which he commends Athens for promoting Panhellenism and condemns Sparta for undermining this cause (Isocrates 399). In contrast to Aristotle, Isocrates was less concerned with precept than objective in his epideictic rhetoric. If the use of print, the employment of both praise and blame within one text, and promotion of shared interests rather than the celebration of individual achievement served his agenda, Isocrates employed these strategies, as would Kansas City girls during the late nineteenth and early twentieth centuries.

Despite the example of Isocrates, Aristotle's conceptualization of epideictic rhetoric long has held sway, as inadequate as it is. Kennedy notes that Aristotle failed "to formulate its role in the instilling, preservation, or enhancement of cultural values, even though this was clearly a major function, as seen in Pericles's famous *Funeral Oration* or the epideictic speeches of Isocrates" (*New History* 4). Kennedy calls for an extension of Aristotle's definition of epideictic rhetoric to include "any discourse that does not aim at a specific action but is intended to influence the values and beliefs of an audience" (*New History* 4). Cynthia Miecznikowski Sheard also takes issue with Aristotle's narrow view of epideictic rhetoric, but she disagrees that epideictic discourse does not encourage action. In her assessment of the public value of this branch, she maintains that

> epideictic discourse can be a vehicle for self-reflection and self-criticism, an expression of critical and rhetorical self-consciousness, both publicly and privately. It can help us to scrutinize our own privately and publicly held beliefs and prejudices, to evaluate them, and to decide whether to reaffirm or reform them. (777)

Takis Poulakis concurs, arguing that epideictic can be understood as "the site of a critique or transformation of the social order" (161). Of the deliberative dimension of epideictic rhetoric, he notes, "Aristotle must have known that the exaltation of familiar values and accepted beliefs was often used by orators before him as an effective strategy for accomplishing their political

5
Girls and Rhetoric

aims" (148). Whether orators sought to advise leaders or participate in public discussions of important issues, they "often defended their political views through laudatory accounts that invoked communal values" (Poulakis 148).

Re-reading Aristotle, Dale L. Sullivan retrieves the historical association of epideictic rhetoric with literature, concluding that epideictic rhetoric is determined not by a "constellation of forms" but by a "constellation of purposes" including preservation, education, celebration, and aesthetic creation (116). Aesthetic creations, such as nineteenth-century landscape painting, constitute epideictic rhetoric, according to S. Michael Halloran, who sees this art form as "an attempt to articulate an American identity" (227). Halloran suggests that the epideictic rhetor may use a paintbrush or pen to declare "who we are" (227).

Drawing on these perspectives, *Praising Girls* argues that the persuasive discourse of young women can be interpreted as epideictic rhetoric that defined their collective identities, influenced public perceptions of their roles and rights, and altered a social order that excluded or dismissed them.[3]

Addressing both sympathetic and resistant auditors, a constraint seldom considered in scholarship on epideictic rhetoric, the young women in this study show that this persuasive category can serve as both a process and a product of identity formation. My use of the term "process" has dual implications. First, each epideictic text that *Praising Girls* assesses enabled a young woman to articulate her vision of community; thus, it serves as an individual example of the process of identity formation. Secondly, whereas studies of epideictic rhetoric tend to focus on isolated performances by individual rhetors, this volume analyzes how groups of young women collaborated through a systematic series of persuasive actions to define their collective identity over time and through shifting rhetorical situations.

The products of these rhetorical processes are the archival sources that Linda Ferreira-Buckley asserts should be the "starting point" for "both our historical accounts and our theorizing" (28). *Praising Girls* is a rhetorical and historical case study of the epideictic activities of girls as documented in the yearbooks, newspapers, and literary magazines of four schools that are representative of educational institutions nationwide during the late nineteenth and early twentieth centuries. These archival artifacts encourage the theorizing and retheorizing of epideictic rhetoric, raising a range of questions: How do gender, race, class, and age influence the production and presentation of this category of persuasive discourse? Why and how do

6
Girls and Rhetoric

epideictic rhetors cooperate to amplify their messages? What strategies do they employ to appeal to heterogeneous audiences rather than homogenous audiences that are assumed to be the mainstay of epideictic rhetoric? How do speakers marginalized by multiple factors inspire group pride? Can epideictic rhetoric broach cultural and social boundaries?

To answer these questions and contribute to epideictic theory, I read primary sources closely and situate them in cultural and historical context. For example, all the girls in this study confronted the constraints of gender and age, which required their assiduous efforts to establish *ethos*, or their credentials to speak—effort that is not required of the male ministers, politicians, or civic leaders who are most often cited as epideictic rhetors. Some girls contended with issues of race and class, as well as gender and age; consequently, they used rhetorical tactics such as *insinuatio* to earn the reader's sympathy. While my subjects are not the first female epideictic rhetors to collaborate over time—the first wave of the women's rights movement can be construed as a seventy-year collaboration in amplification—the insights that they offer are relevant to other long-term epideictic campaigns. Nor has much attention been paid to resistant auditors, an obstacle encountered by the Native American girls in this study who used the technique of dialogism to signal multiple meanings within a single text and thereby speak to different constituents. Last, African American and Native American girls whose texts are addressed in *Praising Girls* help to answer the question of whether epideictic rhetoric truly blurs cultural and social divisions through the girls' participation in the pan-Indian and New Negro movements.

Laying the foundation for the ensuing discussion, this chapter addresses new rhetorical possibilities and obstacles for girls of this period, considers conceptions of young women, and describes Kansas City as a rhetorical site for young female rhetors.

New Rhetorical Opportunities and Challenges for Girls

Although some antebellum academies and seminaries for young women offered rhetorical training and venues for expression, the postbellum expansion of secondary schools provided many more girls with opportunities for rhetorical instruction and epideictic performance. One of the most important educational trends of the late nineteenth and early twentieth centuries is that girls constituted the majority of high school students. In 1890 girls

7
Girls and Rhetoric

comprised 57 percent of high school students in the United States (Tyack and Hansot 114). By 1928 girls accounted for 51.6 percent of white high school students and 62 percent of African American high school students (Tyack and Hansot 173).

Historians offer different explanations for this gendered attendance trend. Correlating a complex set of regional data, John L. Rury contends that boys attended and stayed in school longer in areas of the country where high school diplomas could help them find white-collar jobs or where they could go to college. In contrast, girls went to school in proportionately greater numbers in nonurban areas where employment opportunities were limited (Rury 67–70). David Tyack and Elisabeth Hansot write that "boys often regarded secondary education as irrelevant to their futures, for they could obtain a variety of white-collar jobs without going to high school. The situation was different for girls. They had few opportunities to do nonmanual work" (115). Since the majority of late nineteenth-century high school students were native-born and middle class, according to Tyack and Hansot, the public high school was seen as a

> safe haven for the proper urban girl, a place to spend one's adolescent years preparing to be a better wife and mother. In addition, the high school was a gateway for many young women into teaching careers, one of the few white-collar jobs open to women at this time. (115)

Class was crucial to the school attendance of young people in Reed Ueda's study of two high schools in Somerville, Massachusetts, in the late nineteenth century. Ueda found that white-collar parents tended to send their sons to high school, and blue-collar parents sent more daughters (102).

Taxpayer-supported high schools accommodated girls of lower classes who could not have afforded the tuition of private schools, and girls of color who were barred from attending some of these institutions. In 1879 the U.S. government introduced its program to educate Native Americans in federal Indian boarding schools, such as the Carlisle Indian School in Carlisle, Pennsylvania, which served as the model for other boarding schools, including the Genoa Indian School in Nebraska, the Chilocco Indian School in Oklahoma, and the Haskell Institute in Kansas, the focus of the chapter 3 of *Praising Girls* (Vučković 13). Serving as both institutions of democratization and indoctrination, Indian schools provided girls with formal education while reinforcing restrictive racial and social ideologies. Native American girls

8

Girls and Rhetoric

acquired literacy and rhetorical skills and job training at schools such as the Haskell Institute, but they also were encouraged to disparage their Native cultures and enact the domestic ideals of white women.

Rhetoric was a popular course in coeducational public high schools. In 1900, for example, 39.2 percent of girls and 37.5 percent of boys at public high schools nationwide took rhetoric classes (Latimer 149). In Kansas City–area schools, the rhetorical instruction of girls ranged from the study of classical traditions to application of the "practical" approach of late nineteenth-century composition-rhetoric theorists, such as John Franklin Genung and Fred Newton Scott (Connors, *Composition-Rhetoric* 12). College-bound girls at Miss Barstow's School read Greek and Roman rhetoric, including Caesar's epideictic *Gallic War*, and the orations of Cicero in Greek and Latin classes; they also took elocution lessons ("Catalog c. 1901" 8–11).[4] The Haskell Institute school records do not list textbooks, but the curriculum included composition, and the published texts of girls indicate that they had lessons in persuasive writing and oral presentation. White girls at Central High School and African American girls at Lincoln High School were tutored in the new composition-rhetoric theories. These theories were engendered by industrialization, the larger number of students attending school, and the fact that many of these students were preparing to go to work, rather than to college, according to Lucille M. Schultz (30). Central and Lincoln girls were assigned textbooks by Genung and Scott that were widely used in schools throughout the United States, and thus, their training offers perspective on rhetorical education nationwide during this period. Although the archives that hold Central and Lincoln student publications do not have classroom records, such as teachers' plans, that might indicate how these rhetorical textbooks were used, the books provide perspective on what school authorities expected girls to learn about rhetoric.

The rhetorical affordances of school-sponsored publications also supported the epideictic efforts of girls in the Kansas City area. Picture albums that appeared after the Civil War propelled the popularity of school yearbooks—often called "annuals"—as did the spread of secondary education (Kleine 651). In Kansas City, Central High School started a yearbook in 1899, Lincoln High School reportedly published its first annual in 1900, and Miss Barstow's School launched *The Weather-cock* in 1901. The fact that all of these schools introduced yearbooks within a two-year period suggests institutional peer pressure: schools were aware that other institutions were

9
Girls and Rhetoric

producing these epideictic publications and followed suit in order to uphold their own reputations.

The amateur-periodical trend gained momentum in the early 1900s. By 1910, Allan Abbott referred to "the flood of school journalism spreading the country over," noting a recent exhibition of sixty newspapers, magazines, and yearbooks from New York City schools that represented a fraction of the thousands of similar publications nationwide (657). The chairman of the English Department of the Horace Mann School in Teachers College, Columbia University, Abbott recognized the rhetorical power of student editors and the epideictic potential of school publications. In an article for an educational journal, he writes that editors "gain influence in the school, of a kind frequently monopolized by the athlete" (658). Individual students benefited from producing these publications, according to Abbott, "and for the school at large the paper does as much or more" (658). A student publication disseminated news and kept a permanent record of events. Abbott adds that it also stimulated the activity of student societies

> by their anticipation of "what the paper will say"; it binds alumni to the school; and if conducted with frankness and public spirit, it often reveals to the principal tendencies in student thought and opinion that are worth his consideration and may help to shape his policies. (658)

Abbott envisioned the high school newspaper as an epideictic production that built community by chronicling the history of an institution, inspiring noble behavior among students and unity among graduates, and positively influencing the actions of authorities.

Girls in the Kansas City area were participants in this epideictic enterprise. Before Central High School issued its first yearbook in 1899, it started a literary magazine in 1885 and followed with a newspaper in 1921. The Haskell Institute began to publish a newspaper in 1897, and Lincoln High School did so in 1925. Taking advantage of these new venues, girls articulated their collective identities and constructed community. To do so, however, they had to confront ideas about girls in the late nineteenth and early twentieth centuries.

"What Shall We Do with Our Daughters?"

The epideictic rhetoric of girls in the Kansas City area was affected by the national debate about young women that was inspired in part by demographics

Girls and Rhetoric

and ideologies of gender, race, and class. In 1890 the U.S. Census began counting single young women as a separate category for the first time. That year, girls between the ages of fifteen and twenty-four constituted nearly 30 percent of all women aged fifteen and above, and 72 percent of this group was unmarried. These percentages fluctuated only slightly over the next thirty years (Nathanson 85–86). In a society that promoted marriage and motherhood as the primary goals for girls, the number of young women who were not married and presumably not mothers caused concern.

"What shall we do with our daughters?" asked white suffragist Mary Livermore in one of her most popular lectures, which she initially delivered in 1867 (Livermore 619). The first editor of *Woman's Journal*, a periodical started by the American Woman Suffrage Association in 1870, Livermore espoused education for girls (Weatherford 111). Like many commentators of her time, however, she idealized and objectified young women, describing them as "the fair bright girls who are the charm of society and the delight of home; the sources of infinite comfort to fathers and mothers; and the sources of great anxiety as well" (Livermore 619). Livermore's maternalistic tone and use of the possessive pronoun "our" characterize arguments about girls in the late nineteenth and early twentieth centuries.

The discourse about young women tended to focus on white native-born girls of the middle and upper classes who were seen as the standard of American society, but it also affected Native American, African American, and immigrant girls, who were judged by their adherence or failure to conform to white expectations. Adults expected girls to be obedient, virtuous, even-tempered, well-behaved, and, as the middle and upper classes grew, increasingly idle. Jane H. Hunter writes that "parents of the new bourgeoisie cultivated their daughters to embody the refinement and leisure that they were too busy to practice themselves" (12). Released from household labor that now was performed by servants, who had come to be seen requisite by the middle class as further proof of its economic status, girls filled their time by reading, writing, sewing, playing piano, and going to school (Hunter 21).

Girls of this era also were influenced by different and sometimes competing female ideals: the "True Woman," the "Real Woman," and the "New Woman." Barbara Welter asserts that the True Woman, who was defined as domestic, pious, pure, and submissive, dominated gender ideology in the United States from 1820 to 1860, and many scholars maintain that the legacy of this model extended through the nineteenth century (18). An alternative

11
Girls and Rhetoric

image, the Real Woman, circulated during the mid-nineteenth century, according to Frances B. Cogan. This ideal stressed health and physical fitness, extended education, economic self-reliance, and careful consideration of marriage choices. The mothers of the daughters in this study were affected by these two conceptions, as was the society in which these girls grew up. In the 1890s the New Woman emerged as a third female paradigm; she espoused the right to seek higher education, public activities, and paid work and to delay or forgo marriage and motherhood (Patterson, *American New Woman Revisited*).

Some of these New Women participated in the reform movements of the progressive period, which allowed many women to assume public roles in the late nineteenth and early twentieth centuries, thus offering new models for girls of this era. Flourishing between the 1890s and World War I, the movement known as progressivism is not easily defined. As Nancy S. Dye observes:

> A complex, sometimes contradictory amalgam of social criticism, popular protest, political restructuring, economic regulation, social welfare legislation, and progressive reform embodied a vast array of responses to the changes taking place in American society at the turn of the twentieth century. (1)

Among those changes were the consequences of industrial capitalism and the fact that by 1890, the richest 1 percent of American families owned 51 percent of real estate and personal property in the United States, while the poorest 44 percent of the population owned only 1.2 percent (Diner 4). Rapid urbanization was another factor that propelled progressivism. In 1890, 35 percent of all Americans lived in cities; by 1920, 51 percent of the population lived in cities (Diner 5). The size of some cities also grew astronomically: from 1880 to 1890, for example, the population of Chicago more than doubled (Stebner 50). These shifts and increases of population created myriad problems that progressive period reformers attempted to solve.

Women were at the forefront of this movement. Extending the agendas of the women's associations of the 1870s and 1880s, when groups, such as the women's club movement, the women's foreign mission crusade, the Woman's Christian Temperance Movement, and the Young Women's Christian Association, tackled problems of child labor, alcoholism, and prostitution that they deemed threats to the home, progressive period women reformers took on new projects (K. M. Smith 385). Middle-class women styled themselves municipal housekeepers as they worked to clean up crowded cities lacking

12
Girls and Rhetoric

proper sanitation, adequate housing, and services for families. Working-class women joined labor movements that campaigned for workers' protection and child labor laws (K. M. Smith 381–84). One of the best-known reforms of the era is the settlement house movement, led by white women, such as Jane Addams. In 1889, Addams opened Hull House to serve the mostly immigrant population of the west side of Chicago; six years later, she and a group of Hull House colleagues published a study of the tenements, sweatshops, and exploitation of child workers in the Nineteenth Ward of the city (K. M. Smith 390). Another important project was the anti-lynching campaign led by African American activist Ida B. Wells during the 1890s, which inspired women to take action against racial injustice (K. M. Smith 387). In 1896 African American women organized the National Association of Colored Women (NACW), which pursued political reform on behalf of people of color; the National Association for the Advancement of Colored People (NAACP), founded in 1909, used NACW programs as models for its own (K. M. Smith 389). While these women and these movements made positive differences in the lives of many Americans, progressive period reformers tended to privilege their own perspectives on race, class, and religion and attempted to impose their ideas and ideals on others. For example, white reformers often assumed that the cultural customs and values of immigrants were inferior to their own and sought to teach immigrants the mores of Anglo-Americans (Lissak 1–9).

Addams and Wells also were participants in the campaign for women's suffrage, which Alan Brinkley describes as "the single largest reform movement of the progressive era" (565). Karen Manners Smith notes that between 1890 and 1915 many of the newcomers who joined the campaign for female enfranchisement claimed that women needed the vote in order to help the country solve its problems. Yet the suffrage movement stalled in the early twentieth century: by 1896, four states (Colorado, Idaho, Utah, and Wyoming) allowed women to vote in all local, state, and national elections, but from 1896 to 1910, no new states granted women voting rights. Antisuffragists helped defeat state referendums by arguing that women's subordinate position in society was divinely ordained and that they were ill-equipped to deal with the world of male-dominated politics (K. M. Smith 392–93). Meanwhile, the National American Woman Suffrage Association struggled to reach a consensus on the subject of votes for African American women, who formed their own organizations, and wrestled with the ramifications of allowing immigrant women to vote (K. M. Smith 395). In the 1910s, young activists,

13
Girls and Rhetoric

such as Alice Paul and Lucy Burns, introduced the tactics of hunger strikes and mass demonstrations that they had learned from British suffragettes (K. M. Smith 396–97). More conservative activists did not always approve of the efforts of more radical members of the movement, but through the 1910s, their shared agenda slowly was achieved, as more states granted women the vote. Finally, in 1920, the Nineteenth Amendment was ratified, enfranchising all women in the United States (Weatherford 244).

Progressive period movements led by women helped alter perceptions of and opportunities for girls, but young women still were subject to ideologies of race and class—particularly Native American and African American girls. While whites tended to define these ideologies, these groups' regard for young females should also be considered. Although views of girls were not monolithic among Native Americans, girls generally were held in high esteem. In most traditional Indian cultures of the nineteenth century, young women were seen as important members of the tribe who performed gendered duties that were crucial to the welfare of their communities (Tong 472). In an autobiographical essay first published in the *Atlantic Monthly* magazine in 1900, Native American writer Zitkala-Ša describes the loving treatment and careful instruction that she received as a young Sioux girl growing up on a South Dakota reservation during the 1880s. To illustrate the reverence of Native adults for children, she recounted her inept attempt to entertain a visitor while her mother was away from their wigwam. The visitor, an old warrior, dutifully drank the cold coffee that Zitkala-Ša served, and when her mother returned, "neither she nor the warrior, whom the law of our custom had compelled to partake of my insipid hospitality, said anything to embarrass me. They treated my best judgment, poor as it was, with the utmost respect" ("Impressions" 28–29).

Many whites, however, thought of young Native American women as "savages" capable of redemption through education. In the 1880s, the U.S. government began a concerted effort to assimilate indigenous peoples by educating young Indians at schools such as the Haskell Institute. Benson Tong writes that

> government officials and concerned humanitarians aimed to transform Indian girls into middle-class, Victorian ladies who were domestic, pious, and chaste in line with the "true womanhood" ideology of the late nineteenth century. Female graduates, government officials predicted, would promote a Christian, "civilized" lifeway and support their husbands in the transition from hunters to farmers. (477–78)

14
Girls and Rhetoric

Objectifying Native girls as tools of assimilation, whites denied the autonomy of these young women to formulate their own identities.

African Americans often had pragmatic views of girls, upon whose labor they tended to depend. In the early decades of the twentieth century, 54 percent of African American girls older than ten worked outside of their homes, as compared to 17.9 percent of white girls (Cook and Thompson 28). After the Civil War, the rising African American middle class sent girls to school and expected them to observe Victorian gender codes; upper-class African American girls might attend private academies and boarding schools in the north, take music and dancing lessons, and travel to Europe (Gatewood 248–49). Like middle- and upper-class white girls, these privileged young women of color emblemized their families' social status. Whatever the economic class of African American girls, they often endured the consequences of racism, as Fannie Barrier Williams suggested in 1905. Joining other African American women who championed girls, she argues:

> That the term "colored girl" is almost a term of reproach in the social life of America is all too true; she is not known and hence not believed in; she belongs to a race that is best designated a "problem," and she lives beneath the shadow of that "problem," which envelopes and obscures her. (150)

Williams also criticized African American men who had condescending views of young women: "We have all too many colored men who hold the degrading opinions of ignorant white men, that all colored girls are alike" (154). Delicately alluding to the stereotype of the highly sexualized African American woman, Williams held both men of color and white men responsible for perpetrating that image.

Certainly, white men as well as women promulgated negative opinions of African American girls. In 1889 white historian Philip A. Bruce blamed African American mothers for failing to nurture virtuous and properly domesticated daughters. He opines that African American mothers

> do not endeavor to teach them, systematically, those moral lessons that they particularly need as members of the female sex; they learn to sew in a rude way, to wash, to iron, and to cook, but no principle is steadily instilled that makes them solicitous and resolute to preserve their reputations untarnished. (11–12)[5]

15
Girls and Rhetoric

Patricia Morton notes that Bruce's book was enthusiastically received by white readers and helped to embed the image of the "bad black woman" in the collective consciousness of whites (28–29).

Although these ideologies shaped discourse about girls, other factors, such as postbellum prosperity, a decreasing birth rate and smaller families, and the increase of manufactured goods, also had an impact, especially on public perceptions of white middle-class girls. Hunter and Joan Jacobs Brumberg maintain that these economic and social trends freed many girls from their traditional occupations of tending younger siblings and producing household goods ranging from candles to cloth. Meanwhile, expanding educational opportunities, including the establishment of free public high schools, women's colleges, and state universities, provided girls with new options for their adolescence. Joseph F. Kett contends that middle-class white girls of this era were "the first adolescents" (137). Hunter observes that the term "adolescent" did not come into popular usage until the publication of psychologist G. Stanley Hall's two-volume *Adolescence; Its Psychology and Its Relations to Physiology, Anthropology, Sociology, Sex, Crime, Religion, and Education* in 1904. She argues, however, that an important shift in identification began in the mid- to late nineteenth century, as the age group called "young ladies" became known as "girls." Exempted from adult responsibilities, girls were able to attain and prolong formal education. Hunter cites school attendance as crucial to the construction of girlhood that began in this period and influenced ideas about female adolescence. Her conclusion validates my investigation of how girls created and communicated their identities through school publications during this period.

Response to the changing status and new educational opportunities for girls was mixed during the late nineteenth and early twentieth centuries. Doctors and the new child-study experts questioned whether adolescent females had the intellectual ability and emotional and physical stamina for academics and athletics. Medical authorities who did not fully understand female biology predicted dire consequences for young women seeking advanced academic training. As Brumberg puts it, "according to Victorian medicine, the ovaries—not the brain—were the most important organ in a woman's body" (8). Other commentators promoted the education of girls. In a series of speeches that she delivered in the Midwest in 1880, white women's rights activist Elizabeth Cady Stanton urged girls and their parents to

Girls and Rhetoric

remember that young women had brains as well as bodies. Championing the education, health, and aspirations of girls, she declared: "I would have girls regard themselves not as adjectives but nouns, not mere appendages made to qualify somebody else, but independent, responsible workers in carrying forward the grand eternal plans in the redemption of mankind" (491). Leavening this lofty goal with more practical concerns, Stanton acknowledged that girls needed education in order to secure their "pecuniary independence" (491).

Although Stanton spoke about young white women to white audiences, there was support for advanced academic training for Native American and African American girls. By the early 1900s, numerous Native Americans recognized that education was a valuable commodity. Myriam Vučković comments, "Many Indian parents regarded schooling as a necessity in a rapidly changing world, and like all parents, they hoped their children would have a better life in the future" (48). Tribal leaders encouraged Native girls and boys to attend schools such as the Haskell Institute to acquire the literacy skills that would enable them "to act as cultural brokers between the dominant culture and the tribes," according to Vučković (49). Throughout her long career as an African American scholar and teacher, Anna Julia Cooper advocated education for black girls. Addressing teachers and proponents of racial uplift, she urged,

> Give the girls a chance! . . . Let us insist then on special encouragement for the education of our women and special care in their training. Let our girls feel that we expect something more of them than that they merely look pretty and appear well in society. Teach them that there is a race with special needs which they and only they can help. (86–87)

Both Native Americans and African Americans who supported education for girls saw it as the means by which young women could assist their races.

Clearly, adults of the late nineteenth and early twentieth centuries tended to view girls as both paragons and problems. While African Americans and Native Americans championed their girls, whites tended to ignore or vilify these young women or impose their own agendas upon them. The girl of the period usually was imagined as white and middle class and from the East Coast, and thus girls of other races, classes, and regions were absent from the collective consciousness.

17

Girls and Rhetoric

Kansas City as a Rhetorical Site for Girls

Praising Girls deliberately focuses on diverse girls in what historians call the preeminent region of the nation after the Civil War. Andrew R. L. Cayton and Susan E. Gray contend: "No longer the 'great West,' the Midwest became the place that best exemplified the United States. As it became the physical center of the country, so it also became the literal and spiritual metonymy of the nation" (16–17). Advancing new ideas about young women in a new midwestern city, girls were part of the transformation of what had been an antebellum frontier town at the junction of the Missouri and Kansas Rivers to one of the fastest-growing cities in the nation by 1890 (Worley, *Kansas City* 33). By 1900 Kansas City had emerged as a national center of meatpacking and grain milling with a population of two hundred thousand (Mallea 7). This growth continued in the early twentieth century as the populations of Kansas City, Missouri, and Kansas City, Kansas, nearly doubled between 1900 and 1920. Native-born migrants, foreign-born immigrants, and African Americans from the south contributed to this increase; in 1900 about twenty-five thousand residents of the urban core of Kansas City were foreign born (Worley, *Kansas City* 69).

In 1928, in an article for the *New Republic*, Shaemas O'Sheel called Kansas City "the crossroads of the continent," adding that "every force and current and influence that has made, and is making, America, flows here" (375–76). Cataloging these forces, O'Sheel alludes to industrialization, commercialization, imperialism, Jim Crow codes, and immigration. The girls in the current volume witnessed and were affected by these historical forces; consequently, their epideictic rhetoric was informed by and in some cases responded to issues of national and international import.

The families of girls at Miss Barstow's School, Lincoln High School, and Central High School, for example, helped to drive the industrialization and commercialization of Kansas City. Among the affluent white girls who attended Barstow was the daughter of August R. Meyer, who founded Kansas City Consolidated Smelting and Refining. The corporation employed a thousand workers, and by 1888, its transactions amounted to $15 million annually (R. P. Coleman 25). In 1895 Meyer served as president of the Commercial Club, the most influential association of businessmen in Kansas City. The president of the club in 1898 was another Barstow girl's father, Henry W. Evans, the president of Evans-Smith Drug Company (Green 206–8). Some of the

18
Girls and Rhetoric

parents of African American girls at Lincoln and white girls at Central contributed to the industrialization and commercialization of the city through their jobs as laborers, factory workers, mechanics, clerks, and merchants. While girls in this study observed the imperialism of the United States during the Spanish American War (1898), the annexation of Hawaii and Puerto Rico (1898), and the Philippine War (1898–1902), Native American girls at the Haskell Institute experienced the consequences of imperialism within the country. Amy Kaplan argues that continental expansion and international imperialism were linked in the nineteenth and twentieth centuries: both depended upon acts of conquest and the positioning of colonial peoples within racial hierarchies related to African American slavery and Jim Crow racial segregation (12–22). Haskell girls were part of the first generation of young Native Americans who attended off-reservation government boarding schools where they were encouraged to assimilate to white culture and society through education.

Meanwhile, Lincoln girls contended with Jim Crow law in Kansas City. Although these racially repressive customs and statutes originated in the antebellum north, Jim Crow was institutionalized in Missouri and states of the former confederacy during the 1880s and 1890s (Litwack 97; Jones et al. 579). With the U.S. Supreme Court decision on the case of *Plessy v. Ferguson* (1896), which condoned separate seating for different races on railroads, Jim Crow became the law of the land (Jones et al. 610–11). Certainly, it was the rule in Kansas City. African American journalist Roy Wilkins, who worked during the 1920s as a reporter and columnist for the *Kansas City Call*, one of the leading African American newspapers in the region, describes Kansas City as a "Jim Crow town right down to its bootstraps. Except for the streetcars, which had somehow escaped the color line, neighborhoods, schools, churches, hospitals, theaters, and just about everything else were as thoroughly segregated as anything in Memphis" (60–61). Wilkins uses the phrase "the color line," which W. E. B. Du Bois popularized in *The Souls of Black Folk* (1903). Wilkins, in characterizing the racial climate of Kansas City, contends that "in its feelings about race, Kansas City might as well have been Gulfport, Mississippi. In this respect, the town only practiced what much of the rest of America also believed" (61). He maintains that whites thought that African Americans were "good manual workers" but not "good thinkers" capable of "abstract learning" and that whites believed blacks could "imitate" but not "originate" and had no "geniuses" but were "born rapists and thieves" who

Girls and Rhetoric

owed any progress that they had made "to white blood in their veins" (61).[6] African American girls were aware of these derogatory assumptions and resisted them through their epideictic rhetoric, as the chapter on Lincoln High School documents.

The final national historical trend that O'Sheel cites in his article about Kansas City was immigration, an issue that affected the girls in this study. The proportion of foreign-born Kansas City residents in 1890 did not rival that of midwestern cities such as Chicago, where 87 percent of the population was immigrants, or Milwaukee and Detroit, where 84 percent of the urban populations was immigrants (Brinkley 484). There was, however, a significant number of immigrants in Kansas City. In 1890 the U.S. Census reported that 16 percent of the population of Kansas City, Missouri, was foreign born; by 1920, the percentage was 8 percent (Schirmer 29). Reflecting the national trend of the early twentieth century, increasing numbers of immigrants to Kansas City came from Russia, including Jews from Polish and Lithuanian areas. From 1910 to 1920 there was an influx of Mexicans, and by 1920 there was a large increase in the number of Italians (Worley, *Kansas City* 69).

The children of African American migrants attended Lincoln High School, and the children of recent European immigrants attended Central High School. Some of the girls in this study commented on the changing cultural mosaic of the city. For example, in the early 1900s, upper-class white girls at Miss Barstow's School wrote fiction that perpetrated ethnic stereotypes. In 1906, in an essay for a student publication, a white girl at Central High School articulated anxiety about the influx of Russian Jews and Italians.

The confluence of historical forces that is evident in the Kansas City area at the turn of the twentieth century justifies the geographic focus of this study, as does the presence of diverse young women who were both witnesses and agents of change. Representing the largest faction of the high school population both locally and nationally, the girls who are the subject of this book offer new insights on gender, race, class, and ethnicity as they define and celebrate their collective identities through epideictic rhetoric during an important era in U.S. history.

These Kansas City–area girls share similarities that shaped their epideictic discourse, and as the chapters make clear, each group also is marked by differences that also affected their rhetoric. The common denominators for all of these young women are age and gender: they were adolescent females living in a time of contradictory assumptions about them. Girls were viewed

20
Girls and Rhetoric

as either the angel of the house or the delinquent of the street, as the status symbol of well-to-do families or the bane of patriarchal adult society. Images and discourse of the day privileged white girls, whether they were the elite daughters of business and civic leaders at Miss Barstow's School or the middle- and working-class girls of families who could afford to send their daughters to Central High School rather than to work for wages. If Native American girls could emulate white girls, according to the dominant culture, they might save the "race" and help American Indians assimilate into mainstream society—an expectation that influenced girls at Haskell. In contrast, African American girls at Lincoln High School were neither expected nor invited to join white society, but they were well aware of their designation as members of a racial vanguard in the black community of Kansas City. That is not to say that the black community was unified; in fact, it was divided by class, with Lincoln girls representing the small number of adolescent blacks who had the opportunity to attend high school. That distinction also directed their epideictic efforts.

Although the current volume deals with white girls at both Miss Barstow's School and Central High School, there are significant class and cultural differences between these two groups that merit scrutiny. For example, I have no evidence that Jewish or working-class girls were admitted to Barstow, which had rigid social codes and private-school tuition, but girls of religious minorities and lower classes attended Central. Furthermore, Barstow was an all-girl's school, while Central was a coed school where girls had to compete with boys for rhetorical rights. Barstow girls pursued epideictic aims that are quite different from those of Central girls, and this is a relevant distinction to draw. It is also important to contrast the epideictic rhetoric of African American girls at Lincoln High School to that of white girls at Central High School. In some cases, both the black and white girls were middle class, but the black girls had to confront very different assumptions about their identity than did the white girls. Documenting and analyzing these rhetorical challenges are crucial to this study and to a broader understanding of how race, class, and gender affect all epideictic rhetors.

Filling a gap in narratives of the history of women and rhetoric, this book also contributes to conversations about epideictic rhetoric. It shifts the paradigm of this persuasive category by positing that some of the least powerful members of society in the United States during the late nineteenth and early twentieth centuries found available means for defining and celebrating their

21
Girls and Rhetoric

collective identities. As Ruth Harris, Madeline Haff, and Rebecca Gray suggest in a yearbook of Miss Barstow's School, the epideictic rhetor is not only the solitary man evoking emotion from podium or pulpit on an extraordinary occasion. The epideictic rhetor may be a girl who appropriates the strategies of epideictic rhetoric to reappropriate representations of young women and construct community in print forums on ordinary occasions.

CHAPTER 2

Amplifying Identity:
Barstow "New Girls"

Go at your work with a vim that will make your successors wish to follow in your footsteps; and in your sports win for your class and school such honours as will inspire others to keener competition.
—Rebecca Gray, *The Weather-cock*

To those who have suggested that a dramatic club would take too much time from the regular studies, we can only say "Consider all the advantages—are not they too a legitimate part of a girl's education? What of clear enunciation, training of the carrying powers of the voice, self-possession, grace and ease of movement? ... Our aim is not to "strut and fret our hours upon the stage," but rather the better to carry ourselves through life—"A stage where every man must play a part."
—Madeline Haff, *The Weather-cock*

THE SAME YEAR THAT Ruth Harris depicted the Barstow girl as a herald, as seen in chapter 1, her classmates Rebecca Gray and Madeline Haff confirmed their collective identity as privileged white secondary students in the editorial section of their school yearbook. Countering conventional wisdom that pupils at Miss Barstow's School, the first private female college preparatory school in Kansas City, were frivolous upper-class white girls biding their time until marriage and motherhood, Gray portrayed their rigorous work ethic and ambition to excel in academics and athletics. Haff demonstrated the deliberative capacity of epideictic rhetoric in her endorsement of the school's dramatic club, which trained girls for public performance. Read rhetorically

23
Amplifying Identity

and historically, the epideictic discourse of Gray and Haff defines Barstow girls as "new girls" and models amplification, one of the key strategies of this category of persuasive discourse.

Although Barstow girls did not use the term "new girls" in the epideictic rhetoric that they delivered in *The Weather-cock*, they are part of a cohort that began to emerge in the United States and Great Britain during the late nineteenth and early twentieth centuries. The appellation of new girl was coined in this period, according to Sally Mitchell (3), who notes that British writer Mary Anne Broome used it in her book *Colonial Memories* (1904). Celebrating the new girl, Broome writes of "the superiority of the modern girl," who "is more sure of herself" and believes that marriage is not her "invariable destiny" (293, 298, 300). Contemporary scholars use the term to describe the growing number of young women who envisioned and pursued lives different than those of their Victorian-era mothers. Jane H. Hunter maintains that school attendance "played a large role in the emergence of a 'new girl,' less sober and intellectual than the New Woman, but her significant precursor" (5). These new girls were a larger social group than that of the late nineteenth-century "New Woman," who generally is defined as an unmarried college-educated woman who pursued a profession or paid work outside the home (Hunter 395). Avoiding a narrow definition of the new girl, Hunter suggests that she was middle class, attended high school, was ambitious, played sports, liked to have fun, claimed the right to move in public spaces and garner attention, and found venues for expression in school-sponsored publications. While most Barstow girls came from upper-class families, they exhibited the other traits that Hunter notes. Joining other girls who were altering images of female adolescents, students at Miss Barstow's School represented themselves as academicians, athletes, and public performers planning to go to college at a time when less than 3 percent of young women in the United States were enrolled in institutions of higher learning (Gordon, *Gender* 2).

Proclaiming their collective identity as new girls for two decades in *The Weather-cock*, Barstow girls demonstrate the epideictic device of amplification. While this technique usually is assessed as the means by which an epideictic rhetor develops a claim about a subject in one speech or text, Barstow girls show that amplification can be used by a group of rhetors in a series of texts issued over time to construct community. Consequently, my analysis suggests the re-viewing of other epideictic enterprises, such as the rhetorical campaign for women's rights, as a collaborative exercise in

24

Amplifying Identity

amplification. Beginning with the issuance of the "Declaration of Sentiments and Resolutions," cowritten by five women in 1848, women's rights activists in the United States worked together for the next seven decades to repeatedly praise women. As Elizabeth Cady Stanton, Susan B. Anthony, and Matilda Joslyn Gage claim in the introduction of the first of the six volumes of *History of Woman Suffrage* (1881):

> The leaders in this movement have been women of superior mental and physical organization, of good social standing and education, remarkable alike for their domestic virtues, knowledge of public affairs, and rare executive ability; good speakers and writers, inspiring and conducting the genuine reforms of the day. (15)

In turn, Barstow girls re-formed ideas about young women, identifying themselves as serious scholars, competitive sportswomen, and confident participants in public activities. Distinguishing themselves from young women of earlier generations, Barstow girls also positioned themselves as superior to people of different ethnicities, races, classes, and nationalities.

To frame discussion of the rhetorical and historical insights the epideictic rhetoric of Barstow girls offered, the next section discusses amplification and *The Weather-cock* as a rhetorical venue and then briefly reviews the early years of Miss Barstow's School.

Methods of Amplification

Aristotle notes that epideictic discourse depended on many ways of expanding upon a subject, but he does not describe those ways in detail. In *On Rhetoric*, he writes that appropriate subjects for amplification include

> the only one or the first or one of a few who most has done something; for all of these things are honorable. . . . Amplification [*auxesis*], with good reason, falls among forms of praise, for it aims to show superiority, and superiority is one of the forms of the honorable. (81–82)

Richard A. Lanham notes that rhetoricians created confusion about amplification by using different terms and creating lists of amplificatory devices that in some cases included as many as sixty-four figures. Theorizing this epideictic strategy, Lanham maintains that "amplification collaborates with chance, introducing a seeming synonymy by dividing and particularizing

25
Amplifying Identity

an assertion, creating thereby an expanded set of words for which, in turn, the audience can invent an expanded sense of reality" (9). He contends that if "the new reality is convincing, amplification evaporates, becomes literal description once again when measured against the new reality" (9). The successful epideictic rhetor uses amplification to persuade auditors to entertain a different vision of a person, group, or city and in so doing, moves from persuasion to factual description.

Surveying the history of amplification, Nevin Laib comments that rhetors of the classical period regarded this strategy as "the ability to extend, vary, and expatiate upon one's subject at length, to shape, build, augment, or alter the force and effect of communication, and to repeat oneself inventively" ("Conciseness" 443). He asserts that classical rhetoric and ensuing traditions recognized five forms of this device: magnification; an element of confirmation or proof; emphasis; restatement, varied repetition, or other self-paraphrase; and any enlargement, augmentation, extension, embellishment, or elaboration of a point (450). Laib observes that ancient and contemporary rhetoricians have criticized the use of amplification, but it serves valid rhetorical purposes: "Amplification shows respect for the complexities and importance of the subject. It is patient with those who do not comprehend and generous in explaining the author's point of view. It suggests emotion, openness, and wit" (457–58).

The epideictic rhetoric of Barstow girls relied on all five methods of amplification and is marked by emotion, openness, and wit. To promote the premise that Barstow girls were new girls, successive classes of students developed this proposition in *The Weather-cock* through art, editorials, and accounts of their activities. Early volumes of the yearbook, for instance, magnified the academic acumen of students in witty editorials and the athletic abilities of girls in humorous reports about the Barstow basketball team. Later editions emphasized these points through student drawings that showed Barstow girls as strutting roosters who openly crowed about their achievements and as athletes who proudly displayed the muscles that they developed through sports. To augment their sense of community, Barstow girls disparaged people outside of their community, such as African American and French girls.

Like all high school yearbooks, *The Weather-cock* is a historical artifact and an epideictic performance. Lynn M. Hoffman comments: "The high school yearbook is unique because it serves to document elements of high school culture while being a significant element of the high school traditions

26
Amplifying Identity

it reflects" (25). A yearbook also reflects the self-conceptions of the students who create it and their rhetorical efforts to persuade others to accept these conceptions. In contrast to the yearbooks of the two larger coeducational public high schools in this study, Lincoln and Central, the Barstow yearbook constitutes an exceptional site for examining the amplification of female identity over time. Produced by a small group of culturally cohesive girls at a progressive single-sex institution, *The Weather-cock* reflects the homogeneity of the student body and the philosophy of the school.

The Barstow yearbook also helped to create community by repeatedly reminding students about their shared values. As Joseph Harris observes:

> We write not as isolated individuals but as members of communities whose beliefs, concerns, and practices both instigate and constrain, at least in part, the sorts of things we can say. Our aims and intentions in writing are thus not merely personal, idiosyncratic, but reflective of the communities to which we belong. (12)

Consequently, *The Weather-cock* epitomizes the capacity of periodicals to be both mirrors and shapers of culture, which are functions of these publications (Phegley 11). The messengers changed as the years passed and girls graduated, but the proposition that Barstow girls were new girls remained remarkably consistent for the first two decades of publication of *The Weather-cock*.

Miss Barstow's School

The influence and long tenure of Mary L. C. Barstow, the cofounder of Miss Barstow's School, encouraged Barstow girls to present themselves as new girls and amplify this image through their epideictic rhetoric for twenty years. A New Woman from Maine who was a graduate of one of the first women's colleges, Wellesley, Barstow came to Kansas City in 1884 at the invitation of prominent local families to start a private girl's school (Gilbertson 11; Brayman 7). Barstow's Wellesley classmate Ada Brann accompanied her, and together they established a school in the upscale downtown neighborhood where their first students lived. Barstow specialized in Latin, Greek, and "Anglo-Saxon," and Brann taught English, history, and mathematics (Brayman 12). After Brann left Kansas City to marry in 1897, the school became known as Miss Barstow's School and operated under this name until Barstow's retirement in 1923 (Brayman 24).

27

Amplifying Identity

In contrast to the academies and seminaries that the mothers of some Barstow girls may have attended, Miss Barstow's School by 1901 offered a college preparatory program, as well as academic and postacademic programs. Hunter describes the academic curriculum of mid-nineteenth-century northeastern female seminaries and girls' boarding schools, which set the standard for such institutions throughout the country, as "relatively gentle" (176). The curriculum of Miss Barstow's School could not be described as gentle, and the school also encouraged competitive sports that did not become acceptable or popular for girls until the 1890s. A catalog issued around 1901 describes upper-school courses in Latin, Greek, English, French, German, mathematics, history, and science. Girls in the college-preparatory program took four years of Latin, math, and English; courses in geography, mythology, and ancient history; and electives in Greek, French, or German. The English Department offered classes in elementary and advanced rhetoric, exposition and argument, and literature with readings from Shakespeare, Milton, Pope, Coleridge, Scott, and Eliot ("Catalog c. 1901" 8–11).

The catalog also includes requirements for admission to five East Coast women's colleges—Bryn Mawr, Radcliffe, Smith, Vassar, and Wellesley. These colleges sent recruiters to Barstow; by 1909, Stanford University, the University of Chicago, and the University of Kansas also accepted Barstow students (Brayman 19). Barstow school records for this period were lost in a flood during the 1920s, which makes it difficult to determine how many graduates went to college. During the 1910s, however, *The Weather-cock* introduced an "alumni department" that featured the writing of Barstow graduates at Smith and Wellesley. Classes at Barstow were small: nineteen students comprised the academic department in 1901 ("Catalog c. 1901"). The small number of students helped to create community, as did the fact that only girls attended the upper school during the period that this book addresses. A limited number of boys under the age of ten, however, were admitted to the lower school, as noted in a prospectus for 1885–86 (Gilbertson 3). Significantly, the title of the prospectus, "School for Girls," indicates the intention of Mary Barstow and Ada Brann to create a single-sex institution, so they may have seen the boys as a way to supplement the income of the school, accommodate the young brothers of their female students, or both.

The timing of the debut of *The Weather-cock* in 1901 suggests that Barstow may have had reasons for encouraging this epideictic enterprise other than to keep up with other Kansas City schools that also started student

28
Amplifying Identity

publications around this time. In 1898 the school moved several miles south from downtown Kansas City to a fashionable new neighborhood favored by prosperous families that could afford private-school tuition and followed the recent trend of sending daughters to women's colleges (Brayman 15; R. P. Coleman 33). The new Barstow four-story building accommodated 150 students in kindergarten through twelfth grade and had an assembly hall, gymnasium, studios for art, music, and dance, and living rooms (Brayman 15). It is not coincidental that three years after the new facility opened, *The Weather-cock* appeared. To suggest that the yearbook served as a marketing tool for the school does not negate but, rather, reinforces its epideictic nature: one of the best ways to attract new students is to praise through publication the work of current pupils.

While *The Weather-cock* never named Barstow as its adviser, she encouraged its introduction, suggested the name, and penned its title in graceful calligraphy (Brayman 19, 22). Gauging the degree of influence that she and her counterparts at the other schools in this study exerted is difficult, but educators of the day urged teacher advisers to exercise restraint. In 1910 high school journalism advocate Allan Abbott wrote that the adult

> who takes this office should be the helpful friend, resourceful, ready with advice when wanted, familiar with the paper's past and ambitious for its future. Two things he should not be: one is a censor, the other is an editor-in-chief. (666)

Abbott observed that occasionally, students produced "objectionable matter," but it was best for adult advisers to respond with a tactful suggestion rather than require prepublication approval. He also acknowledged that advisers often became invested in a student publication and might be tempted to dictate its contents, but "the teacher adviser should tell his editors *how*, and not *what*, to write," because the student body was quick to discern adult interference and lose respect for the publication, which then diminished its power in the school (666). There is no evidence in *The Weather-cock*, the limited Barstow School records of the period, or two histories of the school that Mary Barstow usurped the rhetorical authority of Barstow girls in the yearbook.

The stability of *The Weather-cock* staff and the consistency of its editorial content also enabled Barstow girls to amplify their collective identity as new girls. From the beginning of production of the annual in 1901 through the early 1920s, at least one girl worked for two or more years on the staff.

29
Amplifying Identity

Constituting a community of rhetors dedicated to promoting the same message, these girls sustained the epideictic agenda of *The Weather-cock*. Their efforts at amplification were accommodated by the regular features of the annual: editorials, sections for athletics and dramatic performance, student artwork, and creative writing. Editorials magnified their knowledge and abilities as scholars; accounts of sports and reports on the Barstow drama club confirmed their claims that they were avid athletes and public performers; student artwork emphasized their identities as active and articulate young women; and creative writing enabled them to position themselves as superior to people of different races and lower economic classes. These departments reinforced the epideictic declarations of Barstow girls within individual volumes and across time, as successive editions allowed these young women to define their identity as new girls of a new century.

If the business and civic leaders who helped start Miss Barstow's School saw it as a status symbol and regarded their daughters as emblems of their socioeconomic class, Barstow girls claimed authority to create their own vision of community in *The Weather-cock*. Certainly, their vision was informed by their privileged racial, social, and economic position, but Barstow girls rarely mentioned their families or their families' aspirations in their yearbook. Rather, these young women created a utopia where female academic, athletic, and public performance garnered acclaim—not the facts that their parents were listed in social registers and exercised significant influence in Kansas City.

Epideictic Amplification in The Weather-cock

From the beginning of publication of *The Weather-cock* in 1901, its logo was a wind vane in the form of a rooster perched atop a cupola. The weathercock, seen as a symbol of mutability or fickleness, is a cock, an overtly male animal, and would seem an unlikely mascot for a girl's school. Yet the rooster amplifies his message through repetition and is associated with pride and vocal ability—two traits that Barstow girls demonstrated in *The Weather-cock*. Some of those girls appeared in a staff portrait in the first edition of the yearbook (fig. 2.1). Clad in high-collared blouses with their hair upswept in fashionable pompadours, ten young women gaze forthrightly at the camera in a formal black-and-white studio photograph. On the opposite page is the table

Amplifying Identity

Figure 2.1. "Staff of *The Weather-cock*," *The Weather-cock*, 1901. *Courtesy of the State Historical Society of Missouri Research Center–Kansas City.*

of contents listing five works of creative writing, reports on school dramatics and athletics, and the editorial section. A photograph of the school and two photographs of the all-girl basketball team are interspersed in the text. At the end of *The Weather-cock* are eight pages of advertisements sold by the staff to finance its professional printing by a Kansas City company. Advertisers include local merchants and purveyors of services and luxury items ranging from equestrian lessons to fashionable clothing to jewelry. These "commercial texts," as media historian Carolyn Kitch calls print advertising, also register the upper-class standing of Barstow families who displayed their status by purchasing these services and items (181). The first issue is a thirty-two-page publication printed on high-quality paper stock measuring eight and one-half by six inches and bound by dark-green cover papers. While the number of pages of individual issues varied, this format was followed until 1912 when hard-cover editions were introduced.[1]

What did not vary in *The Weather-cock*, however, was the use of amplification by Barstow girls. Laib notes that amplification is useful when an audience is diverse, uninformed about a subject, or sees the subject from a different perspective, and when the rhetor is seen as inexperienced or lacking in authority

31
Amplifying Identity

(*Rhetoric* 274). The audience of *The Weather-cock* included Barstow pupils and teachers, parents, friends, advertisers, and probably prospective students who had different degrees of knowledge about the school and its students. Furthermore, it is possible that not all of these auditors shared the same attitude toward progressive female education that the school espoused. The epideictic rhetoric of Barstow girls took into account these factors, and from the first volume of *The Weather-cock* in 1901, these young women delineated their identity as new girls who were scholars, athletes, and public performers. They then amplified this image through the next two decades, using the techniques of magnification, confirmation, emphasis, restatement, and enlargement. While an epideictic rhetor might use several or even all of these methods of amplification in a long text, Barstow girls generally produced short editorials and commentaries that relied on one form, as the following analysis suggests.

MAGNIFICATION

Magnification is the act of enlarging; to magnify also means to glorify or praise, which are among the objectives of epideictic rhetoric. In his catalog of classical rhetorical devices of amplification, Laib qualifies his listing of magnification with the phrase "when speaking of the magnification and diminution of arguments" ("Conciseness" 450). Laib does not elaborate on this point, but Lanham clarifies it in his discussion of how rhetors create new realities through amplification: "When theorists (Quintilian or Peacham, for example) argue that amplification can either elevate or diminish a subject, the success in creating a new reality would seem to make the difference between the two" (9). Barstow girls used this tactic to magnify their self-representations in their school yearbook. Defying gender codes that relegated young women to the sidelines of society, they created a new reality that depicted girls as students pursuing a demanding course of study, sportswomen who played to win, and performers who were comfortable and competent on public stages.

Barstow girls used magnification repeatedly in the epideictic rhetoric that they produced for the premiere volume of *The Weather-cock* in 1901. That fact suggests that they recognized the need to educate auditors about their abilities and aspirations, refuting assumptions that they were rich girls more accustomed to leisure than labor. For example, the lengthy lead editorial, spanning two pages in the yearbook, magnifies the erudition and leadership abilities of Barstow girls:

32
Amplifying Identity

> This paper is not, as some short-sighted people may suppose from its name, a poultry journal, nor yet is it a dissertation on anemometry. It is a school paper registering the activities of school life as the weathercock indicates the direction of the wind. (Editorials 1901, 19)

The writer uses the term "dissertation" from the lexicon of scholars and "anemometry," the act of measuring the force or velocity of wind, from scientific jargon, to signal the elevated level of academic inquiry at Barstow. The writer then increases the stature of Barstow students by situating them in a historical and universal pattern: "In all ages and among all people, thought has had to be expressed; for without some medium of expression the greatest minds in the world become dwarfed" (19). The writer reasons that just as an inventor must develop an idea and publicize this discovery to the world, the "the thinker . . . must have some way to rid himself of old conceptions and thus make room for new" (19). The implication of this statement was that Barstow girls were intellectuals who rejected conventional wisdom as they acquired new ideas.

Displaying her command of classical rhetoric, the writer continues by discussing the study of oratory in ancient Greece and Rome and the ambition of young Roman men to speak publicly. Modern media has replaced the Forum, she observes, but "many of the girls and boys of this generation are less fortunate than the educated Roman, for they are not taught to think for themselves and to present their thoughts clearly to others" (Editorials 1901, 19). To amplify that Barstow girls were capable of thinking for themselves and presenting their thoughts clearly to others, the writer contrasts the "college-bred man" whose mind is merely a reservoir for received knowledge with the self-made man "who has been accustomed all his life to settle his own problems, to acquire his own information, to act upon his own judgment" (20). The ideal is a fusion of these two paradigms, and

> the only way we can get it is by giving the schoolgirls and boys strong incentives to originality of thought. A school paper supplies this want. It is read by all the members of the school and each one is urged to contribute to its pages. (20)[2]

Creating common ground among ancient orators and self-made Americans, which included some Barstow parents who read this declaration, the editorial positions the young women directing the production of *The Weather-cock* as leaders who model "originality of thought" and provide a venue for younger

33

Amplifying Identity

students to develop the same. Wary, perhaps, of having pushed the point too far and thereby insinuating that Barstow girls were arrogant or overly ambitious, the writer ends with a seeming retraction: "We do not aspire to anything great, we do not wish for renown; our only desire for our paper is that it may be a medium of natural expression for the students of our school" (20). The conclusion of the editorial suggests that the writer realizes magnification must be wielded cautiously lest it be perceived and possibly dismissed as rhetorical hyperbole.

Having established their intellectual aptitude, Barstow girls magnified their athletic ability in the 1901 yearbook. Barstow student Marion Edwards describes her school's basketball game against a Kansas City coeducational public high school, Manual Training High School, in April 1901. Sketching the pregame scene, she reports that five girls from the Manual team arrived on the field and began warming up:

> Then our School, grouped behind the guests, gave the signal, the school yell, and out came our team, shoulder to shoulder, showing the school colors in their blouses and shouting in answer, "Ho, oi, yo, ho! Ho, oi, yo, ho! Barstow!" (15)

The Manual supporters replied, "I yell, you yell, we all yell, Manual!" Barstow boosters repeated their cheer "until everybody was shouting with all her might" (15). An editorial in this issue explains the unusual Barstow School cheer:

> We wished for one that would rouse our girls to deeds of valor upon the basket-ball field. Someone suggested the battle-cry of the Valkyrs, the warrior maidens, from Wagner's "Die Walküre," and an adaption of this was finally made. ("School Yell" 20)

Transforming opera lyrics into a school chant, the Barstow girls identified themselves not as little women but as warrior maidens on the athletic field. The highbrow origin of the Barstow school cheer also distinguished it from the more pedestrian cheer—"I yell, you yell"—of the public high school.

Barstow basketball players heeded this call in their game against Manual. Edwards intensifies the account by reporting that two Barstow players repeatedly outscored opponents who were much larger than they were, and another Barstow girl defended "with all the fury of a tiger" (M. Edwards 16). Comparing an adolescent girl to a wild animal, Edwards stresses that Barstow basketball players were physically aggressive. The Barstow

34
Amplifying Identity

girls won the game 12-10 and celebrated by hoisting their team captain on their shoulders and parading around the outdoor court as their classmates shouted. Edwards magnifies the meaning of the victory in her final line: "Our great game with Manual Training School was over and our team had made a name for itself in Kansas City" (16). Clearly, Barstow girls believed athletic achievement helped to establish their collective identity beyond their campus community.

The significance of these events is heightened in an editorial titled "The Class." Reviewing the history of the class that entered Miss Barstow's School just after it moved from downtown to midtown Kansas City in 1898, the editorial notes: "We have chosen the school pin and the colors, we have originated a yell and have developed a splendid school spirit largely fostered by the work of the basket-ball teams" (21). Athletics fostered school "spirit," or loyalty, that paralleled national patriotism during this imperialistic period. This account of a basketball game established Barstow girls as enthusiastic athletes and authorized their participation in competitive contact sports.

Claiming the right to engage in vigorous athletics, Barstow girls defied gender and class codes dictating rigorous sports as unsuitable for girls of their socioeconomic standing. While medical experts and leaders of the new physical education movement of the late nineteenth century encouraged moderate exercise for girls, particularly to offset the strains of scholarship, competitive organized sports were promoted for men and boys. Susan K. Cahn observes that "proponents of manly sport hoped that sport could renew middle-class manhood" enervated by industrialization that increasingly separated physical labor from paid work (12). Athletic training also was seen as the means to "reinvigorate pampered boys" and channel the energies of young immigrant and working-class males who might otherwise exercise their presumably innate proclivity for sexual and criminal delinquency (12). Several historical developments, however, encouraged young women to engage in rigorous and increasingly competitive athletic activities: the bicycling craze of the 1880s and 1890s, the invention of basketball in 1891, and the rising number of girls in high schools and colleges that offered physical education. Cahn relates that skeptics warned that sports would turn the

> female body into a facsimile of the male. Such corporeal suspicions were often rooted in deeper concerns about the social implications of female athleticism. The female athlete kindled acute anxieties about

35
Amplifying Identity

the erosion of men's physical supremacy and the loss of distinct male and female preserves. (20)

Anxiety arose that the female athlete would join the ranks of suffragists and protofeminists, young working-class women, and mature women pursuing professions. Cahn concludes that "together they formed a threatening cadre of New Women whose public presence prompted shrill calls for a return to more familiar patriarchal arrangements" (20).

As a New Woman, Mary Barstow was an advocate of athletics and competitive sports for girls. She expressed her holistic educational philosophy in the 1909 Barstow School catalog: "The object of the school is to promote sound scholarship and to give symmetrical development to the mind, body, and character" (qtd. in Brayman 21). In *The Weather-cock*, students did not promote activities deemed appropriate for upper-class girls at the turn of the century, such as archery and tennis. Although they participated in gymnastics and swimming, which were recommended for young women, they enthusiastically embraced vigorous contact team sports, such as basketball and field hockey. Putting their bodies on display in athletic events, Barstow new girls emulated the enthusiasm for competitive sports at women's colleges. In her letter from Smith College, which was published in *The Weather-cock* of 1915, Barstow graduate Doris Howes reports on the fervor of her female classmates for basketball, hockey, cricket, volleyball, rowing, and clock-golf ("Weather-cock Letter" 78–80). As college-preparatory students, Barstow girls trained for the athletic as well as academic challenges of higher education. That is not to say that girls at other schools in this study did not also engage in competitive sports, as indicated by the account of the Barstow basketball game against the girls' team of the public coeducational Manual Training High School. The difference, however, is the way that Barstow girls relied on their athletic performance in their identity formation, a reliance that is not evident in the epideictic rhetoric of girls at the Haskell Institute, Lincoln High School, or Central High School.

A third example of magnification from the 1901 volume of *The Weather-cock* registered Barstow girls as public performers. Reviewing a play the Barstow Dramatic Club presented, student Helen Cooper is effusive in her praise of *Bianca*. In a three-page review, she effuses: "It can truly be said that this dramatic effort was a great success, for the actresses not only showed their talent, but also their powers of invention" (12).[3] Cooper highlights the

36
Amplifying Identity

talent and powers of invention of the actresses: "Miss Barbara Allen, as the page, won all hearts by her beauty and sweetness. The villainy of Huon, Miss Alice Rossington, was almost too realistic, while Miss Helen Barton's Hilda presented another aspect of evil with equal force" (14). Significantly, Barstow girls eschewed the popular dramatic genre of the tableaux in which women silently assumed poses that symbolized emotions ranging from fear to mirth. Nan Johnson argues that the women in tableaux "appear not to be using their voices nor to be representing these emotions in the service of any intellectual argument or persuasive, political effort" (38). Barstow girls used their voices as they staged melodrama, literary adaptations, and Shakespearean productions that implicitly argued for their right to seek public attention, a trait of new girls.

In 1918 Mabel M. Knollin magnifies the Barstow "military squad," the first mention of such in *The Weather-cock*. The public high schools of Kansas City introduced military training at about the same time that the United States entered World War I in April 1917. Boys who joined the cadet corps at Central and Lincoln High Schools were issued uniforms and rifles; Central girls who were seniors formed a Red Cross corps and learned to administer first aid and to march in formation ("Cadets," 154; "Red Cross Corps," 158; "Military Training," 16–18).[4] Barstow girls did not organize a Red Cross corps but groups that Knollin calls military squads. Reporting on the completion of a new outdoor basketball court at Barstow, she notes that it provided more than playing space for teams: "As everything is, directly or indirectly touched by the war's activities, so our court, too, has done its part, for have not our military squads paraded with much ardor and enthusiasm upon its smooth surface?" (53). Knollin implies that marching was the main activity of the Barstow squads and goes so far to suggest that these groups may "have a part perhaps in the eventual ending of this world's war" (53). How the squads might help to end the war was left unsaid, but she continues by positing another possibility:

> I believe that our court has done its share in helping to build up girls who will become fine, strong women, ready to play both small and large games; as large perhaps, as re-construction work at some not far distant day. (53)

Magnifying the function of athletic and military training, Knollin predicts that Barstow new girls would mature into women who could help rebuild Europe when World War I was over.

To introduce the idea of Barstow girls as new girls in 1901, young women magnified their abilities and activities as scholars, athletes, and performers.

37
Amplifying Identity

Aware of cultural assumptions about the intellectual and physical capabilities of young women of the period, as well as expectations of their behavior, Barstow girls collaborated to create what Lanham calls a "new reality" that authorized and celebrated female scholarship, athleticism, and public display. Their arguments can be reduced to simple, if rather radical, statements: Girls had intellectual abilities and the stamina to sustain them; they could be competitive athletes; and they could play new roles on both a school stage and in the world. Expanding these statements in the premiere editorial of *The Weather-cock*, Barstow girls demonstrate their rhetorical mastery and capacity for leadership. They heighten their performance as basketball players by aligning themselves with mythological women warriors. They glorify their dramatic performance and assert that they were preparing to participate in the aftermath of the largely male enterprise of World War I. All of these activities were group activities that established and supported the community of the school. The use of magnification by Barstow girls suggests that this strategy lays the foundation for epideictic discourse that can be further developed through means such as confirmation.

CONFIRMATION

In Roman rhetoric, amplification served the purpose of confirmation or proof, according to Laib. Confirmation is an element of the "complete and perfect argument," as defined by the *Rhetorica ad Herennium* (ca. 85 B.C.E.) (Laib, "Conciseness" 451). Aristotle identifies two kinds of proof: inartistic and artistic. Inartistic proof entails evidence, such as sworn testimony, documents, scientific analyses, and laws. The three main types of artistic proof are also known as the persuasive appeals of ethos, pathos, and logos. Barstow girls relied on artistic proofs to commend their collective identity. Their use of ethos, pathos, and logos suggests that these artistic proofs operate interactively in amplification. Barstow girls drew their ethos from the external authority that they acquired through their activities as scholars, athletes, and performers. They then reinforced this authority and, consequently, their credentials through their first-person and eyewitness accounts of these activities that function as logos. Barstow girls also were adept at creating pathos and often used humor to offset the possibility that they might be perceived as bragging about their accomplishments.

The interaction of proofs is evident in two features from early editions of *The Weather-cock*. In 1901, an unnamed contributor compiled a series of

38
Amplifying Identity

translations from Julius Caesar's *Gallic War*. This feature establishes the ethos of Barstow girls as Latin students and offers logos of their valiant attempts to master the language long regarded as the foundation of a classical education. The author employs pathos by deliberately citing humorous mistranslations that disarm auditors who might resist the notion of girls entering the traditionally male domain of Latin studies. Using the enthymeme, she quotes a classmate who translated, "Summum in cruciatum se venturas viderent" (They should be put to the greatest tortures) as "They saw themselves running before the wind in the highest torture" ("Gems" 14).[5] Another line, "Obsides nobillissimi cuiusque liberos posceredere" (To demand as hostages the children of all the principal nobles)—is rendered, "He demanded the children of the noblest as hostages to eat" (14). Readers who could not translate the original lines can get the joke; readers who studied Latin can appreciate the challenge that Barstow girls faced with good humor.

The same strategy of confirmation marks "As the Wind Blows" in the 1902 edition of *The Weather-cock*. Although the column focuses on the mistakes of Barstow girls, it confirms that they studied Latin, French, geometry, rhetoric, science, and ancient and modern history. K. S., for instance, asserts in her U.S. history class, "The Merrimac had a fight with the Minataur" (122). Referring to a Confederate Civil War battleship and a monster from Greek mythology, K. S. may intend to produce a pun about the USS *Monitor*, a Union vessel that fought the CSS *Merrimac*. Or, perhaps, she simply confuses the Minotaur and the *Monitor*. Nonetheless, she supplies proof that Barstow girls were students of both Greek mythology and U.S. military history.

These examples suggest that Barstow girls often used a humorous rather than haughty tone to amplify their identities as scholars, a tactic that reflects their awareness of audience. Some of their readers may have questioned the intellectual capabilities of girls or heeded the warnings of conservative experts who claimed that adolescent girls could damage their bodies through strenuous mental activity. Rather than making antagonistic responses to such arguments, Barstow girls used pathos to persuade their audience that they were capable of demanding scholarship. Furthermore, Mary Barstow may have encouraged girls to temper their rhetoric about their academic abilities in early issues of *The Weather-cock*. A member of the first generation of college-educated women in the United States, she must have been aware of negative images of female scholars. Lynn D. Gordon observes that

Amplifying Identity

Americans often assumed that women who graduated from college between 1865 and 1890 were mannish caricatures of womanhood. Female college graduates were held responsible for falling marriage and birth rates, rising divorce rates, and what Harvard University President Charles William Eliot and President Theodore Roosevelt called "race suicide," the fear that white women would fail to produce enough children to offset the influx and prolific reproduction of southern and eastern European immigrants (Gordon, "Gibson Girl" 215). As a New Woman who went to college, never married, and pursued a career, Mary Barstow may have advised Barstow new girls to avoid appearing arrogant about their intellectual identity in the early years of *The Weather-cock*. Using humor to confirm the caliber of their academic pursuits offset the possibility that they would be accused of bragging.

Such reticence was not required, however, a decade later, judging by Rebecca Gray's confirmation in the 1911 yearbook of the commitment of Barstow girls to academics. In her amusingly assertive poem, "The Legend of the Laboratory," Gray merges ethos, logos, and pathos as she describes the efforts of students who called themselves the "Physics Four" to prepare for exams. Working together to record in their notebooks the results of experiments, the girls energetically argue about their findings:

> She laughed and she teased, the Philosopher did, she teased
> and she argued with zest,
> Till the Teacher rose on the Jabbering Four and the Beautiful
> One had rest,—
> Had rest till the first dispute arose and a fight was about to
> start,
> For the Fusser said that the Weight was wrong by a Gram's
> ten thousandth part. (21)

The fourth girl in the group, known as the "Lazy One," is not interested in debating such minute differences, but each girl recognizes the significance of the all-important notebook: "The tale is old as the Laws of Sound, as true as the Inverse Square, / For each maid knows if to college she goes she must carry a notebook fair" (21). In her comparison of schoolgirl studies and the laws of science and math, Gray does not consider *whether* she and her classmates should attend college but, rather, what they must do in order to go.

40
Amplifying Identity

Offering proof of the academic attitude of Barstow girls, Doris Howes claims in her review of the 1913–14 school year that she and her classmates were happy to return to school after the winter break. In a rare allusion to the social status of Barstow girls, Howes recounts a two-week whirl of dances, luncheons, parties, and teas that she and her classmates attended during the holiday, commenting that these "events were all fun, but too much of it" and that the resumption of classes was a "peaceful release" ("Year" 11). The winter weather prohibited Barstow girls from participating in their usual outdoor activities and allowed them to focus fully on their studies:

> Too snowy for basket-ball, too cold for hockey, too wet for cross-country walks, what restful times we had. Then it was that we turned to our row of poets. We even enjoyed our lessons. It was fun to write stories, fun to read German and French, even fun to translate Virgil. We found we had minds as well as bodies,—and we loved the discovery. (11)

Howe's discovery counters discourse of the day that privileged girls' bodies over their brains—and sought to control their bodies and minds. And her veiled critique of the expectations of her social class—to endure and enjoy endless diversions—refutes the notion that Barstow girls were a group of socialites instead of a community of dedicated scholars.

Athletics remained central to the self-conceptions of Barstow new girls, as they proved through the passing years in editorials and first-person columns. Following the 1901 editorial that magnifies the performance of Barstow basket-ball players, the only editorial in the 1902 volume of *The Weather-cock* proves the growing popularity of sports: "The interest in athletics has been greater and more varied this year than ever before. Basket-ball, stage dancing and tennis have all received their share of attention from the older girls" (Editorial 1902, 112). The editorial recounts several matches between the two upper-school basketball teams, as well as the formation of two teams of girls from the grammar department, or elementary school. The writer also reports that "circumstances" foiled the plan for the Barstow school team, composed of the best players from the upper school, to play the Topeka High School girls and the women of the Kansas City Athletic Club. She adds, "Arrangements may be made for these games next fall, as our players are anxious to try their prowess against other teams" (112). Eager to prove their mettle, as they did against the public high school the year before, Barstow girls welcomed the chance to further enhance their reputation as athletes, as well as the reputation of their school.

41
Amplifying Identity

The testimony of two girls in the 1910s confirms the continuing importance and rigor of athletics at Barstow. In 1914 Susan De McGee exercised her ethos as an athlete to celebrate the renaissance of field hockey and warned would-be players: "I should advise you, if you come to play with us, to come in bloomers and shin guards, and prepare for a rough-and-tumble good time" (56). Five years later, Caroline Shields paid comical tribute to the most essential element of her wardrobe: "My bloomers are my best friends; a dozen or so relations I could spare, but not my bloomers. . . . Few worthwhile things can be done without bloomers. Basketball, hockey, gymnasium, dancing, and even riding would cease" (19). Dancing, one of the physical activities sanctioned by nineteenth-century parents for their daughters, ranked fourth in this new-girl catalog of "worthwhile things," published in *The Weather-cock* of 1919.

The third component of Barstow identity—public performance—was confirmed by a 1910 account of the founding of a permanent dramatic society. Inspired by the success of plays presented in 1908 and 1909, Barstow girls organized a dramatic club that they named "The Pretenders" in honor of "Bonnie Prince Charley," according to Agnes Thompson (25).[6] She reports that ten girls who had demonstrated acting ability were chosen as charter members and that the club also invited alumnae and faculty members to join. Stressing the serious nature of the group, she remarks, "The trial for new active members is made sufficiently severe to maintain the high standard for the dramatic work of the club" (25). That standard called for professional equipment, and the society procured a curtain, scenery, and electric footlights for the hall at the Barstow School where they presented plays during the evening so that parents and other nonstudents could attend. For its first season, the Pretenders performed scenes from three Shakespeare dramas: *The Merchant of Venice*, *A Midsummer Night's Dream*, and *As You Like It*. Judging by the lengthy and fervent reports of the society in subsequent issues of *The Weather-cock*, it was an important organization at the school and enabled students to prove that public performance was appropriate for young women.

To confirm their claim that they were new girls, the young women of Barstow used the artistic proofs of ethos, logos, and pathos, demonstrating how rhetors use them in concert in individual examples of epideictic discourse and over time to amplify the same message. Their proofs were culled from classrooms and playing fields, where they participated in and witnessed rigorous academic and athletic activities, and from stages where they performed

42
Amplifying Identity

dramatic roles. Initially cautious in their epideictic campaign to prove their intellectual abilities, they were consistently bold about their skills as athletes and public performers. And bold was the byword of the visual rhetoric that they created to amplify their identity through emphasis.

EMPHASIS

The Greek root of "emphasis" (*phainein*) means to show, and art can function as visual rhetoric that amplifies an epideictic argument, as Kitch suggests in her analysis of female visual stereotypes in the popular press. She contends that feminine imagery dominated the illustrations of American magazines during the first three decades of the twentieth century and that these images "conveyed ideas about women's nature and roles, but they also stood for societal values" (6). Kitch notes that the United States "traditionally has been depicted as a woman, in forms from Indian princess to Greek goddess. So too has American progress" (39–40). For example, the Gibson Girl, one of the most prolific images of the early twentieth century, embodies the American values of confidence, independence, and material wealth through myriad depictions of a poised and well-dressed young woman whose facial expression and posture indicate her sense of sovereignty.

Participating in this trend, Barstow girls relied on visual rhetoric to emphasize they were new girls. Their artwork represents some of the most persuasive epideictic rhetoric in *The Weather-cock*. The images that they produced for the yearbook depict girls as industrious workers, strutting roosters, and athletes who model fearlessness and good sportsmanship.

One of the first student illustrations in *The Weather-cock* was reproduced on the editorial page of the 1909 volume and shows a girl hunched over a desk (fig. 2.2).[7] A pile of papers covers the table and obscures the girl's face; more sheets litter the floor around her feet. The long length of her skirt suggests that she is in the upper school; the Barstow pennant on the wall indicates where she goes to school. Across the top of the illustration is the word "Editorials." The artist may have intended the figure to represent a yearbook editor or a Barstow girl engaged in her studies; in either case, she clearly is immersed in her work.

The editorial below the illustration accentuates the theme of labor. Retelling the Biblical story of the Garden of Eden, the writer adds a rooster—a coy reference to the title of the yearbook. In Eden, according to this rendition, the rooster's duty was to call Adam and Eve to their daily work. When

Amplifying Identity

Figure 2.2. Editorials illustration, *The Weather-cock*, 1909. *Courtesy of the State Historical Society of Missouri Research Center–Kansas City.*

Adam asked the cock why he always faced the wind, the bird replied that this position allowed him to see the good things coming and fulfill his destiny to alert man about the direction of the wind. The editorial ends with two morals:

> The first is that good things are being blown our way all the time if we only face in the right direction to see them. The second is that if we have as worthy a purpose as the cock and serve it as well we shall be justified in crowing as loudly. (Editorials 1909, 18)

Revising Christian mythology to justify the pride of Barstow girls, the editorial reinforces the message of the visual rhetoric: school was work, and it was acceptable to boast about good work.

A year later, Janet Glover amplified this adage by drawing a strutting rooster with a girl's face to illustrate the editorial page of *The Weather-cock* (fig. 2.3). Merging the symbol of the yearbook and the girls who produced it, she created a unique visual expression of the pride of Barstow new girls. The commentary that accompanies the illustration sketches a barnyard scene, where a rooster known as "The Weather-cock" perches on top of a water barrel and delivers "a magnificent satire on society" (Editorial 1910, 18). Rife with literary references, the editorial portrays *The Weather-cock* as a feisty fighter ready to engage in combat with any other rooster in the yard—a reflection, perhaps, of how Barstow girls saw themselves in the youth culture of Kansas City. Certainly, they expressed competitive feelings toward other schools in their athletic reports.

44
Amplifying Identity

Figure 2.3. Illustration by Janet Glover, *The Weather-cock*, 1910. *Courtesy of the State Historical Society of Missouri Research Center–Kansas City.*

Barstow girls also used art to emphasize their identity as athletes. Blending aesthetics and ideals, Louise Haas illustrated an article about Barstow girls taking swimming lessons that appears in the 1912 yearbook (fig. 2.4). Her drawing reinforces the report on this athletic activity: girls took learning to swim as seriously as learning Latin. Rather than representing a girl floating idly or ineptly paddling, Haas shows a young woman concentrating intensely as she prepares to dive into a pond, a public space where spectators could watch these female athletic exhibitions. Poised on the edge of a diving board with her arms raised in an arc over her head, the girl exudes the confidence of a new girl who was not afraid to test new waters.

Three years later, Hortense Meade altered the familiar female figure of Columbia, the symbol of American liberty, into an emblem of the Barstow athlete. The full-page pen drawing anchors the athletic section of the 1915 volume of *The Weather-cock* (fig. 2.5). Dressed in a middy blouse, bloomers, black stockings, and lace-up athletic shoes, the girl clutches a basketball in her left hand and hoists a Barstow banner above her head with her right arm.

45
Amplifying Identity

Figure 2.4. Illustration by Louise Haas, The Weather-cock, 1912. *Courtesy of the State Historical Society of Missouri Research Center–Kansas City.*

On the left side of the illustration is the motto:

> B a clean player
> a good loser
> a fair partisan
> a true sport
> then you will win your B. (67)

The letter *B* that begins and ends this directive is in uppercase Gothic script, distinguishing it from the smaller-point font used for the rest of the statement;

46
Amplifying Identity

Figure 2.5. Illustration by Hortense Meade, *The Weather-cock*, 1915. *Courtesy of the State Historical Society of Missouri Research Center–Kansas City.*

the final *B* probably refers to the sports letter that participants earned. Meade's illustration reflects the visual rhetoric that would permeate print culture after the United States entered World War I in 1917. Popular magazine illustrator Howard Chandler Christy, for example, created a poster promoting the purchase of war bonds in 1917 that shows Columbia raising the U.S. flag with her right arm and pointing with her left arm to an army of miniature American soldiers. Kitch observes that on World War I posters, the figures of women "were meant to stand for ideas, for larger concepts and values that made war seem noble and necessary" (104, 110). Christy and other artists

Amplifying Identity

pictured Columbia as a young white woman, but Meade transforms her into a schoolgirl who signifies the noble ideals of Barstow students.

A final example of emphasis achieved through visual rhetoric is Ruth Munger's illustration for the athletic section of *The Weather-cock* of 1918, which also features Knollin's article about the new basketball court at Barstow. While Knollin describes the military squads that paraded on the court, Munger depicts three girls wearing middy blouses and bloomers exercising on the court (fig. 2.6). In the foreground, a girl flexes her arm, and her bicep is noticeably pronounced. In the left background, another girl stands by a hurdle, and to the right, a girl aims a basketball at a hoop. The caption reads, "Show how your muscle has grown in forty weeks" (53). The "forty weeks" refers to a school year of athletic training that produced these specimens of muscular girlhood. A compelling articulation of young female physicality, this visual rhetoric underscores the idea that Barstow girls were as devoted to exercising their bodies as their brains.

In Roman rhetoric, emphasis was known as *significiatio* and meant to imply more than was actually stated. One of the ways of achieving signification is to choose an exceptionally strong word or phrase (Lanham 138). Substituting strong images for words, Barstow girls used their original art to emphasize their collective commitment to academics and athletics, as well

Figure 2.6. Illutstration by Ruth Munger, *The Weather-cock*, 1918. *Courtesy of the State Historical Society of Missouri Research Center–Kansas City.*

48
Amplifying Identity

as their pride in their pursuits. In a series of illustrations reproduced in *The Weather-cock*, they showed how their community of new girls looked and behaved. First and foremost, they were active participants in their education and physical training, not passive observers who received wisdom and sat in the stands during athletic events. Dedicated to their studies, as the illustration of the Barstow girl at her desk suggests, they also dedicated themselves to strenuous athletics, such as basketball, swimming, and gymnastics. The visual rhetoric of Barstow girls amplified their written rhetoric in individual issues of the yearbook and through the years created a compelling catalog of their self-conceptions. Communicating their shared values visually at a time when professional artists relied on female images to signal societal values, Barstow girls reclaimed rhetorical authority to define young women, rather than to be defined. Their written rhetoric then restated the messages of their artistically persuasive endeavors.

RESTATEMENT

Barstow girls studied rhetoric, and while school records from this period do not indicate the titles of their textbooks, it is possible that they were assigned John F. Genung's manual, which was used in the public high schools of Kansas City. In a lengthy discussion of amplification, Genung advises that restatement should be used "in cases where the significance of a term is to be fixed, or where an important assertion is to be impressed" (291). Laib concurs: "Restatement helps readers understand the concept. Those who do not grasp an idea when it is first articulated may understand it better when it is phrased differently or when the subject is described from a different perspective" ("Conciseness" 449).

The editorial section of the 1911 *Weather-cock* exemplifies the effort of Barstow girls to fix the terms of their identity as new girls who privileged scholarship, athletics, and public performance. In the first of two columns in the editorial section, senior Rebecca Gray restates the assertion of the 1901 editorial and that of her poem for the 1911 yearbook, "The Legend of the Laboratory," both of which depict the Barstow ideal of independent and industrious female intellectuals. Chapter 1 refers to Gray's column, and an excerpt serves as the first epigraph of this chapter, but Gray had more to say. Addressing younger students, she describes the principles of Barstow new girls:

> In accomplishing our allotted tasks (and some that were not allotted) with a merry spirit and a right good will, we have found that truest joy

49
Amplifying Identity

of being released from the sordid commonplaceness of this work-a-day world, to feel ourselves transported on wings of bliss to isles of contentment, where work becomes play. You need not wait until you have attained our lofty pinnacle of wisdom and advanced years to discover that labor, pure and undefiled, is the only means to any given end which has as its goals success and happiness,—unstinted labor and unbounded enthusiasm. (Editorials 23)

Significantly, Gray describes the pursuits of Barstow girls as "work" and thus infuses their activities with greater importance than some readers might have allowed. Exercising the Barstow ethic, girls cheerfully complete assignments and willingly take on extra work, according to Gray. Their reward is release from daily drudgery and transportation to an intellectual realm where "work becomes play." Gently mocking her own position as the all-wise and aged senior, Gray repeats the necessity of labor as well as enthusiasm to the attainment of success and happiness. What is at stake is not only the achievement of the individual girl but the reputation of the group:

And so we intrust to your safekeeping this priceless treasure—school spirit—and all that goes with it—the honour and good name of the school, that you may never by word or deed, here or elsewhere, do anything to its discredit. (23)

Echoing the slogans of girls' clubs that required members to pledge to uphold the high standards of these organizations, Gray associates school spirit with the ethical actions of Barstow students.

In another editorial column from the 1911 yearbook—also mentioned in chapter 1 and quoted in the second epigraph of this chapter—senior Madeline Haff repeats the proclivity for public performance that was essential to the identity of Barstow girls. Whereas Cooper magnifies the dramatic abilities of Barstow girls in her 1901 review of *Bianca*, and Thompson, in her 1910 article about the Pretenders, confirms their dedication to public performance, Haff impresses upon readers the good reasons for dramatic training at Barstow. Educating skeptics, she says:

To those who have suggested that a dramatic club would take too much time for the regular studies, we can only say "Consider all the advantages—are not they too a legitimate part of a girl's education? What of clear enunciation, training of the carrying powers of the voice, self-possession, grace and ease of movement?" (22)

50

Amplifying Identity

While these skills might be considered the signs of accomplished young women, they also are the tools of public speakers. Haff also remarks that the Pretenders cultivated traits traditionally encouraged in girls, such as self-sacrifice and self-discipline, as participants learned "to take a minor part when one longs to be heroine"; "to sacrifice everything for rehearsals"; and "to go over one's lines patiently until just the right intonation is caught" (22). She concludes by reassuring readers that Barstow girls did not plan to pursue acting careers, but she also makes clear that she they would use these skills in the future "to carry ourselves through life" (22).

Ten years after Barstow girls magnified their self-conception as scholars, athletes, and performers in *The Weather-cock* of 1901, they exploited the rhetorical affordances of this serial publication to restate the primary components of their identity in the 1911 yearbook. At this point in the history of Miss Barstow's School, there was a strong sense of community among students, as evident in Gray's advice to younger students and her allusion to school spirit. The rhetorical restatements of Barstow girls both mirror and reinforce this community. As opposed to the earlier epideictic editorials of *The Weather-cock*, the commentaries of Gray and Haff carry bylines that capitalize on the ethos of the authors as seniors and prominent members of their class. Speaking for and to their peers, as well as other auditors, these girls articulate the beliefs, concerns, and practices of the Barstow community, an articulation that they amplified through enlargement.

ENLARGEMENT

The epideictic method of enlargement entails the augmentation, extension, embellishment, or elaboration of a point. Barstow girls had the benefit of multiple opportunities to enlarge their collective identity in successive volumes of *The Weather-cock*. They elaborate on their athleticism in reports of their cross-country hikes and embellished assumptions about who they were by making clear who they were not through creative writing and essays.

Although the cross-country "run" described in the 1909 and 1910 volumes of *The Weather-cock* cannot be classified an organized sport, Barstow girls included these accounts in the athletics section to amplify their physical stamina. In November 1908, fifteen girls and two women teachers hiked about five miles from Miss Barstow's School in Kansas City, Missouri, to the ruins of the Shawnee Indian Mission in Johnson County, Kansas, according to an unnamed writer. Meeting a farmer driving a wagon along the way, ten of the

51
Amplifying Identity

girls chose to ride. On the return to school, no wagon appeared, "but for athletes it was not weary work to cover the long distance home" ("Cross-Country Run" 20). The next year, Howes reported that fifteen girls and three women set out for the mission. As they tramped through the business district near the school, Howes relates, "people turned to look at the unusual sight of this miniature army of Amazons marching through the street with their packs upon their backs" ("Our Cross-Country Run" 19). The unusual sight of adolescent girls parading publicly and engaging in the kind of physical activity urged upon boys of the time inspires Howes to compare her comrades to Amazons, the fierce women warriors of Greek mythology.[8] Girls also showed their competitive edge on this occasion:

> We gradually divided into two groups and a friendly rivalry grew up between us as to who should reach the destination first. As our detachment turned the last corner, we chanced to look back and saw that the other group had vanished. Suddenly they reappeared, rushing madly across the field in a wild attempt to beat us to the Mission. Of course, we ran, too, and all arrived at once, breathless and hot. (19)

Qualifying the race as friendly, Howes nevertheless captures the Barstow girls' drive to win, taking for granted that, of course, her group did not want to arrive last.

One of the strategies of epideictic rhetors declaring "who we are" is to amplify "who we are not." Gail Bederman contends that community building in the progressive period, an era marked by anxiety about American identity and attendant reactions, such as racially motivated violence, often depended on distinguishing and excluding people deemed inferior to the dominant culture. Bederman argues that during the late nineteenth and early twentieth centuries, white people in the United States often conflated "civilization" or "the achievement of a perfect race" and white supremacism (27, 123). As elite white native-born girls who lived in a former slave state, enjoyed white privilege in a city with strict Jim Crow codes, and studied history and literature under the direction of Miss Barstow, a specialist in "Anglo-Saxon," Barstow students assumed that whites were supreme. Like prominent professional writers and performers of the day, ranging from Jack London, who created condescending portraits of Native Americans, to white comedians who appeared in blackface in minstrel shows in Kansas City, Barstow girls reiterated racial, ethnic, and class stereotypes (Hinds). They wrote short stories that

52
Amplifying Identity

mocked black and Irish figures, characterized Native Americans as noble savages, and chastised a poor boy who would rather return to his dirty hovel than remain in a sanitary charity hospital. Their gestures can be seen as the rhetorical creation of the "Other," a term coined by French feminist writer Simone de Beauvoir (*The Second Sex*) and popularized by Palestinian cultural studies scholar Edward Said (*Orientalism*). Embracing the zeitgeist, Barstow girls solidified their sense of community through repeated acts of rhetorical differentiation.

Embellishing the difference between white Barstow girls and African American girls, Christine Evans composed a story about an enslaved girl of the antebellum South who wanted to be a white ballet dancer. In "Mirabella Ann's Experiment," published in the 1902 volume of *The Weather-cock*, Evans describes the main character as a "little Virginia pickaninny with about the blackest face and kinkiest hair a little pickaninny was ever blessed with" (100). Mirabella Ann helps to care for white children who live in an "old colonial house" where she is not allowed unless "mammy" is present. Lingering in front of a mirror, Mirabella "stood rapt in the contemplation of the little figure the glass reflected. The height of Mirabella Ann's ambition was to become a ballet dancer, and to become white" (100). As she gazes at her reflection, Mirabella Ann envisions twinkling lights, soft music, and the figure of a ballerina with a "lovely rose complexion" dancing on a stage before an admiring audience. Her reverie is interrupted by mammy, but later that night, Mirabella Ann attempts to make her fantasy a reality. Hearing other characters discuss buttermilk as a remedy for stains, Mirabella takes a cup of buttermilk to the orchard beyond the "plantation" where she casts a spell over the liquid and smears her face with it. She then returns to the cabin and is discovered by mammy, who gives the girl a bath, and "the magic buttermilk was ruthlessly washed away and with it went Mirabella's dreams of rose complexion and the brilliant stage" (102).

Echoing "plantation fiction" of the era—literature that tended to portray slaves and former slaves in comical or paternalistic terms—Evans tells this story without a trace of sympathy for Mirabella. Privileged by race, class, and historical period, the author imagines a girl who was fettered by these same factors, but evoking empathy for this pathetic character does not seem her purpose. Rather, Evans uses the character of Mirabella to enlarge the differences between this girl and Barstow girls, whose aspirations were not hindered by the color of their skin or their socioeconomic class. While it is

53
Amplifying Identity

possible that Evans knew an African American girl, as some Barstow families may have employed black servants, it is unlikely that she would have associated with a young woman from the well-educated African American middle-class community of Kansas City during the Jim Crow era. In other words, Evans never encountered African American girls who could be her equals and thus envisions them as unequal.[9]

While Evans uses race and class to differentiate Barstow girls from other girls, Claudia Gaylord uses nationality. Recounting in the 1914 yearbook her semester at a French boarding school, she judges both French girls and French schools inferior to their counterparts in the United States:

> An American girl is independent and ready to take the initiative, while a French girl stands by, waiting for someone to point out the way. The watchword of an American school seems, "Learn to steer your own boat;" and for a French school, "Sit quiet in the boat, little passenger, and let us hold the rudder, we know how, so you never need to." (31)

Such chauvinism was standard among U.S. citizens, who have a long tradition of drawing disparaging distinctions between the New World and the Old World, but what is noteworthy is Gaylord's confident assertion that the American girl enacts the ideals of independence and initiative usually attributed to men. Perhaps, Gaylord was influenced by the popular and prolific model of the Gibson Girl, or she was aware of the claims of early feminists, such as Charlotte Perkins Gilman, who argues that race counted for more than gender in discussions of superiority (Bederman 121). While French girls were envisioned as white, they were not Anglo-Saxon, and thus they were inferior to American new girls.

This sample of epideictic enlargement by Barstow girls includes incidents, fiction, and metaphors that amplify their self-conceptions as new girls who are different from other girls. Discussing amplification, Genung notes:

> Not all illustration is in the nature of example; nor is it always employed merely to make the reader understand more fully. Some material produces its proper effect only by being realized in the imagination, and the amplification applied to it must be of a heightening and vivifying character. (294)

Indeed, Barstow girls exercised their imaginations and called upon their auditors to do the same as they described in vivifying detail their cross-country

54

Amplifying Identity

hikes, transforming schoolgirl outings into evidence of their physical stamina and competitive spirit. Evans created a fictional Other in her poignant portrait of a young African American girl who stood in stark contrast to the powerful girls that Barstow girls imagined themselves to be. And Gaylord invented a nautical metaphor to represent American girls, such as Barstow students as stalwart sailors steering the ships of their destiny, in contrast to passive French girl passengers who relinquished the right to guide the course of their lives. Insisting that they were neither pathetic nor passive, Barstow girls enlarged their collective identity as admirable and active young women. In the process, they constructed community, an important objective of epideictic rhetoric.

Conclusions

In his rhetorical manual, Genung advises that after a writer has determined the main ideas of his text, these ideas "need to be taken up anew and endowed with life; to be clothed in a fitting dress of explanatory, illustrative, and enforcing thought. This is the office of rhetorical amplification" (285). Barstow girls enacted this advice by delivering epideictic rhetoric that defined them as a coterie of new girls. Using five different forms of amplification, they persuaded their audience to regard them as superior scholars, sportswomen, and public performers who were different from earlier generations of upper-class girls—including the generation of their mothers, who did not have the same opportunities or the encouragement to pursue such opportunities. Barstow girls also differentiated themselves from other races and nationalities and suggested new possibilities for girls of the upper class, such as helping to rebuild Europe after World War I. Resisting the appropriation of their school as a symbol of their families' status, Barstow girls reappropriated it as a symbol of their autonomy and achievement.

The epideictic rhetoric of Barstow girls began to change after World War I, signaling an end to the era of the new girl.[10] Girls continued to praise their academic, athletic, and performative abilities, but they also began to address other facets of their identity, such as their appearance, clothes, and personality. This alteration in their self-definitions was cultivated by mass media and mass merchandising of the 1920s, which encouraged girls to think of themselves as a national cohort focused on fashion, fun, and romance, according to Kelly Schrum (18). Another factor may have influenced the

Amplifying Identity

rhetorical self-constructions of Barstow students: after leading the school for thirty-nine years, Mary Barstow retired in 1923 and returned to her family home in Gardiner, Maine. With the departure of this New Woman, girls lost their primary role model at the school, which was renamed the Barstow School (Brayman 24).

Meanwhile, the new girls that Mary Barstow helped to mold took different paths. Haff, for example, graduated from Vassar College and attended Miss Noyse's School of Dance in New York before returning to Kansas City to marry, rear a family, and work for community organizations ("Madeline H. Field"). Harris studied art at the Kansas City Art Institute and in Europe, becoming a professional painter and printmaker whose work is exhibited at the Nelson-Atkins Gallery in Kansas City. Harris also taught at Barstow, where she helped guide the daughters of Barstow new girls as they articulated and amplified their own identity in *The Weather-cock* (Craig).

The most economically and socially privileged girls in this study, Barstow girls did not confront the same rhetorical contingencies that girls faced at other schools in this study, as ensuing chapters confirm. Unlike Native American girls at the Haskell Institute, Barstow girls did not have to justify their credentials to readers who doubted their inherent intelligence and morality. In contrast to African American girls at Lincoln High School, Barstow girls did not have to defend their race. And as opposed to white girls at Central High School, Barstow girls did not have to argue for their right to speak to and for a student body that tended to be dominated by boys. That is not to say, however, that Barstow girls did not face any rhetorical challenges as they articulated their identity. Despite the prerogatives that their race and class afforded them, they were still young women in a time and place that imposed identities upon white girls rather than allowing them to define themselves. That fact is key to their use of amplification in *The Weather-cock* as the means for repeatedly asserting who they were.

CHAPTER 3

Persuading Diverse Audiences: Haskell Girls

> Life is that part of us which is Divine. It was given us by our Creator
> for the purpose of working out his wonderful will. . . . Each of us
> should have an aim in life and work toward it continually, and in
> this aim we should include doing good to those around us.
>
> —Nellie Wright, "Aim in Life"

IN MARCH 1897, NELLIE Wright was the only girl in an oratorical contest at
the Haskell Institute, the second largest off-reservation government boarding
school for Native Americans in the United States, forty miles west of Kansas City. Wright won second place in the competition, and her speech was
printed two months later in the Haskell newspaper, which was distributed
nationally to white and Native American readers. Promoting pride among
her peers, Wright also educated readers who doubted the capabilities and
motives of Native Americans.[1] As the epigraph suggests, she begins her epideictic address by invoking religious and cultural discourse of the day, a gesture that challenges white assumptions that Native Americans are indolent,
self-centered pagans ("Aim in Life" 4). Inspiring group identification among
Indians through her use of the collective pronouns "us" and "we," she avoids
distinguishing among the different tribes of her Native readers. While her
silence on that subject reflected the white campaign to destroy tribal identity,
her tactic also encourages Indian solidarity. Significantly, she is vague about
Native spirituality, leaving rhetorical room to accommodate a range of readers' beliefs. Although she does not declare herself a Christian nor affirm the
Christian ideology that informed Native American education at Haskell, she
cites Christ, whose goal was "the salvation of the human race" (4). Creating

Persuading Diverse Audiences

unity through her use of the adjective "human" to describe race, Wright suggests that Christ acted to save all members of this group, not merely the white ones. Her next assertion—"the best possible way to make life happy is to live for others"—appeals to Native and white readers by merging the communal values of Indians and the self-sacrifice expected of white women, while rejecting American individualism (4).

As Wright continues, she creates common ground with literate Native and white readers by quoting nineteenth-century social reformer Robert Dale Owen and writers Nathaniel Hawthorne and Ralph Waldo Emerson. Toward the end of her essay, she repeats the key verb, "aim," and proclaims: "We should aim high—aim above the common horde of men; we may reach what seems to be the unattainable and by urging ourselves on and on give new impulse and vigor to our lives" ("Aim in Life" 4). Exhorting her classmates to aspire to more than the menial jobs and working-class status that most students were trained to perform and embrace in Indian schools, Wright contradicts claims that indigenous peoples were incapable of achieving as much as whites. She encourages her Haskell classmates to think of themselves as competent citizens preparing to join society, not as ragged refugees forced to leave reservations. At the same time, she informs non-Native readers that Haskell students are neither noble savages nor pathetic remnants of a vanquished race; they are civilized members of society who espouse high ideals.

Reaching a much-broader audience through print than she did when she first presented this speech orally at Haskell, Wright fosters a pan-Indian sensibility among Native readers from different tribes. Like other young female epideictic rhetors at Haskell, she encourages Native Americans to think of themselves as Indians with common cause, rather than as Cherokee or Ponca or Sioux with different and possibly conflicting values and goals. This sensibility, cultivated by other educated Native Americans around the country, led to a national movement and the founding in 1911 of the Society of American Indians (SAI), which addressed industrial, educational, legal, and political issues relevant to all indigenous peoples in the country (Hertzberg 36, 60). Although Native American men dominated the SAI leadership, women, such as Zitkala-Ša, promoted the "Indian cause" through print. While Haskell produced leaders of the pan-Indian movement and cohosted the fifth annual SAI conference in 1915, Wright and her peers were in the vanguard of this epideictic campaign (Hertzberg 48, 135).

58
Persuading Diverse Audiences

Wright also broaches an issue seldom discussed in classical or contemporary theories of epideictic discourse—how an epideictic rhetor persuades an audience composed of auditors who do not share the same beliefs. Usually regarded as homogeneous, epideictic audiences may be heterogeneous, as in the case of readers of two Haskell student publications: the newspaper, the *Indian Leader*, and a folklore anthology, *Indian Legends* (1914). The audience for these publications comprised as many as eight hundred male and female Haskell pupils from eighty tribes in thirty-six states; Haskell alumni and families; tribal leaders; white Indian schoolteachers and administrators; and non-Native readers throughout the country ("Haskell Indian"; Wise). Readers of these Haskell publications included advocates of Native Americans and Indian education, and people who questioned the innate intelligence of indigenous peoples and their future in white society. There also were Natives who supported Indian education but disapproved of the often-harsh methods and assimilationist agenda of the Haskell Institute, which provided English literacy instruction, courses in industrial and vocational work, and for a time, teacher training.[2] To engage this mixed audience, Haskell girls extolled the abilities of students, chronicled Native beliefs, and exalted their status as "progressive Indians" who were preparing to join white society by espousing the attitudes and values of the dominant culture.[3]

This chapter considers how Haskell girls confronted the complexities of their audience through epideictic discourse published in the *Indian Leader* from 1897 to 1924 and *Indian Legends*. Assessing the persuasive discourse of young women from the inception of the Haskell newspaper to the year that the federal government granted full citizenship to all Native Americans, I chart the rhetorical means that Haskell girls used to reconcile skeptics, reassure sympathizers, and rouse support for Indian education and rights. In so doing, these young women confirm Dale L. Sullivan's assertion that epideictic rhetoric is determined not by a "constellation of forms" but by a "constellation of purposes" including education, preservation, and celebration (116). Each facet of this constellation also is part of identity formation: to form its identity, a group must educate its members and outsiders, preserve its history and folklore, and celebrate its successes. To inform readers about Native Americans, Haskell girls wrote about their educational activities and the current practices of Native Americans. To preserve their heritage, they narrated legends and narratives of their tribes. Celebrating their multiple identities as young Native female students training to become clerks, cooks,

Persuading Diverse Audiences

nurses, seamstresses, and teachers, they depicted themselves as model citizens, not social outcasts. Haskell girls often pursued more than one purpose in a single text; therefore, my analysis of their epideictic rhetoric is organized according to the publication that featured it. I begin with texts that were published in the *Indian Leader*; proceed chronologically, which allows for discussion of the shifting historical context that affected the persuasive discourse of Haskell girls; and conclude with assessment of the epideictic rhetoric of *Indian Legends*.

To read the published writing of Haskell girls as epideictic rhetoric is to take their texts seriously, even though I cannot prove that these young women always were responding to their marginalized position or that all of them deliberately tried to promote positive perceptions of Native Americans. Nonetheless, the examples that I provide, analyze, and contextualize can be interpreted as persuasive discourse that defines and praises their collective identity as progressive Indians.

My interpretative strategy also challenges assumptions about the agency of these young women to pursue their own purposes while supporting the official agenda of the *Indian Leader* and the implied purpose of *Indian Legends*. The newspaper announced its objectives in an editorial published in the initial issue of March 1897: "The *Leader* makes its first appearance in public modestly, even shyly. But having a mission to perform gives even youthful and modest persons courage" (Editorial 1897, 2). Evoking the image of a demure girl hesitant to enter public society, the editorial personifies the publication as a young person inspired by duty. The duty of the *Indian Leader* was two-fold: to foster communication between current and former students, "to give them a word of cheer, a helping hand," and to

> win new friends, to enter the homes of many who know but little of Indians and their capabilities, showing them that though of a different race, many of them are intelligent and progressive; that they have for their motto, "Onward and Upward" and are trying to live up to this. (2)[4]

The editorial intimates that the *Indian Leader* creates an association of enlightened Native Americans who reinforce the lessons of assimilation that students learned at Haskell while demonstrating the efficacy of Indian education. Haskell girls helped to build this coalition and confirm the potential of Native Americans, but they also advanced their own visions of their identity and capacities. Disputing white stereotypes of Native Americans as passive,

60
Persuading Diverse Audiences

dependent, and inferior, Haskell girls depicted themselves and their peers as active, independent, and superior young people bridging the gap between the past and the future of indigenous peoples.

The introduction of *Indian Legends* indicates that it was a showcase for the school. As Haskell Superintendent John R. Wise contends:

> Like other primitive peoples, the Indian race has a rich heritage of legendary lore. . . . These students, in their childhood days, heard the stories of their parents and grandparents, as they were related by the camp fires or in the homes. They have been encouraged by their teachers here to put these into written form, and this booklet is the result of an effort to select the best and most striking of their products. (Introduction)[5]

Patronizing Haskell students as "primitive" members of a monolithic "race," Wise also romanticizes the oral tradition of Native Americans and the ways that young people acquired their knowledge of these stories "related by the camp fires or in the homes," omitting realistic details, such as the setting of these storytelling sessions on often destitute reservations and in impoverished homes.

If paternalism guided the white teachers who solicited these narratives, and administrators saw the folklore anthology as both validation and promotion of the school, Haskell girls nonetheless took advantage of new opportunities to educate their diverse audience about the values and traditions of Native Americans while preserving their customs through this publication. Acknowledging this enterprise, I respond to the call of Scott Richard Lyons to focus on "the study of American Indian rhetoric—and the rhetoric of the Indian" (464). My study reveals the rhetorical challenges that Haskell girls faced and suggests that they were neither victims nor victors but young women making the most of their available means to represent themselves and their peoples to multiple audiences. In so doing, they offer insight on epideictic audiences that is relevant to the epideictic performances of other groups.

Perspectives on the Epideictic Audience

Audience is a crucial element of every type of rhetoric. Gideon O. Burton points out:

> All rhetorically oriented discourse is composed in light of those who will hear or read that discourse. Or, in other words, rhetorical analysis

61
Persuading Diverse Audiences

always takes into account how an audience shapes the composition of a text or responds to it. ("Audience")

Considerations of audience are closely linked to *kairos*, "the opportune occasion for a speech," and "thus, sensitive to *kairos*, a speaker or writer takes into account the contingencies of a given place and time, and considers the opportunities within this specific context for words to be effective and appropriate to that moment" (Burton, "Kairos"). Haskell girls encountered an unusual epideictic contingency: an audience that had different and sometimes contradictory ideas about Native Americans.

Although other epideictic orators and writers must have encountered diverse audiences over the centuries, classical and contemporary rhetoricians do not offer much guidance on how to appeal to different factions. Aristotle alludes to the composition of epideictic audiences, quoting Socrates as saying it was not difficult to praise Athenians in Athens, but neither Socrates nor Aristotle advise orators how to praise Athenians in, say, Sparta. Typically terse, Aristotle recommends that the epideictic rhetor should "consider also the audience before whom the praise [is spoken]. . . . And one should speak of whatever is honored among each people as actually existing [in the subject praised]" (*On Rhetoric* 79–80). To put Aristotle's advice another way, effective speakers express in their epideictic performances the values and beliefs of audience members.

Contemporary rhetoricians deduce that Aristotle views epideictic audiences as not merely recipients of conventional beliefs but as observers who actively respond to the messages of rhetors. Jeffrey Walker contends that the poetry of Sappho, the dialogues of Plato, and the argument of Isocrates for Panhellenic unification are epideictic discourse that asks audiences to "form opinions, or even revise their existing beliefs on a given topic" (9). The most famous epideictic speech of Aristotle's time, the funeral oration of Pericles, provides insight on Athenian audiences, according to George A. Kennedy:

> A speaker on a ceremonial occasion is faced with the challenge of trying to say something original and significant rather than to present a series of platitudes. But there are also audience expectations of what is traditionally appropriate, which a speaker should respect. (*New History* 22)

Athenians expected epideictic speakers to claim that their discourse was "inadequate to the occasion," to praise the ancestors of the dead by recounting

62
Persuading Diverse Audiences

important events in the history of the city, and to offer consolation to survivors (*New History* 22).

Brenda J. Child addresses the relationship between rhetors and audience in her cautionary observation about Indian school publications, such as the *Indian Leader.* She asserts: "Newspapers reflected the culture of boarding schools; even articles authored by American Indians were destined for a public audience and must therefore be approached with a measure of skepticism" (xii). Of course, the same can be said of writing in any periodical destined for a public audience. All texts reflect the "culture" of the publication, which may take a particular ideological or political approach to content, such as newspapers of the late nineteenth century that promoted the Spanish American War (Mott 527–45). The culture of Haskell also was more complex and less static than might be assumed. Over the years, it was affected by factors ranging from the unmarried white women who dominated the faculty to changes in Indian educational policy to the composition of the Haskell student population, as graduates began to send their own children and grandchildren to the school. Furthermore, there was not only one public audience for the *Indian Leader* but multiple audiences: current and past students who had both positive and negative feelings about their Haskell experiences, Native families who wanted their children to attend Haskell but worried about how students might be treated and how they might change, older Natives who were suspicious of the educational indoctrination of young Natives, tribal leaders who believed that education would enable young Indians to act on behalf of their home communities, white reformers who sympathized with Native Americans while refusing to acknowledge the cultural integrity of indigenous peoples, government officials and school administrators who debated Indian educational policy, and politicians who evaluated the arguments of administrators to determine Indian school budgets.

The content of the *Indian Leader* mirrored its multiple audiences. The first issue in March 1897, for instance, featured an inspirational poem, reprints of moralistic essays from religious periodicals, a history of the Haskell Institute, national news, reports on Haskell events, notices from other Indian schools, and compositions by two unidentified Haskell primary students. The poem and essays were intended to inspire Native American readers; the Haskell history apprised whites and prospective students about the origin and curriculum of the school; and the national news and reports on activities and people at Haskell and other Indian schools edified Haskell pupils and staff.

63

Persuading Diverse Audiences

The student compositions published in the *Indian Leader* encouraged both proponents and opponents of Indian education to recognize the tangible results of instruction at schools such as Haskell. As the following brief history of the Haskell Institute suggests, this instruction was seen as key to solving the so-called Indian problem.

The Haskell Institute

That problem was created by the defeat of thousands of Native Americans in the final Indian wars of the 1880s. While the U.S. government corralled Indians on reservations and attempted to force them to trade hunting for farming, and tribalism for individualism, white reformers promoted the assimilation rather than the ostracism of Native Americans—a significant difference from the white policy of segregating blacks, as I discuss in chapter 4. These ethnocentric activists regarded education as essential to Indian assimilation and favored boarding schools because they separated children from their families, enforced discipline, and controlled the learning environment (Trennert, *Phoenix* 4).[6]

Founded and financed by the government in 1884, the same year that Miss Barstow's School was established, the Haskell Institute was situated near Lawrence, Kansas. Although official records did not always note the number of male versus female students, it appears that boys usually outnumbered girls, but neither the records nor contemporary historians can fully account for this difference.[7] It seems likely that before Haskell established a reputation among Native Americans, some Native parents were leery of sending their daughters into an unknown environment far from home. Even after Haskell became better known, Native American parents, like white parents, may have felt protective of their girls and hesitated to enroll them. By the late nineteenth century, the gender inequity at Haskell was less pronounced. In 1899, the school counted 300 to 350 boys and 191 to 241 girls; these fluctuating numbers presumably reflect the coming and going of students that year (*Report of the Commissioner* 10, 394). Robert A. Trennert calculates that girls comprised from 40 to 50 percent of the student body at most of the twenty-five nonreservation Indian schools in operation from 1890 to 1910 ("Educating" 280).

The ages and tribal affiliations of Haskell students varied, with students as young as five and as old as twenty-five attending the school until 1909, when an effort was made to limit enrollment to students aged fourteen to eighteen

Persuading Diverse Audiences

("Opening" 2; Vučković 40). To achieve the government's goal of undermining tribal allegiance and fostering individualism, Haskell recruited students from different tribes and different areas of the country, deliberately mixing students who could not speak the same language, in order to force them to learn English. By the mid-1890s, students from thirty-five tribes attended Haskell; enrollment records indicate that the majority of students came from Kansas, Michigan, Minnesota, Nebraska, North Dakota, Oklahoma, South Dakota, and Wisconsin (Vučković 28, 34). By 1914 Haskell registered students from eighty tribes and twenty-eight states (Wise). Upon acceptance to Haskell, students were expected to stay for three years, but some young people were allowed to go home for summers. Not all Haskell students completed full terms, leaving for reasons of health or unhappiness or because their families wanted or needed them at home.

An article in the first issue of the *Indian Leader* in March 1897 describes the school and its programs, proudly noting the four main buildings on campus were three or four stories tall and constructed of stone, "heated by steam and fitted with all modern conveniences and sanitary apparatus" ("Haskell Institute" 2). Haskell required students to attend school half of the day, and "all those large enough do industrial work the other half of the day" (2). Whether "large" referred to age or size is not clear. What is clear is that labor was gendered and supported the operation of the school: girls practiced sewing, cooking, laundry management, and "all manner of domestic work" while boys learned farming, gardening, painting, shoemaking, carpentry, tailoring, harness making, wagon making, engineering, baking, and blacksmithing (2). The Haskell Institute also attempted to domesticate Native American girls through the social and religious activities of the Young Women's Christian Association and through the outing system, which sent Haskell girls to work as servants for white families in Kansas City and towns near Lawrence during the summer. Despite the emphasis on domestic training, the business, nursing, and teaching programs at Haskell were popular with girls and enabled graduates to pursue jobs other than as maids.

Although white reformers saw schools such as the Haskell Institute as crucial for assimilation, and some Native students saw them as the means to a positive end, there were critics of these institutions. One of the most outspoken opponents was Native American writer Zitkala-Ša, who recounts her experiences as a teacher at the Carlisle Indian School for *Atlantic Monthly* in 1900. Her critique of Carlisle cites unprepared and cruel teachers, the systematic

65
Persuading Diverse Audiences

hoodwinking of school inspectors, and the exhibition of Indian children as exotic relics to be viewed by white visitors. Zitkala-Ša ends her indictment of Indian schools by defiantly questioning "whether real life or long-lasting death lies beneath this semblance of civilization" ("Indian Teacher" 99).

Although Zitkala-Ša had grounds for criticism, contemporary historians offer more nuanced interpretations of Indian schools. Clifford E. Trafzer, Jean A. Keller, and Lorene Sisquoc call the boarding-school system of the late nineteenth and early twentieth centuries "a successful failure" (1). These scholars acknowledge that Indian schools in the United States and Canada offered varying degrees of academic, domestic, agricultural, and vocational education, but they failed "to assimilate completely Indian children or entirely destroy the essence of their being Native peoples" (1). The authors also note a consequence that whites did not anticipate: "Ironically, the American boarding school and Canadian residential school experience for many Native American children provided new skills in language, literature, mathematics, and history that strengthened their identities as Native Americans" (1). At Haskell, girls learned to speak and write English, which enabled them to compose tribal histories and conserve legends and traditions that cultivated the collective consciousness and pride of indigenous peoples.

The Rhetorical Contingencies and Responses of Haskell Girls

To perform epideictic rhetoric, Haskell girls confronted the gendered and racial assumptions of whites about Native Americans in general and Native women in specific. Myriam Vučković observes: "On the one hand, Anglo ethnocentrism had led to a vision of Indian women as drudges and slaves, toiling for their idle husbands and fathers in an environment of humiliation, immorality, and sexual exploitation" (115). This widespread white perception dictated that " indigenous girls had to be saved from a life of savagery, and their social standing as well as sexual role needed to be changed" (115). The paradox was that whites "recognized and exploited the important role of Indian women as culture brokers, who exercised great influence on their partners as well as their children" (115). Native American girls were seen as particularly important to achieving assimilation on the basis of racist and sexist logic: girls could be trained to be wives and mothers according to white standards and would then teach their children the lessons of the dominant culture.

Persuading Diverse Audiences

In 1896, the year before the *Indian Leader* was founded, Indian school administrator Mollie V. Gaither wrote in a national report that Indian schools should teach every Native American girl "the strength of character to become an independent, self-reliant woman, capable of assuming any burden that life [with] its manifold chances and changes may lay upon her" (Gaither 64). Like many pronouncements of white middle-class reformers who claimed authority to impose their cultural standards on Native Americans, as well as African Americans, immigrants, and lower classes, Gaither's proclamation is problematic. Acknowledging Native girls as important members of society, she expresses the common belief that these girls lack innate "strength of character," which must be instilled by whites. Gaither also seems to take a protofeminist position, claiming that Native American girls should strive for independence and self-reliance. Yet she implies that Native girls must attain these traits not for personal gain or individual happiness but in order to meet the extraordinary challenges that they would encounter in a society that marginalized them on the basis of race and gender. Gaither maintains, "Educate a man, you educate an individual; educate a woman, you educate a race" (64). Her edict is a variation of the motto of the early nineteenth-century "Republican Mother," who was privileged as the teacher of the boys who would become the leaders of the nation (Kerber 235).

Two years later, the *Indian Leader* reiterated Gaither's position by publishing "the wise utterances" of the white male Commissioner of Indian Affairs:

> The only way we can solve the Indian problem is to educate the girls. We have no objection to your educating the boys; make college graduates out of every Indian boy in the land, but unless you educate the girls, the solution of the Indian problem is as far away as it ever was. The superiority, so-called, of the white race to-day is owing entirely to the condition of our mothers and sisters. ("We Quote" 4)[8]

This ideology supplied the ethos, or credentials, of Haskell girls to speak from the pages of the *Indian Leader* and *Indian Legends*. What these young women say, however, often subverted as well as supported government objectives for Native Americans. Expected to save the "race" by promoting assimilation, Haskell girls also encouraged recognition of Native American achievements, potential, and humanity, through the epideictic rhetoric that they delivered in the Haskell newspaper and folklore anthology.

67
Persuading Diverse Audiences

Although historians have used the unpublished papers, recorded testimonies, and personal letters of Native American students as primary sources in histories of Indian education, and a few scholars have used rhetorical theory to assess the persuasive discourse of adult Native Americans (Enoch; Kennedy, *Comparative Rhetoric*; Stromberg), there is scant scholarship on the rhetorical activities of young Indians.[9] Yet some scholars read resistance as well as accommodation in the texts of Native American students. For example, Amy Goodburn notes that girls at the Genoa Indian School in Genoa, Nebraska, wrote essays in the late 1800s that support assimilation, but these girls also charge that whites helped to create the "Indian situation" by displacing indigenous peoples (89). Amelia V. Katanski identifies a dialectic that she calls "learning to write 'Indian'" created by Native American boarding-school students who used their newly acquired literacy skills to produce a "wide-ranging literary response to their educations, writing back to the institution to claim . . . their voices, cultures, nations, and histories" (6). This dialectic is comparable to Mikhail M. Bakhtin's conception of dialogism, or double-voicing, which Cheryl Glenn detects in the medieval rhetoric of Margery Kempe (108), and Shirley Wilson Logan links to the "multiple positioning" of African American women rhetors of the nineteenth century (177).

Bakhtin articulates his concept of dialogism most fully in "Discourse in the Novel" (Leitch 1073). He theorizes that language is "never unitary" (288) and contends:

> The dialogic orientation of discourse is a phenomenon that is, of course, a property of *any* discourse. It is the natural orientation of any living discourse. On all its various routes toward the object, in all its directions, the word encounters an alien word and cannot help encountering it in a living, tension-filled interaction. Only the mythical Adam, who approached a virginal and as yet verbally unqualified world with the first word, could really have escaped from start to finish this dialogic inter-orientation with the alien word that occurs in the object. (279)

Explicating Bakhtin's rather opaque discussion of dialogism, Phyllis Margaret Paryas avows that he thought of double-voicing in two ways:

> In the first sense, double-voicing is a characteristic of all speech in that no discourse exists in isolation but is always part of a greater whole; it is necessarily drawn from the context of the language world which

68
Persuading Diverse Audiences

preceded it. Because language is a social phenomenon, it can never be neutral and free from the intentions of others. (537)

The "intentions of others" may include the attitudes of auditors who are part of this "greater whole." Bakhtin also viewed double-voicing as "an element discernible in discourse when the speaker wants the listener to hear the words as spoken with 'quotation marks'" (537). Paryas suggests that speakers use these figurative quotation marks to signal that there is an alternative point of view embedded in their discourse.

Native American writer Sarah Winnemucca uses double-voicing in her autobiography, *Life among the Piutes* (1884). Andrew S. McClure argues:

> Winnemucca's blurring of savage and civilized is evidence of dialogism found throughout her prose: it is loaded with double meanings and what M. M. Bakhtin terms "hybrid constructions," indicating a pervasive tension between the conflicting cultural systems she finds herself in the middle of. (47)

To prove his point, McClure cites several passages in which Winnemucca refers to European Americans as "white brothers" or "white sisters," phrases that are surrounded by figurative quotation marks, denoting alternative viewpoints. The idea that whites are the brothers and sisters of Native Americans comes from a Paiute legend that whites and Paiutes were descended from the same forefathers but were separated by a dispute that would eventually be resolved and allow them to be reunited—a belief that made the Paiutes friendly toward whites and thus vulnerable to white abuse. Winnemucca's use of these phrases serve as ironic emphasis that supposedly "civilized" whites seldom acted like "brothers" or "sisters" to the reputedly "savage" Paiutes (McClure 48–49).

Like Winnemucca, Haskell girls used double-voicing to speak to the competing discourses that surrounded their performances of epideictic rhetoric, and to suggest different perspectives within a single text. Wright, for example, evokes the communal sensibility of Native Americans and the white ideal of the True Woman by claiming that "the best possible way to make life happy is to live for others." Her call to aim high above "the common horde of men" carries invisible quotation marks that imply the common horde encompassed both whites and Native Americans who fail to fulfill their potential. As these Native American women suggest, double-voicing is a viable epideictic strategy for responding to kairos, particularly when that occasion involves rhetors and auditors who do not share the same ideas.

Persuading Diverse Audiences

The Epideictic Rhetoric of Haskell Girls in the Indian Leader

The Haskell newspaper provided a platform for Native American girls to deliver epideictic rhetoric to a diverse audience. Produced by male students in the Haskell print shop, the *Indian Leader* initially was a monthly publication; in September 1898, it became a bimonthly, and a weekly in October 1899. Generally, issues were four pages. Marking commencement in June, longer editions identified as the "Annual Number" served as a yearbook until a traditional yearbook was introduced at Haskell in 1923. Beginning in September 1916, Haskell issued a magazine, also called *The Indian Leader*, which replaced the newspaper once a month. The newspaper published announcements by administrators; excerpts from professional periodicals; notices about current and former students, teachers, and supervisors; and the writing of both female and male pupils.

Establishing an egalitarian policy from the beginning of its publication, the *Indian Leader* newspaper features roughly equal numbers of female and male student writers through the course of several issues. For example, the April 1897 issue published essays on the topics of "Providence in History" and "Liberty" by two Haskell boys and no texts by girls. The next three issues, however, privileged girls: Nellie Wright's oration in May 1897; the autobiography of a nineteen-year-old girl in June 1897; and Ada Brenninger's "My First Experience in Housekeeping" on the front page of the July 1897 issue.

This gender parity may have been encouraged by Helen W. Ball, a white Haskell teacher who probably supervised the production of the *Indian Leader* from its introduction in March 1897 and was named as its editor in the June 1898 issue. The newspaper lists Ball as editor until August 1908 (Littlefield and Parins 197). Before she came to Haskell in September 1889, Ball attended the University of Kansas, also in Lawrence. After college, she worked for newspapers in Indiana, Kansas, and Kansas City and reportedly was the best-paid woman journalist west of New York City ("Helen W. Ball" 2–3). Ball played a central, if conflicted, role as editorial gatekeeper of the Haskell newspaper. As a woman, she ensured that young female students were represented in the *Indian Leader*; as a white Indian service employee, she also made certain that Haskell girls did not criticize the school in their contributions. To be sure, young women served the official editorial purpose of the publication by composing narratives, commentary, and essays that confirmed the efficacy of Indian assimilation through education. Yet, in

70
Persuading Diverse Audiences

the next two decades, they also created and commended Native American group identity in this periodical.

In the June 1901 issue of the *Indian Leader*, for example, two girls pursued the epideictic purposes of education, preservation, and celebration in essays about the long histories and sophisticated social systems of their respective tribes. Informing white readers who were unfamiliar with the Pueblo and Munsee, these young women also encouraged Native readers to take pride in the distinguished past and current status of these groups. In her history of the Pueblo, Belle Marmon, a normal-school student from Laguna, New Mexico, describes her tribe's different clans, democratic government, innovative agricultural methods, and religious beliefs. She stresses that the Pueblo were dutiful parents:

> The Pueblo parents are very careful in the bringing up of their children to be useful men and women. And an educated child is the pride of the family. There is nothing the parents would put down sooner than disobedience and disrespect to parents. The mother takes great pride in making home pleasant in every respect. ("Story")

Appealing to whites in her audience, Marmon emphasizes that the Pueblo privilege the dominant-culture ideals of domesticity, industry, and adult authority.

Katie Veix, a Munsee from Ottawa, Kansas, who was in her late teens and a student in the commercial department, or business training program, followed suit in her description of the Munsee. She reports that the main occupations of the Munsee are farming and raising stock and contends that a traveler passing through a Munsee settlement in Kansas "would never know by the appearance of the farms that he was not among white people. The residents are in every sense of the word loyal, intelligent American citizens" ("Munsee"). Praising their peoples, Marmon and Veix preserve the beliefs and practices of their tribes, encouraging Native readers to take pride in their indigenous identity and heritage—despite concerted efforts by whites to erase both. Secondly, Marmon and Veix educate government officials and non-Native readers that American Indians were civilized and fit for citizenship that would not be granted to all tribes until 1924. Pointing out that the Pueblo gained citizenship in 1848 and the Munsee in 1886, these young women imply that all Native Americans should have citizenship. Marmon celebrates the historical autonomy of the Pueblo to counter the notion that Indians were incapable of self-government; Veix commends the successful assimilation of the Munsee to prove their capacity for "civilization."

71
Persuading Diverse Audiences

In appealing to the different factions of their audience, Marmon and Veix demonstrate double-voicing. Mindful that whites expected Native Americans to adopt the practices and perspectives of the dominant culture—or practices and perspectives that whites claimed to value—these young women argue that their tribes already espoused them. Veix's dialogic assertion that the Munsee had proved to be "loyal, intelligent American citizens" undercuts the assumption that only whites could be loyal, intelligent, and worthy of citizenship.

Most of the early epideictic rhetoric of Haskell girls praised Natives and refrained from blaming whites for the plight of indigenous peoples. A noteworthy exception was Minnie Riley's essay "The Returned Student," published in the 1 July 1899 *Indian Leader.* Riley, a Shawnee from Indian Territory who was in her early twenties and a senior in the Haskell normal school, criticized whites for corrupting Native American boys when they graduated from the institute and returned to their homes. She began by pronouncing the potential of these young men to be teachers, leaders, and examples to their race, thus reinforcing group pride among Haskell students and their families. That potential was threatened, however, by the exigencies of reservation life. To prepare her white readers to accept her indictment of whites, Riley creates common ground: "The Indian youth's environment is not entirely unlike that of his white brother, for he is surrounded by two classes of people, the good and the bad." Depicting Natives and whites as members of the same family, Riley construes class in moral rather than economic or social terms:

> But he [the Native youth] is sought after more as a prey by the bad. The young man returns from school; he is kindly welcomed by all. He meets the bad white man who claims to be his friend and tries to entice the youth from his work and lead him away from purity to intemperance. The youth often gives way because he has not yet learned the lesson of self-control. Young men are frequently placed in circumstances in which they require heroic determination to resist the temptation to drink.

Riley alludes to the alcoholism that plagued Native American reservations, but she points out that whites provided the liquor. There are two reasons why Native youths drink, according to Riley. Lack of self-control is one; the other is "circumstances," her euphemism for factors influencing the lives of returning students. Those factors ranged from the often desperate conditions on reservations to racism that limited the economic and social opportunities

72
Persuading Diverse Audiences

of Indian school graduates. Accusing white men of supplying vulnerable young men with liquor, Riley characterizes Native Americans as victims rather than wastrels and educates whites about the reasons for alcoholism on reservations.

Riley also positions young Native American women in the temperance movement led by white women—a dialogic gesture that authorizes her criticism of white men. As Carol Mattingly notes, women who delivered temperance rhetoric in the nineteenth century often emphasized the suffering of the children of male alcoholics (32–37). Riley extends this argument by suggesting that white men caused a new form of suffering by introducing susceptible young Native men to the evils of intoxicating drink. Making white men the Other, Riley uses the same tactic that Barstow girls used in their treatment of the young black girl who wanted to be a white ballerina and the French girl who did not measure up to the American girl.

During the second decade of the *Indian Leader*, the tone of the epideictic rhetoric of Haskell girls became more subdued. One of the possible reasons for this rhetorical shift was a change in curriculum. By the turn of the century, Indian school administrators had decided that Native Americans should be trained for manual, not professional, labor. In 1898, Estelle Reel, the first woman to serve as U.S. superintendent of Indian schools, recommended that Indian schools should emphasize vocational rather than professional training for both young women and men ("Miss Reel" 2). Three years later, Reel introduced a new "Course of Study for Indian Schools," which privileged vocational over academic education. Vučković characterizes Reel as a social evolutionist who

> assumed most Indian children would return to an environment at the periphery of American society, where they would not need extensive academic training. In Reel's view, Indian education was supposed to make the students productive and self-sufficient members of society, who would no longer require the government's support. (93)

Thus, Reel's goal was to acculturate Native Americans to white society through education, not to assimilate them into that society.

In response to Reel's actions, Haskell superintendent H. B. Peairs acquired authorization to establish a domestic science department at the school in January 1899 ("Domestic Science Department" 2). In September 1902, Commissioner of Indian Affairs William A. Jones wrote to Peairs that Indian schools should only offer education to the eighth grade, as in common schools of the

Persuading Diverse Audiences

country. Jones added that the money required to fund the Haskell normal and commercial departments would be better spent on industrial training (Vučković 94). Vučković maintains that white educators wanted Native Americans "to find their 'proper place' in society, a place among other marginalized groups as obedient members of the rural and later urban working class at the bottom of the capitalist hierarchy" (93). The commercial department and the normal department were eliminated in 1903 (94). Ironically, the demand for clerical workers in the Indian Service led Haskell to open a business department in 1906, but the normal-school program was not revived until 1921 (94). As a result, academically inclined students, such as Wright, were steered into courses of study that did not offer the same opportunities for rhetorical instruction and display as did the teacher-training program. One of the possible consequences is that girls contributed less explicit examples of epideictic rhetoric to the *Indian Leader.*

Another change may have affected the epideictic rhetoric of Haskell girls. In August 1908, Helen Ball's name disappeared from the *Indian Leader*, thus ending an anomaly among Indian school newspapers, which usually were edited by the male superintendents of these schools (Littlefield and Parins 197). Ball reportedly relinquished her duties to become librarian of Haskell, but she continued to report for the newspaper until her death in 1924 ("Helen W. Ball" 2). Presumably, Superintendent Peairs became editor of the *Indian Leader* in 1908 and was succeeded by the subsequent superintendents, H. H. Fiske (1910–11), Wise (1911–17), and Peairs when he again served as superintendent (1917–26) (Littlefield and Parins 197–98). While Peairs and Fiske followed Ball's editorial formula, Wise increased the size of the newspaper from four to eight pages on occasion and introduced a monthly magazine issue that replaced a regular weekly issue. The magazine issues were longer, printed on better-quality paper, and offered lengthier features and photographs emphasizing Indian education and "progress." For lack of funding, Peairs discontinued publication of the magazine on a regular basis in 1922 (Littlefield and Parins 197–98).

Reading between the lines, I suspect that the male superintendents wanted to control the editorial content of the *Indian Leader* more closely than had Ball, and thus they ensured that student texts such as Riley's epideictic blaming of white men who corrupted Native American boys were not published. The historical record of Wise, for example, suggests that he was particularly conscious of the reputation of the institute. In 1912 he defended the enrollment of students of less than one-fourth Indian blood in reaction to objections that

74

Persuading Diverse Audiences

Haskell had too many ineligible students; in 1914, he reassured a concerned official that Haskell girls observed female dress codes by wearing corsets; and in 1916, in a letter to the Indian commissioner, he praised the social skills of Haskell students (Vučković 42, 70–71, 146). Although none of this evidence speaks directly to Wise's editorial stance, it suggests his interest in promoting positive images of the institute through regulation of the persuasive discourse of girls in the *Indian Leader*.

Despite these changes in the Haskell program and newspaper management, girls continued to engage in epideictic rhetoric in the 1910s. Their articles about Native musical, vocal, and dance presentations preserved and celebrated traditions that were integral to Indian identity. Accounts of student associations allowed girls to educate white and Native readers about the organizational skills and intellectual pursuits of progressive Indians. The names of club officers and results of elections were carefully recorded, as were programs including debates, readings of literature and original literary works, and performances of both white and Native music and dance. These details alerted readers that Natives had mastered white rules of governance and were capable of appreciating and creating art.

Haskell girls rarely addressed gender overtly in their epideictic rhetoric, even though the suffrage movement was gaining momentum during the 1910s, culminating with the passage in August 1920 of the Nineteenth Amendment, which granted women the right to vote. Like African American girls at Lincoln High School in Kansas City, Native American girls at Haskell were marked literally by their physical appearance and figuratively by the burdens imposed upon their "race" during this era. Consequently, these young women generally privileged race over gender in their persuasive discourse of identity.

Deviating from that tendency, Haskell student Carrie B. Splitlog celebrated young female graduates of the nursing program in the June 1917 *Indian Leader*. Splitlog was a Seneca from Grove, Oklahoma, who enrolled at Haskell as an eighteen-year-old in July 1913 and was readmitted in 1916 for a year to complete her studies. In "Our Vocational Course and What It Provides for Girls," she advises:

> The girl who completes this course can be of great service to her own people as well as to the people of any community where she may choose to follow her calling. She should be able to maintain herself well with the training she receives in this course. (17)

75
Persuading Diverse Audiences

Native American female nurses, according to Splitlog, were qualified to care for whites as well as Indians. They also had the power to choose where they worked and to support themselves with that work. Speaking for Natives who had been treated as dependent wards of the nation for decades, Splitlog demonstrates double-voicing by declaring Indian independence through participation in the workforce, thus appealing to Natives and whites who saw Indian commitment to organized occupations as essential to assimilation.

Meanwhile, some Haskell girls argued for citizenship through epideictic rhetoric that educated a range of readers. The Haskell commencement program in June 1920 featured a student debate by two coed teams on the subject: "That no person should be denied citizenship in the United States on account of his or her race." Emily Washee, a twenty-year-old Cheyenne from Colony, Oklahoma, and a student in the Haskell home economics department, argued for the affirmative. Her full oration is reprinted in the magazine version of *The Indian Leader* of 18 June 1920.[10] Although a debate usually is classified as deliberative rhetoric that attempts to exhort or dissuade an audience on a particular issue, Washee inserts an epideictic element:

> Certain requisites other than race should determine who shall share in our treasured liberties. Courage in the face of difficulty, industry, loyalty to truth and our Nation, sympathy for and courtesy to one's fellow men, and reverence and obedience to God are the requisites for good citizenship. . . . Would anyone here assert that yellow, brown, and red races have not appreciation for these essential things? ("Briefs" 13)

Referring to Asians and dark-skinned immigrants, who were subject to suspicion and restrictive immigration policies, Washee leaves no doubt that she includes Native Americans—the red race—in her statement that justifies the granting of citizenship to these groups. She then reflects her own position as a progressive Indian, claiming that "enlightenment rather than race should be a prerequisite for citizenship" (13). Enumerating the common knowledge of the enlightened—literacy skills, familiarity with U.S. laws, financial self-sufficiency, patriotism, and the willingness to sacrifice life and property if necessary—she defines herself and her Haskell peers as worthy candidates for citizenship (13).

To put Washee's rhetoric into historical context and thus explicate her double-voicing of competing discourses, she wrote during the Red Scare, a period of heightened national anxiety about strikers, radicals, and immigrants

76
Persuading Diverse Audiences

during the economic recession that followed the end of World War I. In 1919 one out of five American workers went on strike—the highest number to that point in U.S. history—to secure better wages and working conditions and the right to engage in collective bargaining. Although many Americans were sympathetic to workers and their efforts to form unions, some people associated strikes with radical immigrants and anarchists who mailed or delivered bombs to thirty-six public figures between April and June 1919. After the rise of communism in Russia, the United States feared communism's spread and deported 249 foreign-born radicals, including anarchist and feminist Emma Goldman (Jones et al. 702). Linking immigration and radicalism, the U.S. Congress restricted immigration in 1921. Three years later, the Johnson-Reid Act banned immigration from East Asia and reduced the quota for Europeans from 3 to 2 percent, based on the 1890 census; the effect was that northwestern Europeans were favored, and southern and eastern Europeans were ostracized (Jones et al. 713–14). Although Washee's rhetoric was published before these laws were enacted, she uses double-voicing to speak to and against discourses that surrounded her championing of Native Americans and other peoples not considered white.

The call for full citizenship for all Native Americans grew louder in the early 1920s, as prominent Natives and "Friends of the Indian" spoke and wrote publicly on this subject. Unfortunately, there is a gap in the record of the rhetorical contributions of Haskell girls to this campaign through the *Indian Leader* because the newspaper ceased publication in December 1921 for nine months to comply with a congressional act that suspended government publications that were not specifically approved by the Joint Committee on Printing (Littlefield and Parins 198). Coincidentally—or not—when the *Indian Leader* resumed publication on 29 September 1922, there was no further mention of Native American citizenship in its pages. Nor were there many examples of epideictic rhetoric by Haskell girls. The publication did not acknowledge the passage of the Indian Citizenship Act of 1924, which granted all Native Americans in the United States full citizenship rights.

Looking back, it is apparent that the turn of the century was a high point for the epideictic rhetoric of Native American girls in the *Indian Leader*. The most compelling examples of persuasive discourse delivered by these young women include Wright's 1897 address, Marmon and Veix's tribal histories

Persuading Diverse Audiences

of 1901, and Riley's pointed critique of whites in 1899. Speaking to myriad members of their audience and using the technique of double-voicing, these girls put to practice the contemporary theory of epideictic rhetoric as a constellation of purposes that can include education, preservation, and celebration. They attempted to enlighten whites about Native Americans and informed Native Americans about progressive Indians. They celebrated Native American history by preserving it in written accounts. Riley made rare use of the blame strategy of epideictic rhetoric: creating unity among her Native readers by forthrightly criticizing whites for causing some of the problems that students encountered when they returned to reservations, she absolved Native Americans of full responsibility for problems, such as alcohol abuse. If the quantity of epideictic rhetoric Haskell girls perform in the *Indian Leader* decreased during the 1910s as the result of the shift from academic to vocational training that limited opportunities for rhetorical instruction and display and of the replacement of the woman editor by the male Haskell superintendents, the quality did not. Splitlog praises the potential of young Native women to serve both Native and white communities, as well as themselves. Washee persuades readers that Native Americans possessed the requisite traits for civil rights and should be judged on their intellectual abilities and moral qualities, not their race.

As these Native girls attend to the contingencies of their rhetorical occasions, they use some of the same epideictic strategies as white women's rights activists and the African American women leaders of the racial uplift movement. Like white women, Haskell girls capitalize on their cultural designation as teachers to instruct readers; like African American women, they privilege race over gender to forge unity among Native Americans and earn the respect of whites. Haskell girls accommodate their classification by white educators as "representative Indians," a phrase Jessie W. Cook, an educator at an Indian boarding school, coined in 1900 to describe well-known boarding-school graduates, such as Charles Alexander Eastman, Francis La Flesche, Carlos Montezuma, Dennison Wheelock, and Zitkala-Ša (Katanski 37–38). Echoing the racial uplift rhetoric of African Americans of the era, Cook contended that these Indians would "pull their race up with them" (qtd. in Katanski 38). Reappropriating the racist connotations of "representative Indian," Haskell girls represent themselves and their peoples on their own terms, an epideictic agenda that they further pursue in their folklore anthology.

78
Persuading Diverse Audiences

The Epideictic Rhetoric of Haskell Girls in Indian Legends

In 1914 Haskell girls demonstrated the epideictic purposes of education and preservation in *Indian Legends*. An anthology of writing by current and former students, the 104-page soft-cover publication features texts by nineteen girls and twenty-five boys who are identified by their names and tribes; seven texts are attributed to "a former pupil." Their contributions include stories about the origins of natural elements and phenomena, such as tornadoes and thunder; accounts of interactions between animals and humans; and essays on social and religious customs. These myths and narratives constitute "epideictic forms" that transmit "cultural values," according to Kennedy (*Comparative Rhetoric* 108).

The booklet was produced by the Haskell printing department and probably to keep costs down had few illustrations: a drawing of an arrowhead is on the cover, and small swastikas, a Native American emblem of abundance and friendship and not yet associated with German Nazis, are printed above the title of each composition (fig. 3.1). As Haskell superintendent Wise indicates in the introduction to *Indian Legends*, these texts are the product of classroom assignments. Most likely, Haskell administrators regarded the publication as proof of the success of the school. The final page of the collection offers information about the Haskell Institute; therefore, it can be seen as a marketing tool as well.

Haskell administrators and teachers also must have been aware of the growing interest in Indian legends—an ironic counterpoint to the goals of Native American assimilation as whites attempted to "kill the Indian to save the man," in the infamous words of Indian-school administrator Richard Henry Pratt (Katanski 3). In 1879 the Smithsonian Institute founded the Bureau of Ethnology to sponsor ethnological and archaeological research in North America, and anthropologists initially concentrated on the oral literature of Native American cultures. As the twentieth century progressed, historians, musicologists, folklorists, and literary critics compiled and analyzed the myths, legends, songs, and other folklore forms of Native Americans (Clements and Malpezzi xiii).

Native Americans contributed to this project. For example, Eastman wrote *Red Hunters and the Animal People* (1904), and Marie McLaughlin composed *Myths and Legends of the Sioux* (1916) (Spack 59). Zitkala-Ša was the first Native to use English to tell Dakota stories without the assistance

Persuading Diverse Audiences

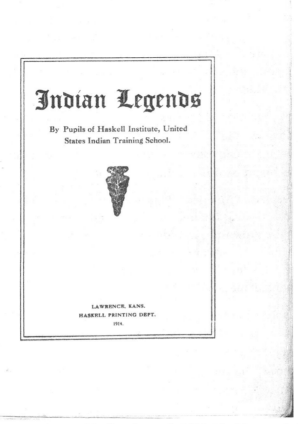

Figure 3.1. Cover of *Indian Legends*, 1914. Used by permission of the University of Missouri–Kansas City Libraries, Dr. Kenneth J. LaBudde Department of Special Collections.

of an interpreter. Talking to elders in her Dakota community and gathering their narratives, she produced *Old Indian Legends* in 1901 (Spack 51, 59). Significantly, the title page of the first edition carries the caveat "Retold by Zitkala-Ša," a double-voicing gesture that credentials the collection for Native readers who might question its authenticity and convinces white readers that Zitkala-Ša is the conduit for the collection, not its creator. In the preface to the book, she comments, "The legends are relics of our country's once virgin soil" (v). Although Ruth Spack does not use the concept of double-voicing to explain the reference to "relics," her remarks suggest that Zitkala-Ša uses this strategy:

Persuading Diverse Audiences

To a turn-of-the-century Anglo audience, the term "relics," penned by a Native author, may have denoted only remnants: surviving traces of a people believed to be vanishing from the American landscape. In the context of Native oral traditions, however, the relics (legends) carry far greater significance, for language and literature hold potent "sacred matter," as N. Scott Momaday puts it. (45)

Spack argues that Zitkala-Ša uses these "relics" to preserve and share the Dakota worldview.

In the preface to *Old Indian Legends*, Zitkala-Ša also implies that she has an epideictic purpose in conserving these stories:

The old legends of America belong quite as much to the blue-eyed little patriot as to the black-haired aborigine. And when they are grown tall like the wise grown-ups may they not lack interest in a further study of Indian folklore, a study which so strongly suggests our near kinship with the rest of humanity and points a steady finger toward the great brotherhood of mankind. (vi)

Persuading both white and Native readers that she shares stories of "America," not merely "Native America," Zitkala-Ša defines the collective identity of the country. Equally noteworthy is her use of the pronoun "they" in the second sentence. The antecedents of "they" are the white "patriot" and the "aborigine"; therefore, she signals her view that the study of "Indian folklore" is important to both of these audiences. She concludes by reinforcing her epideictic assertion that this study leads to recognition of the "great brotherhood of mankind," an inclusive association that does not distinguish members by race. Haskell girls would reiterate this argument by telling stories that helped readers recognize the similarities, rather than the differences, between Native Americans and whites.

Taking a skeptical view of the interest of white Haskell administrators and teachers in Indian legends, Vučković contends that the school

treated Indian cultural expressions as interesting anthropological artifacts of a vanishing race but not as living cultures. The stories Indian students collected were worth preserving for their entertaining and historical value, but they were clearly "superstitions" of a primitive people. (105)

Regardless of the reasons that white Haskell employees published these texts, the stories that girls contributed to the Haskell folklore anthology enabled

Persuading Diverse Audiences

these young women to act as ethnographers who conserve oral narratives through written transcriptions.

Educating white auditors about Native American funerary, medical, and religious practices in *Indian Legends*, the young women countered assumptions that Indians lacked such rituals and knowledge. Reporting on the customs and beliefs of specific tribes, the girls informed whites that there were differences among indigenous people, contrary to the conventional wisdom that all Indians were alike. Drawing a parallel between Native Americans and ancient Greeks, a girl enabled both Indian and white readers to discern the similarities of cultural mythology. Girls also exercised their English literacy skills to preserve Native stories. In an era when many stories were told about Indians rather than by Indians, Haskell girls forged unity among Native readers by conserving their own legends, thus joining adult Native Americans of the pan-Indian movement.

Catering to the anthropological interest of whites in their audience, several Haskell girls describe burial rites in their contributions to *Indian Legends*. Mary Horsechief relates:

> The Indians don't believe in putting shoes on a dead body, because they say that they cannot find their way into heaven, because of their shoes. They don't bury them with their heads to the east because they say they ought to rise with the sun the first morning after death, and go to the land of the hereafter. (30)

Although Horsechief was a full-blooded Ponca from White Eagle, Oklahoma, she does not distinguish among Ponca rites and those of other tribes. She does, however, inform white readers that Native Americans believe in an afterlife and practice their own social rituals as she conserves these practices for posterity.

Julia Bongo, a Chippewa from Ponsford, Minnesota, notes differences as well as commonalities among the burial customs of Native Americans and whites: "The Indians before they ever knew anything about the white people's ways of burial had their way of burying their dead" (56). Having established the fact that Indians had funeral rites of their own, Bongo then carefully recounts rituals, such as shooting arrows "to show that the soul of the dying person is starting on its journey to the other life"—testimony to Native beliefs in the concepts of the soul and afterlife. After the dead person is dressed and wrapped in a blanket that serves as a coffin, Indians "dig a

Persuading Diverse Audiences

grave just as the white people do, but the body is not laid out at full length in it, but it is set up like any living person would sit" (56). One of the interesting aspects of Bongo's account is her use of present-tense verbs, a hint that Indians still observed these customs in her time and that she thus preserved their practices through print.

Along the same epideictic lines, Mary M. Chase reminds readers of another similarity between whites and Native Americans in "The Medicine Man": "The Indians have their doctors, too, as well as the white man, and have their way of healing the sick by roots and different kinds of herbs" (83). Creating common ground among Native and white readers, Chase engages in double-voicing by blurring the significant differences between Native medicine men and white doctors. In 1905 Omaha writer Francis La Flesche relates that Europeans called Native American prophets and priests "medicine men," but they were known in Indian languages as the "Men of Mystery" (273). The duties of the men of mystery were myriad: they dedicated children to the Great Spirit, conducted the installation of chiefs, called leaders to war councils and conferred military honors, appointed tribal officers, designated planting times, and officiated at ceremonies, such as "the introduction to the cosmos of a newly born babe" (273). As La Flesche puts it, the figure whom whites called the medicine man was "the mediator between his people and the Great Spirit" (275)—a role that whites did not typically assign to medical doctors.

Chase may have had personal experience with medicine men: she was a full-blooded Chippewa from the Red Lake Agency in Minnesota, and both of her parents were dead when she applied in her late teens to Haskell in 1907. Omitting the many duties of this important tribal member, Chase continues in educational mode by concentrating on the medicine man's healing rituals. She reports that the medicine man requires a gift of tobacco from the sick person because "tobacco is one of the most pleasing gifts to the Great Spirit, and without it the medicine man could not exercise his powers" (83). Clearly, the medicine man depends on divine assistance as well as human action, which she then details. While whites in her audience may have been disconcerted by her description of the medicine man's singing, dancing, narration of dreams, and self-induced vomiting, some of them must have realized that white doctors of the day engaged in practices that could be considered unusual. Chase also uses present-tense verbs, a double-voicing tactic that suggests the medicine man is not merely a vestige of Native American society but an integral part of it, just as the doctor is an essential part of white society.

83
Persuading Diverse Audiences

Acting as ethnographers, some Haskell girls, to conserve customs, took the epideictic opportunity that *Indian Legends* offered. Julia Seelatsee, who was born in 1887 and was a full-blooded Wasco from the Yakima reservation near Fort Simco, Washington, discusses Native holiday traditions. In "Christmas Festival among Indians," she observes:

> I will try to tell of the way the Indians spend their Christmas on the Yakima Reservation. Of course this only refers to the Indians who have not yet been civilized—those who still cling to their old Indian ways and customs. (87)

Identifying herself as a progressive Indian, Seelatsee appeals to her Native American peers who regarded themselves as the same, as well as whites who supported Indian assimilation. Yet she is neutral in her account of the holiday rituals of members of her tribe who practiced "old Indian ways and customs." Describing the hunting, cooking, and feasting that took place, Seelatsee notes that "after their dinner is over they dance all kinds of dances. Some of them are very pretty to witness, especially when they are dressed in their native costumes. They also sing some pretty religious Indian songs" (88). By preserving Yakima traditions, Seelatsee informs white readers that her tribe has religious practices that are comparable to their own—even if they are a bicultural blending of Native and Christian customs.

One of the more remarkable examples of epideictic rhetoric by a Haskell girl in *Indian Legends* simultaneously educates readers and preserves a legend. Rebecca Turcotte frames her rendition of a Sioux story with a provocative suggestion: "The Indians are said to have been very superstitious in their religious beliefs, somewhat like the Greeks of old" (62). Several aspects of her statement are notable. First, she creates discursive distance between how Indians view their religious beliefs and how their beliefs are viewed by others through her phrasing, "the Indians are said to have been." Next, she crafts a syllogism that argues Native Americans are superstitious, and ancient Greeks were superstitious; therefore, Native Americans are like Greeks. Turcotte's logic calls into question the demonization of Native Americans by whites who revered the ancient Greeks. Elevating Native American mythology to the level of Greek mythology, Turcotte tells "The Story of Little Bear." Like Greek myths, it features a Zeus-like thunder god who had seven brave and warlike sons. Like the Greek gods, they live in the clouds or sky and tend to take advantage of humans. The youngest son, Little Bear, sees a beautiful

84
Persuading Diverse Audiences

Indian maiden and decides to visit her village. Eventually, Little Bear entices the young woman to leave her home to live with him, and then there were no more wars with the Indians on earth (62–64).

Turcotte is identified as Sioux in the folklore collection, and she states that this legend was told by a Sioux woman, leading Turcotte's readers to believe that she may have heard the storyteller. And perhaps, she did, but there is a discrepancy in her tribal affiliation: her Haskell student case file indicates that she was one-half Chippewa from Sandusky, Montana ("Student Case Files"). Turcotte entered Haskell in September 1905 and apparently left in June 1908, six years before her composition appeared in *Indian Legends*, so perhaps the memory of the booklet's editor failed. Possibly, Turcotte was half Sioux or had encountered Sioux in Sandusky and heard the legend. Then again, the blurring of tribal affiliations at Haskell, which was instigated by the school and occurred naturally as Indians from different groups mixed, may have led Turcotte to identify with the Sioux, who suffered one of the more reprehensible acts of Indian repression. Several hundred Sioux were massacred by U.S. troops on the Pine Ridge Reservation in South Dakota in 1890—the last major violent encounter between Plains Indians and the U.S. cavalry (Prucha 726–29; Jones et al. 582–84). In any event, the conclusion of Turcotte's story reflects the reality of her own day: there were no more wars with Indians in the United States because Native Americans had been confined to reservations and sent to schools such as Haskell.

A final example of the epideictic effort of Haskell girls to preserve their cultures in *Indian Legends* is Emily Robertson's long essay, "Customs among the Sioux Indians." Robertson spoke specifically of her tribe, rather than of Native Americans in general, and recounted feasts in honor of babies and people who died. Providing a glimpse of reservation life, she recalls a mourning ritual that she witnessed when "the Indians were all camped in a circle around the station where their rations were issued to them (twice a month)" (81). Robertson qualifies her suggestion that the Sioux maintained their customs even as they adapted to the regulations of the reservation with the caveat that it was so long ago, she could hardly remember it. Given that she reportedly was born in 1897 and entered Haskell in 1907, her memory must have dated from the turn of the century. Shifting between general observation and specific example, Robertson testifies to the intense grief of families upon the death of loved ones, informing whites in her audience that emotion knows no racial boundary. She then reveals her self-conception as

Persuading Diverse Audiences

a "civilized Indian" by renouncing the sun dance, a ritual white reservation authorities banned. During this dance, Native men cut notches in the skin of their shoulders and threaded through the notches a stick that was attached to a pole around which they danced for three days. Robertson observes: "I am glad I have never seen this barbarous way of worshipping, but I have heard of worse things than that" (83). Leaving this titillating prospect unfulfilled—to the disappointment of readers who assumed all Sioux were "savage"—Robertson concludes her account with the benign custom of the "red penny," which required the Sioux to keep a coin in a beaded bag. A committee designated the recipient of the bag, who then was expected to give a feast and offer gifts of horses and beadwork. Ending on a poignant note, Robertson comments, "But even this custom is dying out and soon it, too, will be forgotten" (83). Yet, like the other girls who preserved Native Americans customs in *Indian Legends*, she ensures that this practice would not be forgotten.

Echoing the epideictic purposes of Haskell girls in the *Indian Leader*, the young women who contributed to *Indian Legends* educated white readers while conserving and celebrating, and perhaps even romanticizing, the Native beliefs and practices of their indigenous auditors. If the publication functioned as a metaphorical museum that displayed these texts as cultural artifacts, it also allowed Native American girls to act as curators of their own folklore. One of the striking features of the persuasive discourse of girls in the anthology is that with the exception of Robertson, they do not distinguish between the tribes about which they write and Native Americans in general. Their use of the generic "Indians" may reflect the success of white-directed Indian education to sever cultural and social ties and thus weaken tribal identification. Or this usage may signal the success of the pan-Indian movement to unify Indians as a "race." If the latter is the case, these young rhetors contributed to the movement in ways that cannot be measured by conventional methods.

None of the girls whose texts appear *Indian Legends* or the *Indian Leader* became as publicly prominent as Zitkala-Ša, but after they graduated, they continued to try to influence the perceptions of whites and the collective identifications of their Native American families and friends. Leaving Haskell in the early 1910s, Robertson married in 1915 and became an active member of the community in Martin, South Dakota, where she was a stockholder in the Martin State Bank ("Robertson-Pugh"). After Wright graduated from the normal-school program at Haskell in 1897, she became a teacher at the Grace Boarding School for Native Americans in Chamberlain, South Dakota, and

86
Persuading Diverse Audiences

encouraged her students to attend Haskell (Wright, "From South Dakota" 2). Completing her training at the normal school of Haskell in 1901, Marmon enrolled at the University of New Mexico. She trained and worked as a nurse until her marriage to a Haskell schoolmate, Omar Gravelle, and by 1919, she was living with her two sons and husband, who owned a store, in Red Lake, Minnesota ("What They Are Doing" 3; "Our Alumni" 56). Veix worked as a stenographer and clerk at Ft. Totten, North Dakota, where she married the agency physician ("Our Alumni" 21). As professionals, mothers, and women who moved between white and Native worlds, these young women exemplified the potential of Indians that they had celebrated in their epideictic rhetoric at Haskell.

Conclusions

Helen Ball and the male superintendents who solicited and published the writing of young Native American female students had their own epideictic agenda for the *Indian Leader* and *Indian Legends*: to praise the Haskell Institute by presenting evidence of its success in the form of student writing. No doubt, these white authority figures influenced Haskell girls on topics and stances, encouraging them to produce texts that reflected positively on Indian schools and supported the official objective of Indian assimilation through education. Given the rhetorical constraints that Haskell girls faced, it is all the more remarkable that through their contributions to the Haskell newspaper and folklore anthology, they managed to deliver their own positive portraits of indigenous peoples. These young women were marginalized by race, constrained by gender codes whites established, and subject to the derogatory discourse about Native Americans in the late nineteenth and early twentieth centuries, yet they turned these disadvantages to their own advantage. Capitalizing on their designation as agents of assimilation, they appealed to the diverse audiences of the *Indian Leader* and *Indian Legends*. These girls educated whites about the abilities of indigenous people, preserved Native histories and traditions, and celebrated the achievements of American Indians of the past and the present. In their quest to achieve this constellation of purposes, they demonstrated how epideictic discourse can be the rhetorical means for creating identity and forging group identity.

Gauging the reaction of the multiple audiences of the *Indian Leader* and *Indian Legends* to the epideictic rhetoric of Haskell girls is difficult. Although

Persuading Diverse Audiences

it could have been suppressed, there is no evidence of negative reaction, in either the "Exchange" department of the newspaper or the files of either publication. There is, however, evidence in alumni letters printed in the *Indian Leader* to suggest that former students relied on the newspaper to stay connected with Haskell and their former classmates. As former student Susie Bearchief Jim admits in 1910: "I'm every day thinking of all my schoolmates and friends. I wish through the *Leader* to keep up with all of my friends and what is going on at my old school-home" (1). For Jim and Haskell alumni, the *Indian Leader* constituted a community of Native Americans who imagined new ways of adapting to the incredible changes that were imposed upon them in the late nineteenth and early twentieth centuries.

Haskell girls facilitated this collective identification by praising themselves and their peers through epideictic rhetoric that educated a wide range of readers about Native Americans in the early twentieth century and that preserved for posterity the history and folklore of indigenous peoples in the United States. Using double-voicing, they spoke to and for Native Americans, contributing to the pan-Indian movement of the early twentieth century.

Comparing the epideictic rhetoric of Haskell and Barstow girls, patterns begin to emerge. A sense of optimism pervades the persuasive discourse of both groups of young women as they confront assumptions about their identities, their roles, and their goals. Both groups argue that they are capable of achieving more than society expected of them and work to create community. And both groups use the same epideictic strategies. Yet there are important variations in these epideictic patterns: Haskell girls depict themselves as progressive Indians, privileging race over gender, while Barstow girls take race for granted as they enact the model of the new girl. Haskell girls construct community that transcends tribal differences and encompasses Natives of different ages and genders across the country. In contrast, Barstow girls create a homogeneous utopian community isolated from the outside world. Relying more often on the tactic of praise than blame, both Haskell and Barstow girls contend with the Other. Haskell girls had to counter the notion that they are the Other, and Barstow girls define themselves by conjuring the Other.

Some of these epideictic patterns will be evident in the next chapter about Lincoln High School, where African American girls challenged stereotypes, exuded confidence, and positioned themselves as part of a vanguard that was connected to the wider black community.

CHAPTER 4

Glossing (over) Historical Realities: Lincoln Girls

In Lincoln High, with pen and ink,
Our happiest days were spent,
The teachers trained our minds to think
And we were all content.
                —Hazel Hickum, "Our Future Lies before Us!"

The accomplishments of prominent Negroes are enshrouded in darkness by the white literary press of the world. Largely because of prejudice, the progress of the Negro race is not heralded in the columns of the American newspapers. Men of color who attain any unusual honor are not given the publicity that those of the opposite race are given. This serves to keep the Negro in ignorance of the progress of his races [sic]; it serves to create in the breasts of the young Negro uncontrollable race disinterest, disappointment and disgust.

                —Willa Shaw, "Know Thy Race"

IN THE EARLY TWENTIETH century, African American girls at Lincoln High School joined young people in the Kansas City area and throughout the United States who were delivering epideictic rhetoric from the new podium of school-sponsored periodicals. Like white girls at Miss Barstow's School and Native American girls at the Haskell Institute, who were discussed in the previous two chapters, Lincoln girls praised their peers and defined their collective identity through published accounts of their academic and extra-curricular activities. As pupils at the only public secondary school for African

Glossing (over) Historical Realities

Americans in Kansas City, Missouri, Lincoln girls also used their high school yearbook and newspaper for rhetorical purposes that reflected the epideictic agenda of books, such as *The Work of the Afro-American Woman* (1894), and national and local African American periodicals, such as the *Crisis* and the *Kansas City Call*, which had a circulation of 16,737 in 1927 (Slavens 224). Producing poetry and prose that promoted racial uplift, Lincoln girls attempted to construct community and counter the racism that they experienced in a predominately white city representative of many municipalities during the Jim Crow era.

While all of the girls in this study confronted rhetorical constraints that shaped their epideictic rhetoric, Lincoln girls contended with a particularly complex set of factors. As I argue in chapter 2, Barstow girls, the daughters of elite Kansas City families, challenged assumptions about their socially assigned gender roles and expectations that they would pursue marriage and motherhood rather than higher education and careers. These young white women did not, however, have to deal with the issues of race that Native American girls at Haskell faced, as chapter 3 establishes. In their epideictic rhetoric, both Native American girls at Haskell and African American girls at Lincoln had to refute claims that they were innately inferior to whites. Yet white society authorized Haskell girls to speak, designating them as agents of assimilation who would teach their peers, families, and future children the lessons of dominant culture. Because white society tended to segregate rather than assimilate African Americans in the early twentieth century, Lincoln girls spoke to primarily black audiences whose collective sense of self was negatively affected by derogatory white views of blacks. Furthermore, Lincoln girls addressed auditors who did not always agree about the best way for the race to progress. For example, African Americans debated the efficacy of academic versus vocational education; advocates of academic education argued that black society needed teachers and doctors, while proponents of vocational education maintained that given the limited professional opportunities for African Americans in the early twentieth century, training for trades and industry was more important.

To deal with these constraints, Lincoln girls used two epideictic strategies that are exemplified by the epigraphs of this chapter. Some girls built community by obscuring facts and forces, and other girls emphasized these same elements to achieve this goal. Relying on the first tactic in a poem published in the Lincoln yearbook of 1917, Hazel Hickum portrays the high school as

90
Glossing (over) Historical Realities

an idyllic academic enclave for both girls and boys regardless of their socio-economic class and refrained from reporting that racist educational policies ensured that Lincoln was consistently overcrowded and under-funded. Willa Shaw used the second technique in an essay for the 1923 yearbook, blaming white newspaper editors for deliberately ignoring the achievements of African Americans and thereby depriving young people of proof of racial progress. In the process, these young women enhance our understanding of how epideictic discourse promotes community and register their participation in national discourses of race and racism.

This chapter defines an interpretative framework for analyzing the persuasive practices of Lincoln girls, describes the racial climate of Kansas City in the early twentieth century, and surveys the argumentative aims of African American print culture that influenced Lincoln girls. It then examines the epideictic discourse of Lincoln girls published from 1915 to 1930 in the high school yearbook, *The Lincolnian*, and the newspaper, the *Lincolnite*.[1] Reading the persuasive texts of Lincoln girls within the cultural and historical contexts in which they were composed reveals that these young women responded to their local rhetorical situations by engaging in the national campaign for racial uplift.

A New Lens for Viewing Epideictic Rhetoric

To create a lens for interpreting the epideictic rhetoric of Lincoln girls, as well as the discourse of other marginalized groups of the past and present, I draw upon the theories of rhetorician George A. Kennedy and historian Charles E. Coulter. Analyzing classical epideictic rhetoric, Kennedy comments that the category characteristically "glosses over historical realities" (*New History* 22). He does not consider the negative connotations of the phrase, clarify what he means by "historical realities," or discuss at length the interpretative strategies of epideictic rhetors. Instead, Kennedy notes that Roman orators often resorted to flattery when speaking to emperors and concludes that

> by holding out an ideal as something real the speaker hopes to make it true in the future belief or actions of the addressee and the audience. The basic function of epideictic oratory is to enhance belief in certain moral and civic values and thus to increase social bonding and the solidarity of the cultural group. (22)

91
Glossing (over) Historical Realities

To fulfill this function, however, epideictic rhetors must choose what information about their subjects to share and what information to withhold when addressing audiences. These choices may be influenced by the historical realities that surround an epideictic act. For Lincoln girls, those realities included the repressive effects of Jim Crow laws, the negative assumptions of whites about African Americans, and differences of class and opinion among African Americans. Consequently, the persuasive discourse of Lincoln girls provides the opportunity to interrogate the interplay of interpretation and historical realities in epideictic rhetoric.

In their epideictic rhetoric, Lincoln girls depicted themselves and their peers as part of a group that was distinct from and not inferior to white society. Helping to form a coalition that they styled as separate *and* equal, Lincoln girls joined adults who formed what Coulter describes as the "parallel community" of African Americans in Kansas City. In his study of African American neighborhoods on both sides of the Missouri and Kansas state line from 1865 to 1939, Coulter contends that citizens of color subverted segregation by establishing their own businesses, churches, and professional organizations that sustained the African American community and empowered its members to fight for integration (6–7).[2]

Lincoln girls participated in this project by praising the efforts of younger members in an institution that was integral to the African American community on a local as well as a national level. As William C. Hueston, an African American lawyer in Kansas City, told 550 Lincoln students at an assembly on the first day of class in September 1919:

> This high school represents our race in the contest that we are to have in this country and let it be understood that a contest is in the years to come and you must decide for yourself whether or not this test is to be won by you. (Peebles and Smith 1)

In a speech a local African American newspaper reported, Hueston urges Lincoln students to recognize the communal consequences of their individual efforts:

> You are not here to get an education for your own use. It is for something in which we all are interested and the question is whether or not you as representatives of the race of ours are going to measure up. (Peebles and Smith 8)

92
Glossing (over) Historical Realities

Assigned the task of representing their race, Lincoln girls produced epideictic rhetoric that proved young African Americans were doing their part to meet such expectations. Of course, as chapter 3 notes about Native American girls at the Haskell Institute, I cannot claim that all of the African American girls whose rhetoric is analyzed in this chapter consciously responded to their marginalized position. Racial uplift was not necessarily always on their minds. Yet Lincoln girls were reminded regularly of their duty to represent the race, were surrounded by adults committed to that project, and were aware of the professional print campaign for racial uplift.

While the interpretive lens described affords perspective on the epideictic discourse of Lincoln girls and the rhetorical activities of African Americans in communities beyond Kansas City in the early twentieth century, it may also allow us to see more clearly the persuasive pursuits of other groups, such as urban ethnic enclaves. Historical realities and the reasons why communities are established as parallel rather than as part of the broader community will vary, but acknowledging and exploring the impact of historical realities and parallel communities on rhetorical constructions of identity may guide other inquiries.

Historical Realities for African Americans in Kansas City

The epideictic rhetoric of Lincoln girls was affected by racism and racial segregation in a city divided by a color line. The state of Missouri did not enact segregation laws concerning public places, but "custom" prohibited African Americans from joining whites in hospitals, hotels, restaurants, and theaters (Greene et al. 107). In 1913 white researcher Asa E. Martin published a study of African Americans in Kansas City, Missouri, that testifies to the local color line and its negative effects. Using the 1910 census, he reports that African Americans constituted 9.7 percent of the total population of the city (25) and that sixteen of the twenty-five "typical" families in his sample had annual incomes of less than $500, which he estimated as the minimum "to permit the maintenance of a normal standard" (84). Although as a white scholar Martin often was biased in his analysis of the economic status of African Americans, he acknowledged that white discrimination limited the occupations that they could pursue and consequently the wages that they earned.

Some Lincoln girls came from the working-class families that were most representative of the African American community of Kansas City, Missouri,

Glossing (over) Historical Realities

during this period. Dovie Brown, who composed an epideictic poem for the 1930 Lincoln annual, shared a rented house with ten people, including her stepfather, a salesman, and her mother, a hotel maid. The other adults in the household worked as laborers in laundries and hotels (United States, Census Bureau 1930). In contrast, Lucile Bluford, who wrote epideictic editorials for the Lincoln newspaper in 1926, came from a family that was part of the 3 percent of African Americans in Kansas City who could be classified as middle class during this period (Coulter 8). She was the daughter of Addie and John H. Bluford, who taught chemistry at Lincoln from 1918 to 1944 ("J. H. Bluford"). Whether they came from working-class or middle-class families, Lincoln girls represented the few African Americans who attended high school in the early twentieth century. During this period, only 10 percent of adolescent African Americans went to high school in Missouri (Anderson 190–91).[3]

From the beginning of secondary public education in Kansas City, Missouri, the color line extended to schools. In 1869 the city opened Central High School for whites, but Lincoln High School was not established until 1888 and was the only local high school for blacks until 1936 (Worley, "Historic"). The decision of the U.S. Supreme Court in the *Plessy v. Ferguson* case of 1896 established the "separate but equal" principle, which endorsed racial segregation in public institutions including schools (Anderson 192). In practice, the "separate but equal" rule meant that African American students in Kansas City attended segregated schools that seldom were equal to those for whites. By 1921 Lincoln High School served 750 students in a structure built to accommodate 250 pupils, according to an editorial by Nelson C. Crews in the *Kansas City Sun* (Coulter 187).

While white school officials in Kansas City justified such educational inequities through claims about the intellectual inferiority of blacks, the Lincoln High School curriculum and the credentials of its teachers refute such racist reasoning. In 1915 the four-year course of study at Lincoln concentrated on academics and included a few vocational courses. Freshmen took classes in arithmetic, algebra, English, Latin, physiology, civics, domestic science, and manual training; they could also take drawing and music classes. Seniors studied chemistry, English literature, political economy, domestic science, and manual training; electives included geology, German, music, Virgil, and astronomy ("Course" 10–11). In 1916 the school began to increase its vocational training options, adding mechanical, masonry, and home economics departments in which students could learn carpentry, construction,

94
Glossing (over) Historical Realities

gas engine work, cooking, sewing, and hat making ("Vocational Training" 35–40). Taking the middle ground in the debate over African American education and the question of whether it should focus on industrial training, as Booker T. Washington had contended for years, or liberal education, as W. E. B. Du Bois asserted, Lincoln offered both options to students (Gatewood 266).[4] The Lincoln yearbook of 1915 lists the "the corps of teachers": of the fifteen instructors, ten had bachelor's degrees; two had master's degrees; and three teachers did not list any degree ("Lincoln High" 9).

Clearly, African Americans faced daunting historical realities in Kansas City during the early twentieth century. Jim Crow codes dictated what jobs they could fill, the low wages that they would earn, and where they could live. Racism drove the segregation of schools and assured inadequate funding for black schools. Yet these realities also included the efforts of educators and students at African American schools to challenge the consequences of the color line. Lincoln girls participated in this initiative by producing persuasive discourse that echoed the epideictic rhetoric of African American professional print culture.

The "New Negro" and African American Print Culture

To rhetorically construct a parallel community, Lincoln girls espoused the "New Negro" principles of race pride, self-help, racial solidarity, and the development of a middle class that were promoted by the epideictic rhetoric of African American print culture (Dagbovie 134). The term "New Negro" often is associated with African American culture of the 1920s, but it was in use much earlier and became popular in print culture by the mid-1890s, according to Henry Louis Gates Jr. He sees the New Negro as the metaphorical means for promoting positive images of black collective identity (130–31).

In 1894, for example, African American journalist Gertrude Mossell cataloged the achievements of women artists, businesswomen, composers, dramatists, educators, journalists, missionaries, physicians, and writers in *The Work of the Afro-American Woman*. Of her epideictic agenda, she acknowledges:

> The value of any published work, especially if historical in nature, must be largely inspirational; this fact grows out of the truth that race instinct, race experience lies behind it, national feeling or race pride always having for its development a basis of self-respect. (9)

Glossing (over) Historical Realities

Mossell invokes the New Negro principle of race pride in a book that was one of several of its kind published during this period, including *A New Negro for a New Century: An Accurate and Up-to-Date Record of the Upward Struggles of the Negro Race* (1900), by Booker T. Washington, N. B. Wood, and Fannie Barrier Williams.

Meanwhile, the African American periodical press engaged in epideictic rhetoric. Michael Fultz finds that the most prominent black magazines published in the United States from 1900 to 1930 were dominated by the new middle and professional classes, which were "decidedly race conscious, and they forcefully advocated self-help, character building, social uplift, and race patronage and solidarity" (130). Collaborating in print, African American writers, editors, and publishers publicized New Negro principles through publications such as the *Crisis: A Record of the Darker Races* (1910–present), the official publication of the National Association for the Advancement of Colored People (NAACP), which Du Bois edited from its inception until 1934 (Daniel 139). An epideictic enterprise aimed at African American women, *Half-Century Magazine* (1916–25) was founded by Kathryn E. Williams in Chicago and claimed seventy-five thousand readers by the early 1920s (Daniel 193).

Locally, there was the *Kansas City Sun* (1914–25), a newspaper edited by Nelson Crews. Coulter remarks that Crews vowed to address concerns "that tend to inspire and uplift the race" (103). Enacting the New Negro ideals of self-help and middle-class values, Crews campaigned through his editorials for the establishment and support of businesses owned by African Americans. Crews figures among the New Negroes of Kansas City, a faction that Coulter defines as "the more politicized, more assertive, and more militant African Americans," contending this definition describes "many of the men and women who drove black Kansas City in the first three decades of the twentieth century" (11). Among these women were Josephine Silone Yates and Anna H. Jones, who cowrote an epideictic account of the Kansas City Colored Women's League in 1894 for the premier issue of *Woman's Era*, the first periodical owned and published by African American women (Logan 132). Jones joined the faculty at Lincoln High School in 1916 and taught there for three years, and she may have influenced the rhetorical performances of her female students (Coulter 40).

While both women and men delivered epideictic rhetoric celebrating the New Negro in African American print culture, girls produced most of the epideictic rhetoric at Lincoln High School. Demographics may account for

96
Glossing (over) Historical Realities

this fact: girls constituted the majority of Lincoln students from 1888 to 1930 (Kansas City Board of Education: *Forty-Sixth Annual Report* 135, *Report of the Superintendent . . . 1921–1927*, 55, *Report of the Board of Education . . . 1928–1930*). Considering their numbers, it is not surprising that girls also dominated the student discourse of the school. Exercising their ethos to speak to and for their peers, Lincoln girls fulfilled the epideictic assertion of African American educator Anna Julia Cooper, who praised African American girls as the source of a "staunch, helpful, regenerating womanhood on which, primarily, rests the foundation stones of our future as a race" (61).[5] Emulating New Negroes in Kansas City and nationwide who performed epideictic rhetoric in print, Lincoln girls published poetry that promoted race pride and self-help by suppressing historical realities.

Glossing over Historical Realities

Although Aristotle does not recognize poetry as epideictic rhetoric, as did later rhetoricians, he acknowledges the persuasive affordance of the genre. In his *Poetics*, he maintains that it is "the function of a poet to relate not things that have happened, but things that may happen, i.e. that are possible in accordance with probability or necessity" (12). Aristotle suggests that poetry posits possibilities, and audiences expect poets to take license with literal and historical truths. Lincoln girls turned these assumptions to their own advantage, using poetry to gloss over historical realities in order to engender group pride and self-help, as the following close and historically contextualized readings of three poems demonstrate.

Hazel Hickum's tribute to Lincoln High School in the 1917 volume of the yearbook, one of the epigraphs of this chapter, is typical of the epideictic poetry of Lincoln girls. Provoking emotional response through the rhetorical figure of *paenismus*, an expression of joy for blessings obtained, she avoids addressing the history and consequences of separate and unequal education for African Americans. Instead, she imagines a community of young scholars resolved to succeed:

> In Lincoln High, with pen and ink,
> Our happiest days were spent,
> The teachers trained our minds to think
> And we were all content.

97
Glossing (over) Historical Realities

In nineteen thirteen we entered here
Our purpose plain to all,
It was to leave a record clear
In every study hall.

'Tis true, the path was often rough,
And failures seemed the end,
And some would fain have said "enough"
When cares with joys did blend.

For though we oft our tasks would shirk,
As youths we knew no better;
But now, as we begin life's work,
To these tasks we're the debtor.

We shall go away to college,
To a place of learning rare;
To obtain a better knowledge
From the courses offered there.

For our future lies before us,
May it be a pleasant one,
One to make the world respect us,
As our schoolmates here have done. (1)

In the first stanza, Hickum idealizes Lincoln as a serene site of scholarship where instructors do not merely impart information or drill students in academic catechisms but teach them to analyze and reason. Setting a celebratory tone, she continues by characterizing the class of 1917 as intent on making its mark and excelling in every subject. Hickum then makes oblique reference to the challenges that she and her classmates face: "'Tis true, the path was often rough, / And failures seemed the end." Given the economic and social conditions for African Americans in Kansas City, it is likely that she alludes to more than problems of too much homework or failed exams. The cares of Lincoln students might have included limited financial resources that prevented them from going to school properly fed and attired, as Asa Martin suggested was often the case for African American pupils, or that forced them to leave school to go to work. Class histories published in the

98
Glossing (over) Historical Realities

Lincoln yearbook suggest that not all students were able to complete their high school educations. For example, Hickum's class started with 115 freshmen and ended with 52 seniors; if all of the seniors earned diplomas, the graduation rate at Lincoln that year was 45 percent (Robinson 4–5). Yet, considering that the national graduation rate for all high school students was 16.8 percent in 1920, the percentage of Lincoln students that finished high school was high (Snyder 55). Nor does Hickum refer to the travails of students who came from different parts of the city. Girls and boys from the Leeds neighborhood in eastern Kansas City traveled more than two miles by foot and streetcar, enduring the jeers of white riders, to attend Lincoln, where some of their peers ridiculed them for living in an area without electricity, running water, and paved streets (Kremer 269).

Using the conditional tense—"And some would fain have said 'enough'"—Hickum bolsters the race pride of Lincoln students by implying that while "some" students might have been daunted by the challenges that she and her peers face, they are not. Lest she sound smug, she quickly acknowledges that Lincoln students caused some of their own problems:

> For though we oft our tasks would shirk,
> As youths we knew no better;
> But now, as we begin life's work,
> To these tasks we're the debtor.

Resisting assumptions that African Americans were lazy, Hickum insists that youth, not race, is the reason that Lincoln students sometimes avoided their responsibilities. Furthermore, their newly attained maturity allows them to perceive the importance of tasks that they once avoided.

Hickum makes her boldest assertion in the fifth stanza, declaring that Lincoln students were college bound at a time when only 2 percent of young African Americans were enrolled in institutions of higher learning (Work 243). Determining how many Lincoln graduates went to college is difficult, but certainly some did. Hickum, for example, went to Kansas State Normal School in Emporia ("Class of 1917"). In September 1921, seventy-six Lincoln graduates were starting their semesters at institutions ranging from the University of Kansas to the Conservatory of Music in Ithaca, New York (Coulter 196).

The last stanza of Hickum's poem supplies its emphatic title, "Our Future Lies before Us!" The exclamation point that punctuates the title does

99
Glossing (over) Historical Realities

not appear in this line in the poem, but it transforms the title into a cry that rallies students to persevere in communities outside of Lincoln. Although it was not certain that the future would be pleasant for Lincoln graduates, it does not further Hickum's epideictic agenda to elaborate on the obstacles that they might face as young people of color in a racist society. Rather, she reminds her peers to recall with pride the respect that they paid each other as they move into a world that often did not respect African Americans.

In 1925, the year that Alain Locke's epideictic anthology, *The New Negro*, was published, Gladys Smith composed a Pindaric ode to Lincoln that encouraged race pride. Often used for epideictic purposes, the Pindaric ode is marked by passion, bold vision, and elevated diction (Abrams 206, 277). Students of Greek, Lincoln girls may have studied Pindar and used his odes as a model for their own. Smith effuses in "A Tribute to Lincoln":

> O, Lincoln High, to thee we give
> The praises that within us live,
> Thy name on every lip shall be
> To sound throughout eternity.
>
> O, Wondrous School, O, Matchless art,
> We, too, are proud of thy great part,
> In every meadow, nook and lea,
> Let forever swell thy plea.
>
> O, Lincoln High, on thee we look
> To find Ethiopia's future booked,
> In letters writ in words of flame,
> Blot out all ignorance and shame.
>
> O, Lincoln, let thy colors fly,
> Till in glory they reach the sky,
> May thy motto ever be,
> Faith, Hope, and Liberty.

Employing the rhetorical figure of the apostrophe, a direct and explicit address to a nonhuman object, Smith envisions Lincoln High School as an entity

100
Glossing (over) Historical Realities

worthy of worship. She endows the school with divine stature through her use of the archaic pronouns "thee" and "thy" and her phrases "O, Wondrous School, O, Matchless art." Alluding to the "great part" and "plea" of Lincoln, Smith suggests that the education the school offers young African Americans, who are signified as "Ethiopia's future," enables them to prove that they are neither ignorant nor ashamed of their race. This young poet's reference to Ethiopia is rooted in African American interpretations of a Biblical prophecy: "Princes shall come out of Egypt; Ethiopia shall soon stretch out her hands unto God" (*King James Bible*, Ps. 68:31). Discussing the complex and multiple meanings of the Ethiopia concept, Shirley Wilson Logan notes that nineteenth-century African American women speakers, such as abolitionist Maria W. Stewart, used it as a figure of communion to encourage audiences to perceive a common past. Logan explains that "the prophecy of Ethiopia stretching out her hands became the standard trope of salvation in sermons preached from black pulpits during the nineteenth century" (28). For Smith, Ethiopia represents the future as embodied by Lincoln students.

As her final epideictic gesture to instill race pride, Smith proposes a new motto for Lincoln: "Faith, Hope, and Liberty." Melding religious and political discourse, she draws upon the Bible and the Declaration of Independence. The New Testament advises: "So faith, hope, love abide, these three; but the greatest of these is love" (*Revised Standard Version Bible*, 1 Cor. 13.13). The Declaration of Independence asserts that among the "certain inalienable rights" of British colonists was "liberty." Altering the Biblical injunction, Smith substitutes "liberty" for "love." Smith clearly was well-versed in religious as well as political ideology, and she may have attended one of the more than forty churches that served African Americans in Kansas City by the late 1920s. Local ministers spoke regularly at Lincoln, appearing at both student assemblies and the Sunday forum that the school hosted weekly. In 1920, the Inter-Denominational Ministerial Alliance endorsed a petition for a new Lincoln facility that was presented to the school board (Coulter 184, 196, 199). Significantly, Smith's poem duplicates the meter of hymns that were sung in churches. Using a classical poetic form to promote race pride among her readers, this young woman intertwines allusions to the Bible and one of the most treasured texts of the United States.

The final example of the epideictic poetry of Lincoln girls is Dovie Brown's occasional poem "Parting," which was published in the Lincoln yearbook of 1930:

101
Glossing (over) Historical Realities

Our course at Lincoln is now complete;
And into the world we all must go
To meet with victory or defeat,
But memory of Lincoln will not grow old.

We leave with sorrow in our heart
Because we'll miss you so.
But even then we must depart
To reach our coveted goal.

To take our place among the rest,
The place where we belong.
And strive to make ourselves the best,
Thus we face the future with a song. (40)

Paying homage to the high school in the first two stanzas of her poem, Brown summons the sadness that graduates feel upon leaving the Lincoln community. Like Hickum, she portrays the school in a positive light and does not report that by 1929, it accommodated 1,100 students in space designed for 800 pupils (Coulter 197). Brown then devotes the last four lines to reinforcing the race pride that this community had helped to instill in Lincoln students who had been trained to see themselves as what Du Bois calls the "Talented Tenth," the educated vanguard that would lead the advancement of all African Americans (*Dusk of Dawn* 70). Joining that group, denoted by "the rest," is the "coveted goal" of Lincoln students. Brown's line, "And strive to make ourselves the best," alludes to the "Best Men" paradigm. Whites created this model during Reconstruction as the means of restricting the political influence of African Americans. Only the Best Men—African American men who were benevolent, fair-minded, and genteel—should be allowed to vote and hold office, according to this ideology. Some African Americans appropriated this restrictive concept, historian Glenda Elizabeth Gilmore contends, because it resonated with their own ideas of merit, which were based on education, marriage, religious piety, and social reform (62–63). Although the term was gender specific, Brown does not suggest that only Lincoln boys were capable of enacting this model.

Ending her poem on a seemingly upbeat note, Brown concludes: "Thus we face the future with a song." What song did she have in mind? A popular

Glossing (over) Historical Realities

tune played in the jazz district of Kansas City that was near Lincoln, a hymn sung in the churches that students attended, or a folk song that linked these progressive young people to the resilience of earlier generations of African Americans as they faced the deprivations of the Great Depression? By the time that Brown's poem was published in the spring of 1930, Kansas City, like the rest of the country, was six months into the Depression. A year after the stock market crash of October 1929, the industries that employed the majority of African Americans in Kansas City—railroads, stockyards, packinghouses, and stone quarries—had faltered. African American workers who lost these jobs had trouble finding suitable new jobs, and many found no work at all. As African American men found fewer work options, African American women who had not worked outside their homes were forced to do so to support their families (Coulter 272–75). Suggesting that the Lincoln class of 1930 might meet with victory or defeat, Brown nonetheless urges graduates to call upon their collective esteem "and strive to make ourselves the best."

Although the tone of their epideictic discourse varies from confident to assertive to poignant over the course of thirteen years, Hickum, Smith, and Brown do not waver in their purpose to promote race pride and self-help through poetry. Muting the facts of segregation and economic and social inequities, Lincoln girls imagined a community of confident and capable young African Americans undaunted by these forces. Their omissions can be interpreted as a form of silence, which Cheryl Glenn recognizes as a powerful rhetorical tool: "Silence is not necessarily an essence; it can also be a position—a choice" (177). By choosing to remain silent on issues that could create despair and disunity in the parallel community that they were helping to build, these young Lincoln poets encouraged hope and unity. Their tactics illuminate the epideictic construction of a parallel community, which imagines itself as autonomous rather than dependent on the community of the dominant culture. As Kennedy notes, the goal of epideictic discourse is to encourage the acceptance of specific values in order to strengthen the solidarity of a social group. While some values, such as frugality and propriety, may be encouraged through negative reinforcement that delineates the costs of imprudence and impropriety, the values of pride and self-help are more readily cultivated through positive reinforcement. People are proud about their accomplishments, not the obstacles that they face; they support the principle of self-help when they believe that their efforts will not be thwarted

Glossing (over) Historical Realities

by factors beyond their control. Effective epideictic rhetors, such as these Lincoln girls, perceive these human tendencies and respond accordingly. Thus, their silence is a form of glossing over of historical realities that can be seen as an act of rhetorical agency, rather than as acquiescence to these realities.

Glossing Historical Realities

Whereas Lincoln girls took license with historical realities in their poetry, they accentuated specific facts and factors in their prose to promote racial solidarity and middle-class values. They offered tangible evidence of the ascension of Lincoln graduates to the middle class of Kansas City, documented their participation in middle-class institutions, such as the Young Women's Christian Association (YWCA), charted the achievements of African Americans nationwide, joined the campaign for the building of a new facility for Lincoln, and reported that young African Americans could find common ground with white youths in Kansas City.

To inspire racial solidarity and middle-class values, Lincoln students Arzethyr Franklin and Stella Williams recorded the specific achievements of individual Lincoln graduates in an article for the 1915 volume of the yearbook. Listing the names and pursuits of students from the classes of 1897 to 1914, Franklin and Williams prove that Lincoln alumni were helping to create a cadre of African American businesspeople and professionals in Kansas City. They note, for example, that "William House, '97, Dr. E. J. McCampbell, '04, and Dr. T. T. McCampbell, '98, are in business as a drug company in our city" (28). Another early graduate,

> Mr. G. W. K. Love, '01, is one of Kansas City's most prominent and most energetic business men. He supplies all kinds of regalia and badges of best quality to various lodges and orders throughout the states of Missouri, Kansas, Oklahoma, Nebraska, and many southern states. (28)[6]

As Franklin and Williams make clear, Lincoln graduates were joining the ranks of the Talented Tenth, and some were cultivating the middle-class community of Kansas City, Missouri.

One of the lengthiest entries in the 1915 alumni report commends Lorraine Richardson of the class of 1907 as an orator. Franklin and Williams report that Richardson,

104
Glossing (over) Historical Realities

now Mrs. Wendell Greene made a speech at the Federated Alumni banquet given at the Y.M.C.A. on "The Record of the High School." It was easily the best effort of any and placed in clear light the achievements of our school. (28)

Their description is notable for several reasons. Observing conventions of the day, these Lincoln girls refer to Greene by her marital title and husband's name, which denotes her status as a middle-class woman whose propriety parallels that of white women. They also applaud Greene's oratorical abilities, thereby positioning her within the tradition of African American activists Josephine Silone Yates and Anna Jones of Kansas City. Furthermore, Franklin and Williams suggest the epideictic nature of Greene's address: the record of Lincoln High School. That record represents more than the academic accomplishments of the elite young African Americans who attended Lincoln; it also was testimony to the significance of the high school within the wider African American community of Kansas City, Missouri.[7]

Proving that Lincoln girls embraced the middle-class values of the African American clubwomen's movement, Helen Wheeler contributed an epideictic article in 1917 about the part that girls played in starting a YWCA chapter. The clubwomen's movement emerged nationally during the 1890s and was a "manifestation of black women's race *and* gender obligations," according to Beverly Guy-Sheftall (24; original emphasis). Ostracized by white women's clubs in most regions of the country except New England, African American women joined together to pursue issues and activities of import to citizens of color. Deborah Gray White relates that

> black clubwomen believed they could help solve the race's problems through intensive social services focused on improving home life and educating mothers. Some programs aimed at increasing the skills and intellectual abilities of club members, while others sent members into local neighborhoods. Most clubs did both. (27–28)

Collaborating with the Kansas City Colored Women's League, Lincoln girls formed a club at their school that contributed to the construction of the parallel community of African Americans in Kansas City.[8]

In the 1917 yearbook, Wheeler states, "For many years the women of our city have longed for the formation of a Young Women's Christian Association, and will be glad to know that a beginning is being made among the girls of Lincoln High School" (32). The objective of the Lincoln chapter of

105
Glossing (over) Historical Realities

the YWCA, Wheeler reports, was a middle-class goal, "the making of better young women, both physically, mentally and spiritually" (32). Wheeler emphasizes the autonomy of young club members, who elected their own officers, with Wheeler serving as vice president. Weekly meetings were carefully organized, she notes, and devoted to different activities, which included a social entertainment meeting, a program day, a new member meeting, and a social service meeting during which girls sewed clothing for needy children. Wheeler commends the club's first year, declaring that

> the Y.W.C.A. of Lincoln High School is making great progress and we hope that in a few years our organization will be greatly increased and that we shall have a Y.W.C.A. building in this city. We feel that the work rests mainly with us girls to make it a success. (33)

Taking responsibility for racial uplift, Lincoln girls helped to channel community momentum to establish a physical facility for the YWCA. That goal was achieved in 1919 with the opening of the Paseo YWCA in the African American neighborhood of Kansas City, Missouri (Coulter 140).

By the mid-1920s, the tone of the epideictic rhetoric of Lincoln girls became more strident, as these young women contended with national developments, such as the increasing impatience of African Americans who fought for democracy in World War I but suffered the failure of democracy in their homeland. Although Kansas City did not record race riots or any of the 416 lynchings of African Americans that occurred from January 1918 through 1927 in the United States, such events affected the rhetoric of Lincoln girls (Schirmer 122; W. White 20).

To forge racial solidarity in these tumultuous times, Willa Shaw contributed a remarkable epideictic essay to Lincoln yearbook of 1923 that is quoted in the second epigraph of this chapter. The title of her composition, "Know Thy Race," alludes to the ancient Greek aphorism, "Know thyself." That motto is carved on the temple of the shrine of Delphi, where a female prophet answered the questions of pilgrims (Powell 167). Acting as oracle, Shaw lists twenty-seven important contemporary African Americans who testified to the historical reality that people of color were accomplished and active members of society. To create unity among African American readers, Shaw uses the epideictic strategy of blame, charging that white publishers fail to treat African Americans equally in the press, thereby denying young blacks knowledge that would engender racial solidarity and middle-class values. Yet

106
Glossing (over) Historical Realities

she points out that African Americans shared some of the responsibility for their exclusion because "Colored Journalism," dominated by "men of meager literary training," also neglected to celebrate notable African Americans (44). Part of the problem was that Howard University, "the most advanced educational institution of the race," had not yet established a school of journalism that could properly train editors and reporters, according to Shaw (44). Consequently, African American readers did not always support the "colored press" as they should. Shaw may have been criticizing local African American newspapers, such as the *Kansas City Call*, which regularly featured lurid crime stories (Wilkins 58–59). In fairness, however, white newspapers often did the same. Historian Thomas D. Wilson writes that "black publishers, like white publishers, shared a penchant for attention-grabbing headlines; as businessmen, they had not missed the value of Hearst-style sensationalism" (223). Implicitly challenging African American periodicals to raise their standards, Shaw models the kind of uplifting narrative that she thought they should offer.

Shaw then resumes her praise of African Americans: "The Negro has achievements in every line of human endeavor—in the arts, in religion, in science, in everything that serves to promote a better spirit of humanity" (44). Exercising interpretative authority, she explains that her list "of the most prominent and of the most accomplished men of color today" includes only figures of national and international renown (44). Shaw does not disclose how she chose to order her candidates or why there is only one woman on her list. Her ranking, however, reveals a hierarchy that reflects her identity as a fledging member of the Talented Tenth. First on her list are scholars, followed by artists, businessmen, politicians, writers, and athletes. Assigned fifteenth place is the only woman, Bessie Coleman, "aviatrix, internationally known, is the only woman given permits by the European governments to fly within their boundaries" (45). Although Coleman certainly merits a place on Shaw's list, there are other worthy female candidates, such as educator Anna Julia Cooper, activists Fannie Barrier Williams and Mary Church Terrell, and journalist Alice Dunbar Nelson. Perhaps, the dearth of women in Shaw's catalog reflects the historical reality that while African American women were central to the racial uplift movement, many of them did not seek nor garner the public attention that their male counterparts received.

Top on Shaw's list are leading proponents of racial solidarity, Du Bois and Locke. In her description of Carter G. Woodson, a pioneering scholar of African American history, Shaw notes, "He is the editor of 'The Negro within Our

Glossing (over) Historical Realities

Gates," a book severely criticized in an editorial by The Kansas City Star" (45). Shaw's reference to the approbation of a local white newspaper undercuts her argument that white publications ignored African Americans, but her epideictic tactic is to bolster unity through resistance to white criticism of Woodson.

One of Shaw's most extensive entries addresses the fact that African Americans did not agree about the best way for the race to progress. Of Marcus Garvey, she comments that he was "the originator of the Garvey movement to rehabilitate the continent of Africa with Negroes, and organizer of the U.N.I.A. (Universal Negro Improvement Association), which is exceedingly antagonistic to the N.A.A.C.P. and to W. E. B. Du Bois" (45). Garvey came to the United States from Jamaica in 1916 and launched a movement that espoused African American education, militant resistance, and Afro-American religious nationalism. By the early 1920s, the UNIA had thousands of members and Garvey's international following may have exceeded one million in the United States (Franklin 196–201; Hahn 468–74). Shaw is confident that her audience knows that the NAACP stands for the National Association for the Advancement of Colored People, which had a Kansas City chapter supported by events held at Lincoln High School. She continues that Garvey "is a force greatly feared by white America and greatly hated by many Negroes. His movement has been criticized as being too fantastic. The United States Secret Service has had Garvey under surveillance for more than two years" (45). Although Shaw seems intent on offering a balanced assessment of Garvey, suggesting that he created symbolic solidarity among both whites and blacks who opposed him, her final lines elicit sympathy for this controversial figure: "The government has at last brought him to court under charges of having received money under false pretense" (45). The best that the government could do, she insinuates, was to pursue Garvey on dubious charges. Judging that Garvey belonged among the "most prominent and most accomplished men of color of today," Shaw encourages her audience to reconsider him in the context of his unfair persecution by the white government (45).

To end her epideictic essay, Shaw announces:

The Negro has received from America the Christian religion, western civilization, education, the industrial arts and business and professional life. The Negro has given to America labor, blood, folk lore music, patriotism and loyalty, and the Christian virtues: Humility, meekness, devotion, fidelity, patience and kindness. (45)

108
Glossing (over) Historical Realities

The parallel structure of Shaw's statement initially seems to suggest an equal exchange. Yet her second sentence is longer and more specific as she charts the contributions of African Americans to American society, noting that they had supplied their labor and shed their blood as both slaves and soldiers, proving their patriotism most recently in World War I. Furthermore, although they "received" the Christian religion from whites, they show whites how to enact Christian virtues. Shaw's final line is vehement: "The Negro race is the greatest of all races and, comparatively speaking, the most progressive of all humanity" (45). Countering dominant culture discourse that denigrated African Americans as inferior and passive, Shaw praises them as superior and active, moving from deprivation and slavery to achievement and leadership in a few generations.

The same volume of the yearbook that published Shaw's radical pronouncement features an article that salutes the efforts of Lincoln students to promote racial solidarity by studying African American history and starting a junior branch of the NAACP at the school. Bernice Harvey, the president of the Negro History Club of Lincoln High School, collaborated with reporter Reginald F. Fisher to chart the formation of the new organization, which was founded in February 1923 to "to study prominent men and women of the race, Negro literature, and the progress of the Negro in all his achievements" (52) (fig. 4.1). Harvey and Fisher report that after club members met Walter White, assistant secretary for the NAACP, they decided to form a junior branch of the NAACP. A year later, Nina R. Lawrie, president of the Negro History Club for the 1923–24 school year, notes that the club inspired the Lincoln faculty to offer a class in "Negro History" for full credit. In her article, Lawrie adds that the club donated African American histories to the Lincoln library and compiled information at the African American branch of the Kansas City public library "as an index for lovers of race achievements." These reports on the Negro History Club document the engagement of Lincoln students in the early African American history movement, which began in 1915 with the organization of the Association for the Study of Negro Life and History (Dagbovie 1, 3). The Lincoln girls who wrote about the Negro History Club did not aspire to alter the perceptions of whites, who probably did not read the Lincoln yearbooks, but the students did aim to positively influence the perspectives of their peers by informing them of their illustrious past.

THE LITERARY DIGEST CLUB

HISTORY CLUB

Figure 4.1. "History Club" (*bottom*), *The Lincolnian*, 1923. Used by permission of the University of Missouri–Kansas City Libraries, Dr. Kenneth J. LaBudde Department of Special Collections.

110
Glossing (over) Historical Realities

While Shaw persuades Lincoln students to imagine themselves as part of an international contemporary community of African Americans, and Harvey and Lawrie urge students to acknowledge their ties to the historical community of African Americans, Lucile Bluford advocates racial solidarity in the parallel community of Kansas City through her editorial for the 4 November 1926 issue of the Lincoln newspaper. Displaying the persuasive skills that she would later use as the activist editor of the *Kansas City Call*, she was blunt in "New Schools":

> Everyone knows that the Negroes of Kansas City need better schools. A new high school is especially needed. The present building is not large enough to accommodate the pupils who attend it. The opposite race has six high schools, in which to educate its children. The Negroes, however, have but one inadequate building and that in an unsuitable location. The board of education is going to give us a new building with better equipment and in a better location, but when? "When?" is the question. They have been going to do this for the last two or three years. Surely it cannot be thought the Negro citizens do not deserve a new school. Has not Lincoln as large a percentage of pupils attending college as any high school of the city? Are not two of Lincoln's graduates on the University of Kansas Honor Roll? Still with these facts we are neglected. We must make the best of it, however, and hope that some day we will have a building as fully equipped and as ideally located as any in the city. (2)[9]

Demonstrating the deliberative capacity of epideictic rhetoric in her editorial, Bluford supports adult leaders of the African American community of Kansas City who had been campaigning for a new school for years. In March 1920, a statement endorsed by the major African American organizations of Kansas City, Missouri, was presented to the school board. The report notes that the Lincoln facility served more than twice the number of the 250 students for which it was built and that it had not been expanded for fifteen years. Six to eight classes had to be held on the stairs, seventeen teachers had no desks, and there was no library, librarian, gymnasium, study hall, or art department. The physical science department lacked equipment and laboratory space, and the domestic science department stove leaked gas so badly that windows had to be open during class regardless of the weather. The statement also charges that Lincoln compared poorly to schools for African Americans in other cities.

111
Glossing (over) Historical Realities

A year later, the school board decided to seek voter approval for a bond issue for new school construction. Nelson C. Crews, editor of the *Kansas City Sun*, urged African American voters to reject the school bonds unless the board of education guaranteed that a share of the bond money would be allotted for the improvement of black schools. The bond issue passed, but Lincoln did not benefit; two new schools for white children were built, and a new white high school was planned (Coulter 184–87).

Four years later, Bluford took up this unresolved issue in her editorial, which aims to build racial solidarity that would lead to collective action for a new school. Significantly, the editorial carries her byline, which was rare in the Lincoln newspaper and probably signified the controversial nature of its subject—or the authority of its writer. Taking a defiant tone, she begins by asserting, "Everyone knows that the Negroes of Kansas City need better schools"—a sweeping statement that implies that whites were as well aware of this need as African Americans. Announcing her specific agenda in the second sentence, she builds a case for a new high school. As Bluford puts it, the Lincoln building was not large enough for its enrollment and was situated in an "unsuitable location." Rather than dilute her argument with details, she uses the epideictic tactic of creating opposing groups: whereas African Americans had only one high school, whites had six. Bluford continues to forge African American solidarity by demonizing the board of education. It went without saying, of course, that the board was white. Noting that this group claimed it would "give us" a new and properly equipped school on a site removed from the brothels, saloons, and gambling houses that surrounded the school at its current location, Bluford casts doubt on the sincerity of that promise by repeatedly asking, "When?" (Schirmer 126).

Bluford then shifts from the epideictic technique of blame to that of praise to extol the achievements of Lincoln alumni as proof that "Negro citizens" deserve a new school. Her use of rhetorical questions reinforces the authority of her statements: "Has not Lincoln as large a percentage of pupils attending college as any high school of the city? Are not two of Lincoln's graduates on the University of Kansas Honor Roll?" Her diction reiterates her epideictic agenda, as she relies on facts to persuade her peers to think of themselves as a coalition denoted by the collective pronoun "we." In closing, she counsels patience, a trait that in her 1923 yearbook essay, Shaw identifies as emblematic of African Americans as a group. Promoting patience, both Bluford and Shaw enact Kennedy's contention that epideictic rhetoric holds

112
Glossing (over) Historical Realities

"out an ideal as something real the speaker hopes to make true in the future belief or actions of the addressee and the audience" (*New History* 22). While African American epideictic rhetors were not always patient, they certainly were perseverant in their racial-uplift campaigns.

A final example of the epideictic prose of Lincoln girls is an editorial published in the 7 December 1927 issue of the school newspaper. Although the opinion piece does not have a byline, it must have been written by Bluford or one of the other members of the all-girl editorial staff listed in the masthead. Simultaneously candid and conciliatory, the editorial is titled "The Color Line," the first use of Du Bois's famous phrase in the Lincoln publications surveyed in this chapter. The writer or writers begin by frankly addressing this historical reality at a local level: "It has often been thought and said that the students of the white high schools of Kansas City look upon the Negro students of Lincoln High School with contempt" (2). The editorial then takes an unexpected turn:

> This assumption was contradicted several days ago when four Negro delegates along with eighteen white delegates represented Kansas City at the Maryville Conference of the Boys' Hi-Y Club. The Negro boys ate at the same table with the white boys, Negroes and whites sat side by side; engaged in jovial conversation with each other, disregarding, perhaps even forgetting, the color line completely. This tends to emphasize the spread of the Christian spirit of the Hi-Y Club. It shows that the purpose and aim of the National Organization have been realized. The fact that a group of boys, composed of two seemingly unfriendly races can associate with each other disregarding the ever-present question of color, shows that the modern youth is just one step further toward sublimity than was his father of a generation ago. He will be more successful, too, than was his father, for complete success can be gained by one who is full of brotherly love for all his fellows with whom he comes in contact, regardless of race, color or creed. (2)

Praising young male Christians for their efforts to erase racial divisions, the editorial asserts that the modern youth was more likely to achieve racial reconciliation than members of the older generation. The editorial ends with a deliberative gesture not uncommon to epideictic rhetoric, as the female writers encourage boys to join the Hi-Y:

113
Glossing (over) Historical Realities

Every junior and senior boy of Lincoln High should become a member of such an uplifting, inspiring organization, and perhaps the future Negro would so far surpass the Negro of today that the opposing race would forget all of its prejudices. (2)

Action and racial solidarity among Lincoln boys, the editorial suggests, could lead to racial equality. Assuming authority to advise their male peers, Lincoln girls imagine an equalitarian, integrated community and reject the separatist movements of race leaders, such as Marcus Garvey, and white racists who supported segregation. That integrated community, of course, would be a long time in the making, as historical narratives of Jim Crow in Kansas City and throughout the country demonstrate.

Conclusions

This chapter has analyzed the published writing of girls at Lincoln High School as epideictic rhetoric that defines and celebrates the collective identity of African Americans in the early twentieth century. Challenging white prejudice, the consequences of Jim Crow, and divisions of class and ideology among African Americans, these young women praise their peers as progressive and unified members of society. My analysis relies upon reading the epideictic rhetoric of Lincoln girls through a new lens that merges rhetorical and historical theories about epideictic discourse and parallel communities. This lens may also bring into clearer focus the published epideictic rhetoric of other groups, such as the Italian immigrant press, which helped to invent "an Italian-American ethnicity" in the late nineteenth and early twentieth centuries, according to Rudolph J. Vecoli (22).

Aligning themselves with adults who advocated New Negro principles, Lincoln girls echo and contribute to the epideictic rhetoric of African American print culture. As they interpret historical realities through poetry and prose, they champion race pride and racial solidarity by celebrating Lincoln High School and chronicling the achievements of African Americans locally and nationally. They advocate self-help and upward mobility by citing the movement of citizens of color into the middle class through economic venues and social organizations, such as African American–owned businesses and the YWCA. They encourage African Americans to regard themselves as a

114
Glossing (over) Historical Realities

group that deserved a better high school and urge young people to recognize their ability to blur the color line. Glossing historical realities, they demonstrate how epideictic rhetors attempt to alter those realities.

Like privileged white girls at Miss Barstow's School and Native American girls at the Haskell Institute, Lincoln girls tried to delineate their collective identity in an era and a society that tended to position particular groups as "problems" and "questions." As U.S. citizens pondered how to deal with the "girl problem," the "Indian question," and the "Negro problem," these girls responded rhetorically, arguing in the pages of student publications that they were neither problems nor questions but active agents intervening in discourses of gender, race, and class. Using the same epideictic strategies as Haskell girls, Lincoln girls use both praise and blame, connect their efforts to broader national initiatives, and counter their designation as the Other.

As the next chapter shows, white working- and middle-class girls at Central High School used epideictic rhetoric to mediate conflicts created by factions at one of the largest secondary schools in the country. Despite their differences and their different agendas, all of these girls inform and productively complicate our understandings of epideictic rhetoric in the past and the present.

CHAPTER 5

Creating Consubstantiality: Central Girls

Launched in the pride of youth and of beauty.
Alike was it free from
Contention and frats, the vice of all schools.
Neither rival had it in the town nor in the country surrounding;
Clear was its title as heaven, to the best of all high schools.
There the youth of the city gleamed, and in gleaming gained
    knowledge.
        —Gwendolen Edwards, "Central High School"

THE LARGEST AND IN some respects the most socially complex school in this study, Central High School offers opportunity to assess the epideictic efforts of girls whose rhetorical occasions were different from those of young women at Miss Barstow's School, the Haskell Institute, and Lincoln High School. A prototype for the modern public high school in the United States, Central provided taxpayer-supported education to the white sons and daughters of the working and middle classes of Kansas City, Missouri.[1] The school was founded in 1869 and reportedly was the largest coeducational high school in the United States by 1900, inspiring one observer to call it "a small city within itself" (Kansas City Board of Education: *Twenty-Ninth Annual Report* 81; *Twenty-Fifth Annual Report* 20). With an enrollment that ranged from 1,800 pupils in 1895 to 2,376 in 1925, it is not surprising that students formed affiliations based on gender, grade level, and aptitudes (Kansas City Board of Education: *Twenty-Fifth* 51; *Fifty-Fourth Annual Report* 69). Three school-sponsored publications reflected and reinforced the perception that

115

116
Creating Consubstantiality

the Central student body was fragmented into factions: girls, boys, freshmen, seniors, literary societies, and athletes. Of course, all Central students identified with the markers of gender and grade level, and some students were members of multiple groups. And while relationships between these alliances often were friendly, friction was not uncommon.

In the school year of 1898–99, for instance, competition between Central literary societies and acrimony among three fraternities divided students. There was a controversy after the male winners of a debate between two literary societies refused to face representatives of an all-girl literary society that was excluded from the competition. The female Philomatheans protested the incident in the Central yearbook of 1899:

> When we made bold to challenge the winners on the Plato–C.L.C. [Central Literary Club] contest, you should have heard the petty excuses, the laughs from our worthy fellow colleagues. And why? Because of the fear the boys hold for us sisters. ("Philos" 25)

Possibly punning on the word "fellow," the Philomatheans criticized boys who belonged to the all-male Platonian Society and the coed Central Literary Club for preventing girls from displaying their oratorical abilities—if not their superior command of these skills. Meanwhile, the antics of the male members of Phi Sigma, Phi Lambda Epsilon, and Delta Omicron Omicron were so disruptive that Central administrators vowed to ban the fraternities if they continued to squabble at school.[2]

Exercising her ethos as a yearbook editor, Gwendolen Edwards sought to mend the breach caused by these divisive events through epideictic rhetoric. In a tribute published in *The Centralian* of 1899, she created the image of Central as a venerable institution:

> This is the grand Central High School. The wide-spreading
>   wings of the building,
> Darkened with dust, and in age advanced, most distinct in
>   the sunlight,
> Stretch from Eleventh and Locust half-way to much travelled
>   Twelfth street,
> Stretch like strong-holds old, with gates forever unyielding.
>   ("Central High School" 68)

Creating Consubstantiality

Emphasizing the grandeur and age of the school, Edwards describes its location at the heart of downtown Kansas City. She continues by sketching the academic activities in the building in the present as students labored to master their lessons, and she then turns to the past, recounting the founding of Central in a stanza that serves as the epigraph of this chapter.

Like ancient epideictic rhetors and nineteenth-century nativists who envisioned historical golden eras and promoted these visions as paradigms for their own troubled times, Edwards imagines an era of equanimity at Central. Charting the rise of nineteenth-century nativism, Eric P. Kaufman writes that the romantic nationalist "views the present as an age of decline and seeks to use the myth of an idealized past to revive virtues that supposedly characterized the national ethnic group during its Golden Age" (23). Edwards emulates the tactic of Lincoln girls in chapter 3 by glossing over historical realities: Central was the only public high school in Kansas City, Missouri, from 1869 until Lincoln High School was established for African Americans in 1888 (Worley, "Historic"). From the beginning, Central was racially segregated, and African American students could not attend a local high school until Lincoln opened. Central students, however, rarely mentioned Lincoln, and the two schools did not meet in athletic contests or extracurricular activities, such as debate. Furthermore, the racist climate of Kansas City did not encourage white students to regard African American students as equals, the requisite for rivalry. The second public high school for whites, Manual Training High School, did not open until 1897; therefore, Central had no rival in the city for thirty years because none existed.

Such facts, however, did not further Edwards's epideictic agenda, which was to counter animosity and cultivate unanimity among students. Insisting that factionalism did not exist in the early days of Central, she acknowledges that it had developed and adversely affected the current state of affairs at the school:

> Each year the frats have grown stronger, 'til at last they create
> Much discord, even as the insect of the summer
> Disturbs the dreamer at eve-tide. Now has been issued
> A stern decree, and banished the *Greeks* are forever,
> If into old Central's sacred realm they bring their quarrels
>   and contentions.

118
Creating Consubstantiality

> Societies still reign supreme and strive to outrival each other,
> Claiming each for itself all glory and power literary,
> But by the school at large, in regard to these declarations,
> Addison-like, 'tis opinioned, "There's much to be said on all
> sides." (71)

Comparing fraternities to insects, Edwards diminishes the stature of the groups that troubled the "sacred realm" of Central. She also acknowledges the discord created by the Philomatheans, the Platonians, and the Central Literary Club, but she suggests that like eighteenth-century English essayist Joseph Addison, Central students had the collective good sense to keep such petty matters in perspective. Conjuring an image of Central as a serene sphere, Edwards promotes consubstantiality, an essential aspect of epideictic rhetoric.

Conceptions of Consubstantiality

Most discussions of consubstantiality begin with the theory of Kenneth Burke, who maintains:

> A is not identical with his colleague, B. But insofar as their interests are joined, A is *identified* with B. Or he may *identify himself* with B even when their interests are not joined, if he assumes that they are, or is persuaded to believe so. . . . To identify A with B is to make A *consubstantial* with B. (20–21; original emphasis)

Creating an equation to define a rhetorical concept, Burke clarifies his meaning:

> A doctrine of *consubstantiality*, either explicit or implicit, may be necessary to any way of life. For substance, in the old philosophies, was an *act*; and a way of life is an *acting-together*; and in acting together, men have common sensations, concepts, images, ideas, attitudes that make them *consubstantial*. (21; original emphasis)

Burke does not explain how these doctrines originate and evolve or give examples of the elements that make people consubstantial, but he suggests that people identify with each other "in terms of some principle that they share in common" (21).

119
Creating Consubstantiality

Burke was born in 1897 and attended a public coeducational high school during the same period as the girls in this study. Like some Central students, he was the working-class grandson of immigrants—his maternal grandparents were from France and Germany, and his paternal grandparents were from Ireland and Germany (Kostelanetz 1–2). Burke was one of six hundred students in the first class of Peabody High School in Pittsburgh, Pennsylvania, where he took six years of Latin and two years of Greek, reading Aristotle and Roman rhetors in their original languages ("Our History"; Rountree 20). At Peabody, Burke began his lifelong friendship with the future literary critic Malcolm Cowley and "was part of a literary crowd that rebelled against the school curriculum and the adolescent interests of other students," according to Ross Wolin (9). In a 1987 interview, Burke praised Peabody as "a great public school" and recalled his Harvard-trained teacher of Greek (Kostelanetz 3). Although neither Burke nor his biographers suggest that his high school experiences shaped his concept of consubstantiality, as the intellectually inclined son of an office clerk who urged him to give up his literary aspirations and become a banker, Burke clearly found commonalities with other students and teachers at Peabody (Wolin 9).

Burke refers to the antecedent of consubstantiality as the "old philosophies." Historicizing consubstantiality, Cheryl Glenn links it to the ancient Greek ideal of *homonoia*. Glenn notes that Pythagoras of Croton, who organized a school that admitted female and male students in the sixth century B.C.E., espoused a program of moral reform that "aimed to eliminate discontent among the citizens and to produce, instead, a state of *homonoia*, or union of hearts and minds" (31). A century later in Athens, homonoia was understood as "being of one mind" and was cultivated through epideictic rhetoric (Glenn 35).

Among contemporary rhetoricians who theorize the process of consubstantiality, Chaim Perelman and Lucie Olbrechts-Tyteca observe that the epideictic speaker "tries to establish a sense of communion centered around particular values recognized by the audience" (51). Elaborating on the role of the rhetor in building consubstantiality, Dale L. Sullivan comments:

> Because the epideictic rhetor is attempting to bring people fully into the same tradition of which he or she is a representative, and because the listeners are considered at least initiate members of that tradition, the rhetor treats them as though they are already within the pale and attempts to increase the intensity of their adherence to those values held in common. (126)

120
Creating Consubstantiality

Jerry Blitefield acknowledges Burke by defining consubstantiality as "an identification with others that does not claim to erase differences but rather attempts to build upon those shared segments of disparate lives about which people feel a commonality of concerns" (258). Blitefield then uses this concept to assess the tactics of twentieth-century community activist Saul Alinsky, who organized the Industrial Areas Foundation (IAF) in Chicago in 1940 to assist communities seeking change. The IAF worked "to achieve consubstantiality through defining issues for collective community concern" and "corporealized" this concept "by finding occasion during which community members can experience each other en masse," Blitefield states (258). For Alinsky, those occasions included public demonstrations that allowed people with common causes to experience solidarity while protesting injustice. In summary, epideictic rhetors create consubstantiality by encouraging auditors to recognize the ideas and ideals that unite them—or may unite them—rather than focusing on the differences that do or could divide them.

Such acts of communion are particularly important in times of cultural and social change, when accepted ideas may be challenged and new ideals may emerge. The late nineteenth and early twentieth centuries were a time of change for many young people in the United States, as unprecedented numbers of diverse girls and boys of the lower and middle classes convened in coeducational public institutions, such as Central High School. These schools served as sites for interrogating beliefs that secondary education should be limited to boys and the economically elite, that girls were intellectually inferior to boys and physically incapable of the demands of advanced academics, and that girls and boys should be educated separately in gender-differentiated courses of study. Coeducational public high schools also allowed young people to formulate new ideals, such as the young female scholar, and to resurrect the Greek ideal of the erudite male athlete. Most important, Central and other similar schools enabled young people to construct their own communities, which required them to create communion.

As this chapter will show, Central girls built consubstantiality to counter factionalism and thus promoted community at their high school. Contributing poetry and prose to the Central yearbook, literary magazine, and newspaper, these young women illustrate Burke's tenets by endorsing the image of a venerable institution, the attitude of inclusivity, and the sensation of school spirit to counter factionalism at the high school during the late nineteenth and early twentieth centuries, discussed in the next section.

121
Creating Consubstantiality

Central Factions

A faction often is defined as a contentious minority within a larger group and tends to be associated with politics. Social scientists note, however, that the term also describes groups that compete for dominance and that factionalism is a form of social organization in contexts ranging from peasant villages to schools (Datnow 205). Reed Ueda recognizes factions and factionalism in late nineteenth-century public high schools: "The turn-of-the-century high school was a community with a high degree of social organization and differentiation. Through voluntary choice of coursework and extracurricular activities, students sorted themselves into specialized groups" (146). At the two East Coast coeducational public high schools in Ueda's study, these specialized groups included sororities, fraternities, scholars, male athletic teams, and the staffs of school-sponsored publications. Ueda writes that "a sense of social hierarchy was produced through the exclusivity of the fraternities and sororities, and the subordination of lower classmen to upper classmen" (147). The same held true at Central High School, although there were differences in these specialized groups. At the schools in Ueda's study, fraternities and sororities were local organizations modeled on the Greek societies of colleges; one of the sororities described its members as the "wealthy, curled darlings of the nation," which suggests that they were economically elite students (121). The Central female literary societies also may have looked to college groups as models, but there is no mention of sororities in Central student publications. The Central fraternities that existed in 1899 apparently were chapters of national groups. For example, the Phi Sigma section of the 1899 Central yearbook lists chapters in eight other cities, including Chicago, Detroit, Los Angeles, and San Francisco ("Phi Sigma" 61).[3] And while economic class may have been a criterion for membership, that issue never was broached in Central student publications. Furthermore, fraternities disappeared at Central in the early 1900s.

One of the remarkable features of the factionalism at Central is that it did not pivot on the cultural distinctions of the student body—at least in public discourse. The first public high school in Kansas City, Missouri, Central was racially segregated, but its students were from different regions of the country and of different ethnicities. In 1895, the school district recorded the birthplaces of its 19,189 pupils. The largest group (6,471) was born in Kansas City, followed by Missouri (4,584), central states (4,204), western states and territories (2,116), and Atlantic states (821). (The central, western, and Atlantic

122

Creating Consubstantiality

states are not named, and the south is not listed as a category.) The total of foreign-born students is 723: "German states" (175), Great Britain (142), Ireland (47), and "other foreign countries" (359). The birthplaces of 270 students were unknown (Kansas City Board of Education, *Twenty-Fourth Annual Report* 58). The 1907 roster of Central seniors includes Edna Bimmerman, whose maternal and paternal grandparents were German; Philip L. Epstein, the third child of Russian immigrants and the first of their six children to be born in the United States; Ethel Kapy, whose mother was from England and whose father was from Hungary; Ione McCahon, whose paternal grandparents were Irish; and Arthur Stein, whose father was Austrian and whose mother was German (U.S. Census 1900, 1910).[4]

Despite the diversity of the student body, Central students rarely discussed their cultural differences in school-sponsored publications, even during World War I, when some Americans of Irish and German ancestry did not support the Allied cause. In fact, the German Club of Central High School, an organization founded in 1903 for students who studied German, continued to meet through the war. The German Club disappeared from the Central yearbook in 1919 and must have disbanded after the defeat of Germany in World War I; it was not reorganized until 1927.

One of the exceptions to the Central rule of silence on ethnic differences is an essay by Judith Connelly, who addresses the influx of Italians and Russian Jews to Kansas City in "Our Foreign Cousins," published in the Central yearbook of 1906. Referring to the debate on "the immigration question" in Congress and a plethora of magazine articles about eastern cities crowded with newcomers, Connelly claims, "It behooves the people of Kansas City to study the quota of strangers within their own gates." In fact, as noted in chapter 1, foreign-born residents constituted only 11 percent of the population of Kansas City, Missouri, in 1900, and 9 percent in 1910, but the 1910 percentage represents a 27 percent increase and helped to propel the anxiety that Connelly expresses in her commentary.

The most prominent factions at Central from 1895 to 1925 were based on gender—girls versus boys. Jane H. Hunter reports similar findings in her study of East Coast public high schools comparable to Central:

> The gender segregation of nineteenth-century society reached deep into coeducational high schools. Students may have shared classes and competed for awards, but they were slow to lose their consciousness

123
Creating Consubstantiality

(if they ever did) that they belonged to two opposing corporate bodies, distinguished by culture and loyalty: the boys and the girls. (223)

The demographics of coeducational public high schools fortified this trend. At Central, like other schools throughout the country, girls outnumbered boys through 1925. In 1895, the enrollment comprised 1,078 girls and 567 boys ("Class of '95" 19). By 1925, the school district had stopped publicly recording the number of girls versus boys who attended Central, but the composition of the senior class indicates that the disparity continued. That year, there were 334 girls and 261 boys in the senior class (Kansas City Board of Education, *Fifty-Fourth Annual Report 1925* 69). During the early years of the school, Central publications listed honor rolls that showed girls also academically outranked boys.

Yet girls did not unequivocally rule the school: boys consistently were elected class president until the 1920s; they formed the interschool Central debate teams until 1914; they dominated the competitive athletics that were a focal point of high school culture from the 1890s; and they acted as editor of the yearbook every year from 1899 to 1925, except for 1915 and 1924. In contrast, girls were elected to the supporting positions of class vice president, secretary, and treasurer; they debated within their single-sex literary societies, but they did not represent their school in competitions for more than two decades; and they had far fewer athletic options that received much less attention than those of boys. Girls fared better on the staff of the literary magazine, serving as managing editor for issues published in 1895, 1900, 1914, 1915, and 1924. Hunter's contention that "high school classes demonstrated a penchant for patriarchy" is pertinent to Central (228). The culture of Central mirrored adult society, which viewed leadership, public oration, and physical displays of prowess as male prerogatives—as opposed to the culture of Miss Barstow's School, which contested these views. The Central administration reinforced the idea that men were leaders: the school had male principals and vice principals from 1873 through 1925. Yet women exercised influence as teachers, serving as mentors and role models for both girls and boys. In 1895 there were seventeen female teachers and fourteen male teachers; in 1925 there were fifty-six female teachers and thirty-four male teachers ("Class of '95" 19; "Faculty" 18).

Clearly, gender politics affected school politics at Central, encouraging girls and boys to see themselves as different groups and to portray their differences in three publications: *The Luminary*, a magazine that was introduced

124
Creating Consubstantiality

in 1885 and was issued on a varied schedule over the years; *The Centralian*, the yearbook first released in 1899; and a weekly newspaper, also called the *Luminary*, that made its debut in 1921.[5] For example, the May 1895 issue of *The Luminary* magazine features student Paul J. Leidigh's essay, "The New Man." Leidigh mocks two popular models of women: the New Woman, who eschews marriage and domesticity for college and paid work, and "the angel in the house," who lives to serve her husband and children.[6] In turn, L. Julia Berger portrays high school boys as vain, shallow, and silly in her poem "The Evolution of the Freshman: In Four Chapters," published in the 1899 *Centralian*. Berger hints that high school boys were neither manly nor masculine. As Gail Bederman documents, "manly" signified the nineteenth-century ideal of the honorable and dutiful man, and "masculine" denoted a new male paradigm that emphasized physical vigor and activity (23, 27).

This "gender sparring"—Hunter's term for the battle of the sexes conducted in high school publications—continued at Central as the decades passed. In November 1914, Helen J. Tann, the female managing editor of *The Luminary* magazine, speaks directly to girls as she celebrates her authority over an all-male staff:

> It is with fear and trembling that the editor takes up her pen (doesn't that "her" sound fine, girls?) to write this editorial. Shades of Walter P. Brown and David N. Ross! To succeed these physical and intellectual giants, is no small task for one who is under five feet and whose brain is built in proportion. (Editorials 5)

Referring to two former male editors of the magazine, Tann begins in a humorously self-deprecating tone that she quickly alters:

> However, the editor has two great advantages; viz., belonging to the superior sex and to the Woman Suffrage Party. This, added to the fact that she is assisted by eleven noble, handsome, and talented Worms of the Dust, should assure the success of the 1915's Luminary. (5–6)

The "Worms of the Dust" refers to the boys serving as business managers and associate editors (fig. 5.1). By 1920 *The Luminary* had introduced a section called "Girls" that offered reports on girls' debate and sports and may have reflected special sections for women in professional publications aimed at mixed audiences. While this section of *The Luminary* ensured coverage of girls' activities, it also symbolized the division between girls and boys.

Creating Consubstantiality

Furthermore, there was not a "Boys" section—an editorial gesture that rendered boys the normative Central students.

Academic class inspired the second most important set of student factions at Central. High schools such as Central borrowed higher-education terminology to classify students as freshmen, sophomores, juniors, and seniors. Imitating college and university students, who assigned specific and often derogatory traits to each group, Central students often characterized freshmen as naïve, sophomores as self-assured, juniors as all-knowing, and seniors as smug. The unnamed author of a yearbook account of the junior class of 1899 capsulizes the class competition:

> The historian wishes to place before the public a correct journal of this noble class, without any of that sneering and deriding, that raillery and eulogism that are so much indulged in by ignorant Seniors and others of unmentionable insignificance, Sophomores and Freshmen. ("Juniors" 16)

Figure 5.1. Helen J. Tann and the "Worms of the Dust," *The Centralian*, 1915. Used by permission of the University of Missouri–Kansas City Libraries, Dr. Kenneth J. LaBudde Department of Special Collections.

126
Creating Consubstantiality

Amplifying the insult, the junior continues: "We blush with shame to say that we were once Freshmen. Yet that blush wanes when we look at the examples of that class now before us" (16). As sophomores,

> we held in memory all that had proven valuable to us in the past, and, being endowed with better developed minds than the present Sophomores have, we were enabled to add much more to our already large stock of understanding and scholarship. (16)

Defying the logic of high-school hierarchy, which ranks seniors first, the writer triumphantly concludes: "But now we are Juniors; we have reached the highest pinnacle that can be attained in High School. In this position we are the loftiest and most envied" (16).

An anonymous member of the freshmen class of 1899 retorts:

> Recipients for all anti-diluvian jokes, unspared objects for jests and jibes so called, milk-drinking, candy-eating, sand-pile-playing Freshmen, we want to state right now that we are here, four hundred strong, patiently, serenely abiding the time when the hated name of Freshmen will be relegated to the past and we shall be Sophomores, rampant in name and deed. ("Freshmen" 19)

Class histories were a regular feature of *The Centralian* through 1920, but their tone generally was not as vehement as these examples from 1899. Nonetheless, their regular inclusion confirms the significance of academic class factions at Central. By the 1920s, the senior class was privileged in the Central yearbook. *The Centralian* of 1920, for example features a forty-five-page senior section of student photos that includes club affiliations and a slogan for each senior; the senior section in the 1925 yearbook is a seventy-seven-page photo gallery that lists students' affiliations and clubs.

A third set of Central factions was founded on the intellectual and physical aptitudes of students: literary societies and athletic organizations. Although membership rules for the first Central literary societies were not recorded in student publications, comparing the number of members to the total student enrollment suggests that these were selective associations that may have had certain requirements, such as high grade averages, and admitted members through application or invitation. The unspoken criteria, of course, may have included the prominence, popularity, ethnicity, and economic class of applicants. In 1899, for example, 1,187 girls attended Central, but only 38

127
Creating Consubstantiality

girls belonged to the Philomathean Society (Kansas City Board of Education, *Twenty-Eighth Annual Report* 42; "Philos" 25). In a yearbook report, a representative of the group that took its name from the Greek words for "loving" and "to learn" counters the notion that academically inclined girls were a stodgy bunch:

> We are jolly girls, too. We do not believe in devoting a lifetime under the tree of knowledge, but often turn down the broad path of pleasure. Now and then we stop for a party or feast, yet return ever and anon to the protection of our wisdom tree. ("Philos" 25)

The male counterpart to the Philomathean Society was the Platonian Society, which had 32 members during a year school when 609 boys were enrolled at Central (Kansas City Board of Education, *Twenty-Eighth Annual Report* 42; "Platonian Society" 27). The two coed societies, the Central Literary Club and the Society of Literature and History (SLH) had 45 members and 40 members, respectively ("Central Literary Club" 30; "S.L.H.'s" 33). The competition among these four groups is evident in their 1899 yearbook reports, and the SLH account charts other rivalries. The SLH asserts that before its founding in March 1892:

> Central High School dragged on a wearisome existence with a fortitude and perseverance that was truly remarkable. To be sure, the Glee Club pounded their guitars and sang most dolefully, the Platos and C.L.C.'s held their insomnia-curing contests, yet there was no real life to be seen, no S.L.H. to keep things going. ("S.L.H.'s" 34)

Encouraged by pupils and teachers, twenty-five of the "best pupils in the school" organized this society, which won the Interstate Oratorical Contests in 1894, 1895, and 1896. The SLH reporter comments: "Since then the other societies have deemed it wisest not to compete with the S.L.H., but to hold little contests of their own, in which they can get at least even honors" ("S.L.H.'s" 34). Over the years, societies came and went, but the rivalry continued, encouraged by an annual competition that pitted these organizations against each other in contests of oration, extemporaneous speaking, declamation, essay, verse, and story. *The Centralian* reinforced this rivalry by naming and picturing the winners of these matches.

The athletic faction at Central was a boys' club open to a small number of males who received an inordinate amount of attention in school publications.

128
Creating Consubstantiality

In 1899 there were two football teams with twenty-five boys, a baseball team with nine boys, and a track team with fourteen boys. Despite the limited number of male athletes, as compared to 149 literary society members, the Central yearbook of 1899 devoted eight pages to boys' athletics—and none to girls' athletics. A year later, the newly formed Girls' Athletic Association merited two pages in the yearbook, as compared to seven pages for boys' sports. The disparity in yearbook coverage continued through 1925. In 1910 boys' teams were allotted twenty-four pages and girls' teams, two pages; in 1920 boys got eight pages and girls, three pages; in 1925 the boys' sports section was seventeen pages and the girls' section was six pages. The quality of coverage, as well as the quantity, also varied by gender: individual photos of male football and basketball players often appeared, while female athletes were pictured in smaller team photos. This trend was due to the predominance of boys' sports at Central and possibly to the fact that boys acted as yearbook editors every year other than 1915 and 1924—once again, a radical difference from Miss Barstow's School.

The rise of factions at Central High School had mixed consequences. Involuntary coalitions, such as those based on gender, required members to negotiate issues that they would face in the future and to challenge stereotypes and restrictive ideologies. Voluntary coalitions, such as literary societies and athletic teams, offered students the opportunity to join together to pursue specific interests and to exercise shared abilities. Yet both forms of factions separated students and presented the occasion for epideictic rhetoric that created consubstantiality. The same discursive venues that recorded and bolstered Central factions provided girls a platform for countering their divisive effects. Of course, the factional interests of girls who wrote for Central student publications may have affected their epideictic rhetoric, but they seldom publicly promoted their own agendas.

Girls Creating Consubstantiality

A survey of Central student publications from 1895 to 1925 reveals that girls were more likely than boys to try to create consubstantiality through epideictic rhetoric. Boys rallied students to show school spirit by supporting the male athletic teams, and they occasionally produced testimonials to the school. In contrast, Central girls composed a significant body of epideictic rhetoric that encouraged students to act together, as did Haskell and Lincoln girls.

129
Creating Consubstantiality

The question, of course, is why more girls than boys assumed this rhetorical responsibility. Gender socialization played a part. As Linda D. Kerber and other historians attest, nineteenth-century women and girls were encouraged to think of themselves as the morally superior teachers of the nation (Kerber 235). Hunter notes that late nineteenth-century parents and commentators taught girls to "be good," which included pursuing "moralist projects" (100). Merging these cultural edicts with the educational function of epideictic rhetoric, Central girls assumed authority to instruct the student body in the doctrine of consubstantiality. That doctrine, according to these young female epideictic rhetors, encompassed the image of Central as a venerable institution, the attitude of inclusivity, and the sensation of school spirit that did not depend solely on the performances of young male athletes.

THE IMAGE OF VENERABLE INSTITUTION

Burke observes that Aristotle contends that people could not think without images, and Burke suggests that "imagery could be said to convey an invisible, intangible idea in terms of visible, tangible things" (86, 90). There were both positive and negative images of public high schools in the late nineteenth and early twentieth centuries. On one hand, schools such as Central were seen as an egalitarian enterprise that educated girls and boys who would not join the minority of young people attending colleges and universities in the United States during this period. In 1900, for example, only 30 percent of high school graduates had taken the necessary courses to attend college, and most likely a smaller percentage actually enrolled (Latimer 160). On the other hand, public high schools sometimes were regarded as the domain of the affluent. In the 1870s, newspapers in Kansas City waged a campaign against Central High School, calling it "a school only for the children of the rich" ("History" 193). By the 1890s, however, school demographics indicate that most Central students came from working- and middle-class, rather than "rich," families. Meanwhile, racist and class-conscious parents thought of public high schools as places where their offspring would be forced to mingle with the children of immigrants and members of religious minorities, even though some of these parents believed that the caliber of education provided by coeducational public high schools was superior to that of private single-sex schools (Hunter 196).

In the imaginations of Central girls, however, their public high school was a "sacred realm," as Gwendolen Edwards declared in 1899 (fig. 5.2). Using idyllic images, they transformed a literal space into a figurative site of

130
Creating Consubstantiality

consubstantiality. In 1907 Beatrice Hill personifies the school in her poem "A Tribute to Central," published in the yearbook:

> You stand near the crest of the bluff; and below it
> The muddy Missouri swirls ruthless and free.
> Behind you the hills gently slope to the valley
> Where once rolled the Kaw on its way to the sea. (17)

Addressing the school as "you," the speaker of the poem alludes to the location of the school on the cliffs overlooking the conjunction of the Missouri River and the Kansas River (the Kansas River known locally as the Kaw), near downtown Kansas City. Hill takes poetic license by implying that the Kansas River "once" rolled and thus no longer did through this area. Central sits like a Greek temple, towering over the unruly rivers, far removed from the ordinary activities in the valley. The next two stanzas summarize the swift passage of time, as "Each day brought its knowledge of life's dross and life's treasures / Which lightly we culled o'er within thy dear walls" (17). Describing lessons in algebra, history, and literature as the sorting of the worthless from the valuable—"dross and treasure"—the poet elevates the nature of the intellectual labor that took place at Central before reflecting:

> Now at the end of our course we are pausing
> Yet a moment, to ponder what strength we have won;
> What power you've given; what light you've thrown over us;
> What knowledge of deeds which earth's noblest have done. (17)

Representing all Central students through the collective pronouns of "we" and "us," the speaker of Hill's ode portrays the school as the benevolent dispenser of wisdom, rather than as the location of fractious factions jostling for preeminence. Although girls and boys have "won" strength through their studies, the school acts as a deity, bestowing power, light, and knowledge of noble deeds upon its disciples. The poet concludes her tribute by merging the present and future:

> A moment we pause from our work to salute you;
> To write you on leaving one last farewell line,
> To say that one rose in the garden of memory
> Will, dear old Central, forever be thine. (17)

Creating Consubstantiality

Figure 5.2. Central High School, *The Centralian*, 1910. Used by permission of the University of Missouri–Kansas City Libraries, Dr. Kenneth J. LaBudde Department of Special Collections.

Roses have thorns, but Hill's imagery encourages her peers to associate memories of their time together at "dear old Central" with the flower that long has symbolized beauty and love.

Three years later, senior Margaret Hanley imagines Central in ethereal terms that transcended the mundane realities of contentious factions. Summoning her study of literature in "To Central," Hanley evokes Shakespeare's imagery of life as a stage and a dream:

> Thou art a hall of youthful dreams
> Where budding hope
> Of ever changing scenes anew
> Where thousands come and go.

The speaker intimates that everyone is entitled to dream and hope at Central, a theater where actors and scenes constantly shift. What does not change, however, is the shelter that the school provides:

132
Creating Consubstantiality

And when they've left thee, silence soft,
When scarce is gone that hour,
New echoes wake thy sacred walls
New ones thou dost embower.

Reminding readers that time passes quickly and their happy days at Central would end, the speaker reassures them that they could always return "in memory sweet of yore." Hanley's vision of the school emphasizes its positive impact on students and ignores the negative consequences of factions and factionalism. In so doing, she imitates the rhetorical practice of nation builders. Joyce Appleby, Lynn Hunt, and Margaret Jacob articulate the perspective of British anthropologist Mary Douglas that "nations need to control national memory, because nations keep their shape by shaping their citizens' understanding of the past" (154). Extending this observation, Appleby, Hunt, and Jacob remark that "national leaders try to control the collective memory in order to forge a civic identity" (155). As epideictic rhetors, Hanley and her fellow female poets forge Central group identity by influencing the collective memory of their classmates.

Reviving the epideictic tradition of the ancient poet Pindar, Central girls use it for different purposes than Lincoln girls. Whereas Lincoln girls produced odes to encourage racial solidarity in a homogeneous student body, Central girls used this poetic form to create consubstantiality among a more heterogeneous collective. Endowing the physical facility of their school with admirable traits, they surpassed the divisions created by student factions. Hanley's ode is the last to appear in *The Centralian*, which rarely published any form of poetry after 1910. Whether verse fell from favor among Central girls as a medium for encouraging communion or the predominately male editors of the yearbook did not choose to publish it is unclear. What is clear is that Central girls continued to remind their peers to act together by promoting the consubstantial attitude of inclusivity.

THE ATTITUDE OF INCLUSIVITY

The turn of the twentieth century was an era of exclusivity in Kansas City—and many other cities in the country. Jim Crow laws and codes excluded African Americans from white schools, neighborhoods, and business districts. Private and parochial schools, such as Miss Barstow's School, separated students of different genders, races, classes, and religions. New residential

133
Creating Consubstantiality

developments south of downtown restricted Jews from buying property. The advent of social and country clubs ensured that affluent whites could avoid fraternizing with members of ethnic and religious minorities. And professional organizations limited membership on the basis of gender, race, and class.[7] To some degree, the factionalism at Central reflected this broader trend, which girls sought to counter by advocating inclusivity as a consubstantial principle.

During the school year of 1899–1900, Central girls reacted to the factionalism that Edwards notes in her poem for the 1899 yearbook by launching a campaign for inclusivity. In general, the year was a banner year for the construction of consubstantiality by young women at the school. That fact is due in part to the composition of *The Luminary* staff, which at that time comprised members of the four Central literary societies on a rotating schedule. It is unclear if this editorial practice was imposed by adult advisers or initiated by students, but its purpose may have been to limit the influence of particular factions. Girls acted as the editor for six of the seven issues of the issues of the magazine that year, and they were clearly conscious of their rhetorical roles as community builders. Edwards was editor in chief of the first issue of *The Luminary* in October 1899, and although the editorials in Central student publications did not carry bylines, it is likely that she wrote the editorial that positioned the magazine as a mouthpiece for the school. If she did not write it, as editor she probably assigned it, indicating her commitment to the topic. Acknowledging the duty of the editors, the writer invites all students to transform this discursive space into a consubstantial site:

> We, upon whom rests the personal responsibility of the LUMINARY ask the co-operation of the school. This paper is not to be edited for the sole pleasure and benefit of the four literary societies. It is the desire and aim of the editors to make it a paper of the school; for the school and especially one by the school. Let all pupils—Freshman or Senior— realize that the more locals they hand it, the more stories or essays they write the greater will be the interest taken in the LUMINARY and therefore its circulation will be increased. (Editorial, October 1899, 23)

In an astute epideictic gesture, the writer directly challenges the assumption that the periodical serves only the egos and agendas of the elite faction of students who produced it. The third sentence echoes the Gettysburg Address (1863), when Abraham Lincoln declared that "government of the people, by

134
Creating Consubstantiality

the people, for the people, shall not perish from the earth" (18). Alluding to the most famous example of epideictic discourse of the day, which would have been well known among her peers, the writer elevates the effort to forge unity by invoking Lincoln's eloquent call for national reconciliation during the Civil War. The writer also blurs distinctions among academic classes, calling for everyone, freshman or senior, to contribute news, creative writing, and essays to the magazine. Although the writer's ulterior motive, to increase circulation, might seem suspect, a wide readership enhanced the consubstantial function of the magazine.

Four months later, the staff of *The Luminary* changed, and Ruth Mosher, who was a literary editor in October 1899, became editor. She continued the campaign for consubstantiality by addressing academic class factionalism— or ensuring that it was addressed. Although freshmen usually were the object of the condescending humor of upperclassmen, and students who began school in January, rather than in September, earned more than the usual measure of scorn, an editorial in *The Luminary* of February 1900 salutes these newcomers:

> To the Freshmen who have entered Central at the beginning of the new term, we extend a hearty welcome. Although in some respects, the middle of the year is an unfortunate time to begin High School life, affairs being in such smooth running order that it now seems difficult to find a place in the complete system, things are now on a different basis for the "half-Freshman." (Editorials 6)

Making veiled reference to the cliques and routines that constituted the "complete system" of Central, the writer concedes that newcomers face challenges—and subtly reminds established students to be sensitive to their situation. The writer then alludes to a new plan that allowed students to avoid making up work or endure the indignity of remaining freshmen for another semester. Ending on a positive note, the editorial observes:

> Some splendid classes have been opened to the new members and we foresee no reason why those hitherto considered "irregulars" should not become a strong and influential unit. The LUMINARY wishes them a most successful and enjoyable High School course. (6)

As director of the editorial section and probably the author of this commentary, Mosher was a mature member of the "culture" of Central and promotes

135
Creating Consubstantiality

inclusivity as one of the consubstantial principles of the school. While the editorial speaks explicitly to new freshman, it implicitly addresses students who already were a part of the Central culture, subtly censuring the use of the term "irregulars" for students who could constitute a "strong and influential unit"—or, in other words, a faction.

Perhaps, the idea that factions could be a positive rather than a negative fact of high school life explains why there was a dearth of persuasive discourse about inclusivity after 1900. Certainly, factions did not disappear, as confirmed by the Central yearbook, which records both voluntary coalitions, such as clubs, and the imposed associations of academic classes. By 1920, Central students could join twenty clubs and societies ranging from the Shakespeare Club to the Shorthand Club, three male athletic teams, and four female athletic organizations. The increasing number of special-interest groups may have thwarted the attitude of exclusivity by limiting the power that any one group could wield and by offering every student a social cohort. Furthermore, there were four other public high schools in Kansas City by 1920, and Central competed against all of these schools, other than Lincoln, in sports and activities, such as debate.[8] The growing number of rivals may have encouraged Central students to channel intraschool competition into interschool rivalry. In any event, inclusivity seldom was discussed in Central student publications from 1900 to 1924, when a female editor of the school newspaper revived the campaign for fostering this consubstantial attitude.

Ruth Tinsley conducted the most intensive campaign for consubstantiality during the span of this study in the October 1924 editorial sections of the *Luminary*. By this time, the magazine had been transformed into a weekly newspaper of four to six pages that featured an editorial section with four to five editorials. The editorship of the *Luminary* rotated among four students for the school year of 1924–25, and the masthead lists their names in different order, suggesting which student served as the main editor for each issue. During the month that Tinsley was listed first, the editorial section repeatedly encourages camaraderie and school spirit and discourages cliques and snobbery. It is impossible to ascertain if Tinsley wrote all of these editorials, which do not have bylines, but as editor, she ensured their inclusion. A prominent and popular student, she was president of the Student Council and earned the honor of "Girl Who Has Done Most for Central" in 1925. A glowing inscription accompanies her long list of achievements and

136
Creating Consubstantiality

affiliations in the Central yearbook of 1925: "Remarkable initiative and an inherent ability of leadership explain why she is the outstanding girl of her class" ("Ruth Tinsley" 26).

Under Tinsley's direction, the first rhetorical injunction to communion is the leading editorial of the *Luminary* for 2 October 1924. Starting with a sociological assessment, "Be Friendly" explains the inevitability of factions:

> In a school as large as Central, where we daily come into contact with so many people it is difficult for the students to become acquainted with each other. It is impossible for the entire student body to have the social relationships which are possible in a smaller school. (2)

This observation is based on fact, not rhetorical fancy: the first edition of the newspaper version of the *Luminary* on 18 September 1924 announces that Central was the largest high school in Missouri, with 2,413 students in the high school and 1,491 students in the junior high program ("Central Leads" 1). The junior high school program was introduced in 1919, when seventh-grade students began attending classes at Central ("History" 199–200).

The size of the enrollment, however, neither lessens "our need for friendliness nor does it offer an excuse for the lack of that same spirit. On the contrary the need is increased, the fault made greater by our large numbers," according to the 1924 editorial that Tinsley either wrote or assigned (2). Shifting between observation and explanation, the editorial avoids an accusatory tone and uses collective pronouns to emphasize that this problem was created by the entire student body and could only be solved by that same group. The editorial observes:

> Outside the circle of our immediate friends and some casual acquaintances who are in our classes, we know but few of our fellow students. Nor do we make any effort to know them. We are content to leave this great field of friendship untilled. We are unwilling to sow the seeds which might result in a rich harvest of worthwhile companionships. ("Be Friendly" 2)

This agricultural imagery—inspired perhaps by the industry of the region or the theme of reaping and sowing in the Bible—conveys the consequences of such short-sighted behavior. Moving from rhetorical generalities to local issues, the editorial directs the attention of auditors to its primary topic, new students at Central:

Creating Consubstantiality

There are many who come to Central this year for the first time. They hail from other schools, other localities. Perhaps they have been leaders in their school activities and outstanding students. Now they are cast into the midst of this great body of Centralites, most of us rather self-satisfied, quite content to remain with our own "crowd" with no thought of reaching out to make new friends. Yet in these new students we have offered to us a splendid opportunity for discovering real talent, students who, if drawn into the school activities, might prove to be leaders with valuable contributions to make to the life of our school. Let us seek out these people, strive to make them our friends and to help them feel at home in our great school. We who have been here, perhaps all our high school life, and who have our own groups of friends, let's show the true Central spirit. (2)

Using the rhetorical appeal of pathos to elicit the emotion of readers, the editorial cultivates empathy through the image of strangers stranded in a foreign setting where the natives are not particularly welcoming. Then it calls upon the reason of readers to argue that new students are an asset that could infuse the student body with talent and leadership—not a burden to be avoided by students who are already established at the school. Investing students with the agency to create community, the editorial also assigns them that responsibility. What made Central great was not its record in academics, athletics, or any achievement by its factions but its commitment to inclusivity—the "true Central spirit." As this close reading of "Be Friendly" reveals, the epideictic rhetor builds consubstantiality by defining the orthodox values of a community and then inviting community members to celebrate that tradition through their attitudes and actions.

The *Luminary* of 16 October 1924, still supervised by Tinsley, considers the discord produced by another set of factions: junior high and senior high students.[9] The crowded conditions at Central created ill will among students, as the leading editorial, "Be Considerate," makes clear: "The right feeling has not been existing between the students of the senior and junior high schools. The students of each school seem to consider those of the other as intruders" (2). The editorial acknowledges that the activities of each group of students sometimes hindered those of the other group, but it urges students to recognize their crucial commonality: "In most cases the students either will be, or have been enrolled in the other of the two schools. This should lead them to feel that they all have somewhat the same interests" (2).

138
Creating Consubstantiality

The "same interests" advocates the convergence instead of the divergence of different groups.

To counter the trend of exclusivity, Central girls espouse the attitude of inclusivity in their epideictic rhetoric. Edwards authorizes the description of the Central literary magazine as a collaborative consubstantial space that depends on the contributions of all students. Mosher endorses the welcoming of new freshmen to Central and suggests that they could constitute a faction of students that would strengthen the student body. Tinsley commissions the analysis of factors that led to cliques—the large size of Central, the influx of students from other schools, and the presence of junior high students—to underscore the importance of friendliness. As these young women make clear, the true Central spirit depended upon a unified, rather than divided, student body.

THE SENSATION OF SCHOOL SPIRIT

Tinsley's emphasis on school spirit evokes an epideictic issue that would be discussed by other girls as they worked to create communion at Central. School spirit is a common phrase in Central publications, as well as in other public high school periodicals of the era. Assessing this sensation at public high schools in Somerville, Massachusetts, near Boston, Ueda comments that "the unique sense of community felt by students was expressed by the invocations of 'school spirit.' It was the analog of boosterism practiced by parents who promoted Somerville's civic virtues" (123). Ueda observes that student factions deterred the development of school spirit and that "school leaders struggled constantly to create a broader, abstract concept of school spirit that though lacking the power of intimacy might embrace all by its common symbolism and ritualism" (123). As was the case at Central High School, the editors of the Somerville school magazine assumed responsibility for fostering school spirit. Ueda also notes that high school athletics and male sports teams were the most powerful catalyst of "school patriotism." Hunter links school spirit and nationalism, engendered by the Spanish-American War, in her discussion of school spirit at Concord High School in Milford, New Hampshire:

> The birth of "school spirit" was an energizing source of collective fun, but it centered around boys' sports and the boys' cadet corps and often left girls in auxiliary positions as chief cheerleaders or as members of the girls' cadet corps. (253)

Creating Consubstantiality

The Concord High School newspaper reinforces the notion that the activities and achievements of boys created school spirit.

The association of school spirit and male pursuits suggests gender politics: girls outnumbered and often academically outranked boys at public high schools throughout the nation, but girls did not have as many opportunities to play competitive sports, which were promoted for boys by adults anxious about the alleged "feminization" of high schools. Athletics for boys were seen as a way to keep young men in school, channel their energy, and diminish the deleterious effects of the women teachers who dominated the faculties of public high schools (Tyack and Hansot 198). Sports and military groups also provided boys the opportunity to win attention and accolades that they might not earn in classrooms. If the nationalism of the period depended upon the performance of male soldiers in imperialistic actions, such as the Spanish-American War, it follows that school spirit could be construed in the same masculine terms—especially by high school boys. Such was the case at Central, where boys celebrated male athletic accomplishment as the source of school spirit. That was not the practice, however, of Central girls. Taking gender politics into their own hands, they emphasize the consubstantial function of this sensation, suggesting that all students were responsible for creating and sustaining school spirit. Some girls even go so far as to suggest that school spirit enabled sports teams to win, thus contradicting the belief that male athletic exhibitions inspired this feeling of collective pride.

In October 1899, the first editorial of *The Luminary*, under the leadership of Edwards, makes no mention of boys' sports as it promotes school spirit. Although the editorial does not have a byline, it refers to the "editor," which suggests that Edwards wrote it:

> In this, our first issue of the year, we wish to express our good-will and good fellow-ship to all students gathered beneath the friendly roof of Old Central. We are the mouthpiece of the whole school, therefore it is our duty to give utterance to the sentiment which lies at the heart of every pupil in the building. For several years past we have mourned the death of the school spirit. But the time has now come when we should lay aside our mourning; for the spirit has crept back to haunt us, preparatory to returning in all the pride and strength of former existence. Hence, this feeling of friendliness. We know that every editor of the LUMINARY has sung his little dirge over the dear departed, until the

140
Creating Consubstantiality

subject has grown almost as ancient as the moss-covered bucket you read about. But school spirit is essential to school success; therefore let us woo the timid spirit back to life and render it unnecessary for this paper to add another verse to the mournful hymn of its predecessors. (Editorial 22–23)

From the first sentence, Edwards articulates the esprit de corps that she wishes to inspire among Central students. Addressing "all students," she endorses cordiality and collectivity, reiterating the image of the school as an affable and venerable institution. Edwards then reinforces her credentials to create consubstantiality by pointing out that *The Luminary* represents the sentiments of the entire student body, which include the desire for school spirit. This ineffable essence dies without proper cultivation, flourishes with cooperative coaxing, and is imperative to "school success." Calling for goodwill and good fellowship, Edwards produces what Sullivan describes as a "successful epideictic encounter." Such an encounter, he writes,

> is one in which the rhetor, as a mature member of the culture, creates an aesthetic vision of orthodox values, an example (*paradeigma*) of virtue intended to create feelings of emulation, leading to imitation. As such, epideictic instructs the auditors and invites them to participate in a celebration of the tradition, creating a sense of communion. (118)

Central tradition, according to Edwards, relies upon the shared sensation of school spirit.

School spirit is the subject of Tann's editorial in the February 1915 issue of *The Luminary*. Tann, who gloated over her position as the managing editor and only girl on the staff in the November 1914 issue, takes a different approach to school spirit than either her female or male predecessors. Edwards avoids gendered activities altogether in the 1899 editorial on school spirit, and the boys who subsequently served as magazine editors often claim that the performances of boys' athletic teams roused this sensation among Central students. In contrast, Tann insists that Central school spirit existed independently of the achievements of the male athletic team and that spirit actually inspired the boys to win the interscholastic basketball championship in the school year of 1914–15.

Tann begins to build consubstantiality in her editorial column with an irreverent invocation:

141
Creating Consubstantiality

O for the tongue of a Daniel Webster, Daniel O'Connel [*sic*], Daniel in
the Lion's Den, or some other of those famous old chaps to put into
words our unalloyed rapture at having brought home that Pennant!
Interscholastic Champions? Well, rather. ("Cock-a-Doodle-Do" 6)

Her catalog of Daniels may have been an inside joke or a compilation of characters culled from history and religion classes, but her choice has rhetorical
significance: all of these figures are accomplished orators who promoted
unity. Daniel Webster was the famous nineteenth-century proponent of U.S.
nationalism; Daniel O'Connell was a nineteenth-century Irish political leader
known as "the Liberator" and "the Emancipator," who campaigned for the
right of Catholics to sit in Parliament and the repeal of the act that united
Ireland and Great Britain; and Daniel of the lion's den fame was a Jewish
nobleman who became a prominent statesman in Babylon during the sixth
century B.C.E. What is most significant, however, about Tann's opening line
is that the Central victory evoked "our unalloyed rapture." In her view, and
the view that she wants her readers to share, the triumph of the team is not
cause for celebration by only the athletic faction but by the entire student
body, as denoted by her use of the pronoun "our."

She then comically recounts the feats of the Central team against "our
honorable opponents," the three public high schools for whites in Kansas
City—Manual Training High School, Northeast High School, and Westport
High School. Echoing news accounts of World War I, she writes that in the
battle for the basketball championship, these schools

did their best, too, but none could administer the anaesthetic. We were
too strong for them. In fact, we believe it appropriate at this juncture
to offer, if not our sympathies, at least our services, in answer to the
S.O.S. call of Manual, Northeast, and Westport. Relief is now on the
way, the German and French Clubs having united in sending bandages,
lint, and heart balm. ("Cock-a-Doodle-Do" 7)

Tann aims to nurture consubstantiality among her readers by suggesting
that the rival schools were the vanquished enemy, but as the noble victor,
Central would answer their cries for help by sending supplies collected by
the language clubs. The rather twisted humor of the passage, of course,
ignores the fact that Germany and France were fighting each other during
World War I.

142
Creating Consubstantiality

Finally arriving at her main point, Tann declares:

> In closing, we wish to voice the sentiments of every Centralite—it is needless to modify the word with loyal—that victory was known to be almost inevitable. How could it be otherwise when Central holds that most priceless of heritages—a spirit? What else could keep her in the first rank with the smallest attendance of all four schools? Nothing but her undying spirit. ("Cock-a-Doodle-Doo" 7)

Positioning herself as the representative of all Central students, Tann contends that students were in communion before they assembled for the basketball championship. Her rhetorical strategy of posing questions that she then answers leaves little room for debate on this topic—although her claim that Central had the smallest enrollment contradicts district records. Anticipating possible resistance to her assertions, she directly addresses her auditors:

> You must and do admit that these "spirited" allusions are true, so continue to live up to them in the future. Display, gentle readers, that fighting spirit beneath the "gentle." Don't sell your birthright of sharing Central's glory, but try out for anything and everything. (7)

Invoking the discourse of World War I, as some Americans rooted for France and Great Britain to protect their birthrights and fight with undying spirit the Germans, Tann urges her peers to do their part to preserve Central school spirit by participating in "anything and everything"—not merely boys' athletics.

The fact that Edwards wrote about school spirit in the aftermath of the Spanish-American War, and Tann promotes this consubstantial sensation during World War I, supports Hunter's assertion that nationalism and school spirit were linked in this era. Yet nationalism does not depend only on war, as evident in the early 1920s, when the United States reacted to the perceived threat of communism, prosecuted foreign-born radicals, and passed restrictive immigration acts (Jones et al. 713). This historical context informed Ruth Tinsley's crusade for consubstantiality in the Central newspaper in October 1924 as she delivered or assigned two editorials on school spirit. The epideictic rhetoric of "The Central Spirit" follows the deliberative discourse of an editorial that dissuades misguided social ambition and another editorial that persuades students to seek the advice of

Creating Consubstantiality

teachers. Echoing the treatment of school spirit by other girls, "The Central Spirit" is not linked to the athletic performances of boys but to the behavior of every student. That spirit is manifested by "a cheerful smile of greeting and a hearty handshake," by supporting the school in all of its endeavors, by cooperating with teachers, and by determining if any deed is "worthy of Central" (2). Like the poetry that personifies Central, the editorial envisions the school as a female entity with a stalwart reputation that must be guarded: "Be eager to help in upbuilding Central's standard. Let's keep her fair name as bright and beautiful as ever before. All that combines to make the Central spirit" (2). Enumerating the ways that Central students should act together, the editorial holds every pupil accountable for creating communion at this illustrious institution.

Tinsley's second editorial action about school spirit resurrected the theme of the "fighting spirit" of Central that Tann promoted in her 1915 editorial. The gist of the 1924 editorial is that some students were not doing their best in class and thus not demonstrating the standard of excellence and initiative that defined Central. Rather these pupils wait, like lobsters stranded on rocks as the ocean tide retreats, for "some great billow of good fortune to engulf them and set them afloat" ("Fighting Spirit" 2). The editorial asserts that the school "is on the rocks of life," and it was up to students to set it afloat with their ambition to excel: "It can all be summed up in the words, 'Have the Fighting Spirit.' Then Central will win in anything she attempts" (2). Here the school is not portrayed as a nurturing maternal figure that sheltered students like a mother protects her children but as a female competitor intent on winning, perhaps a reflection of the shifting status of Central girls, who now viewed themselves as entitled to vocalize their competitive spirit.

Vaguely defined by Edwards in 1899, the sensation of school spirit is more fully developed as a principle of consubstantiality by Tann and Tinsley. All of these young female epideictic rhetors separated school spirit from male activities, suggesting that it superseded the actions of any single faction. It was the cause, not the effect, of male achievement, according to Tann. Tinsley offers or sponsors the most comprehensive discussion of school spirit, contending that it depends upon how students treat one other and their teachers, support their school, and enact the Central credo. The ongoing construction of school spirit as an element of consubstantiality also offers insight on the evolution of this doctrine.

Creating Consubstantiality

Conclusions

In epideictic theory, consubstantiality is an abstract concept that seldom is discussed within a specific rhetorical context. In the practice of Central girls, it became a concrete tool for unifying students at an increasingly large and fragmented high school that was significantly different from the much smaller and more culturally cohesive Miss Barstow's School, the Haskell Institute, and Lincoln High School. Responding to the factions and factionalism that threatened the solidarity of the student body, Central girls transformed poetry and prose into epideictic rhetoric that urged their peers to recognize their common interests. Their poetry presented the image of Central as a venerable institution that transcended time and petty rivalries, a place where all students could dream as they gained strength, power, and wisdom. Their prose sanctioned the attitude of inclusivity that deterred the impulse of exclusivity evident at Central and the world beyond its campus, and the sensation of school spirit, which did not depend upon the achievements of students but made those achievements possible. Denouncing cliques and disdain of newcomers, these young women argued that the large enrollment required students to sustain old friendships and reach out to new students who had the potential to make important contributions to the school. Above all else, girls imagined Central as a community where differences were accepted, but commonalities were privileged.

Issues of audience are another important difference between the epideictic efforts of Central girls and those of young women at Barstow, Haskell, and Lincoln. Although teachers, administrators, and families may have read the persuasive discourse of Central girls, the girls directed their commentary toward their peers in a large and heterogeneous setting. Secure in their status as the children of the dominant class, Central girls did not need to defend their race to outside auditors. They did, however, have to establish their credentials to speak as young women in a patriarchal site. Their actions to counter factionalism within their audience are relevant to those of other consensus builders, both female and male, who try to persuade auditors to believe that their interests are joined. Burke's theory of consubstantiality and the application of this theory to specific rhetorical situations by Central girls create a paradigm that may inform our understanding of the epideictic strategies of other historical or modern group leaders and nation builders.

Conclusion:
Rhetorical Ramifications

THE GREEK WORD "EPIDEICTIC" means "fit for display," and consequently, this rhetorical branch is sometimes called "demonstrative." Demonstrating that they were fit for display, the girls in this study produced persuasive discourse that can be construed as epideictic rhetoric to define their collective identities and construct community in an era of changing conceptions of young women and new impetus for building coalitions. Representative of the growing group of girls who attended secondary schools that provided new opportunities and new challenges for female adolescents in the late nineteenth and early twentieth centuries, Kansas City–area girls reflected, refuted, and revised assumptions about gender, race, and class. They responded rhetorically to issues of the day that influenced their lives and those of their fellow Americans: the capacity of women to pursue advanced education, the propriety of upper-class girls developing and exhibiting their athletic and dramatic abilities, Native American assimilation and the resistance of indigenous people to the erasure of their identities, Jim Crow laws and codes that institutionalized racism, and the advent of the large, socially fragmented public high school that reflected urban factionalism.

While all of the girls in this study depicted themselves as progressive young women, differences of race, class, and ethnicity inflected their identity formation. White girls at Miss Barstow's School did not have to defend their race, but they did have to persuade their readers through amplification that girls of their social standing could be serious scholars, competitive athletes, and public performers. Native American girls at the Haskell Institute had to convince whites in their mixed audience that they were not savages and drudges and to reassure Native readers that they would preserve, not forsake, their heritage and values as young progressive Indians. African American

145

Conclusion

girls at Lincoln High School had to deal with the historical realities of Jim Crow laws that attempted to repress them economically and socially. White middle-class girls at Central High School promoted consubstantiality to confront gender politics that denigrated young women and often deprived them of positions of authority.

As time passed, the epideictic rhetoric of some girls remained stable while that of other young women accommodated new developments and trends. Barstow girls were remarkably consistent in promoting their group identity as new girls, and they amplified this image for two decades in their school yearbook. The discourse of Haskell girls reflected changes of educational and editorial policy, such as the closing of the teacher training program in 1903 that reduced their opportunity for rhetorical training, and the replacement in 1908 of the white woman editor who may have ensured that the voices of young women were heard in the Haskell newspaper. Central girls diligently promoted the doctrine of consubstantiality for thirty years, but they relinquished their reliance on the image of the school as a venerable institution and concentrated on promoting inclusivity as an attitude and school spirit as a gender-neutral sensation that solved problems caused by factionalism. The most dramatic alteration in the epideictic rhetoric of the young women in this study took place at Lincoln, where in the 1920s, girls began to espouse radical leaders, such as Marcus Garvey; radical causes, such as a new school facility; and radical ideas, such as the possibility that young African Americans and whites could blur the color line of Kansas City.

Rhetorical constructions of community also varied among these young epideictic rhetors. Barstow girls imagined themselves to be a community of female scholars. Haskell and Lincoln girls focused much more rhetorical energy on creating racial solidarity, with Native girls representing themselves as part of the pan-Indian movement and Lincoln girls registering young people as members of the middle-class African American community of Kansas City and participants in the national epideictic print-culture endeavors of adults. Envisioning a united school community, Central girls urged their peers to think of themselves as bound by common cause rather than divided by competing agendas.

Despite these differences, all of the girls in this study revised ideas about young women of this period. Largely rejecting the nineteenth-century model of the submissive and domesticated True Woman, they merged the ideals of the Real Woman and the New Woman. Like the Real Woman of the

147
Conclusion

mid-nineteenth century, they espoused education and self-reliance; like the New Woman of the 1890s, they pursued public activities, and some of them prepared to attend college. These girls rewrote cultural scripts that designated young women as silent and submissive, recasting themselves as articulate and active members of early twentieth-century society. Delivering epideictic rhetoric in school publications, they alter our understanding of epideictic rhetoric as the province of extraordinary men seeking to build nations, by demonstrating how ordinary girls can use this form of persuasive discourse to build local coalitions.

Defining themselves, these young women helped to define the twentieth century as teachers, nurses, artists, community activists, and mothers. Of the girls in this study, the young woman who became the most publicly prominent is African American student Lucile Bluford of Lincoln High School. Graduating first in her class in 1928, she earned a bachelor's degree at the University of Kansas and joined the staff of the important African American weekly newspaper the *Kansas City Call*, becoming editor in 1955. In 1939 Bluford applied to the graduate program of the School of Journalism at the University of Missouri, but when MU administrators discovered that she was African American, they refused to allow her to enroll. She then filed suit against the university, but she lost and never attended MU (Coulter 113). In 1989, the university awarded Bluford an honorary doctorate, which she accepted "not only for myself, but for the thousands of black students" that MU had discriminated against for years (Trout).

While *Praising Girls* documents the rhetorical activities of a group that has not been recognized by scholars of the history of women and rhetoric, it also suggests new lines of inquiry and methodologies for assessing the epideictic efforts of other collectives of the past and present. I suggest, for example, in chapter 1 that the first wave of the women's movement in the United States could be interpreted as an exercise in epideictic amplification like that used by privileged young white women at Miss Barstow's School. The model that Native American girls used to appeal to diverse epideictic audiences, as described in chapter 3, might inform investigations of a range of initiatives, such as the organized labor movements since the late 1800s and the Civil Rights Movement that some historians contend began well before the 1950s. As chapter 4 notes, Rudolph J. Vecoli has assessed how the Italian immigrant press constructed social reality from 1850 to 1920, and the publications of many ethnic groups await exploration that could be conducted

148

Conclusion

from the perspective of parallel communities and historical realities that I used to analyze the epideictic rhetoric of African American girls at Lincoln High School. The recent national political polarization might be considered a failure of rhetors to create consubstantiality that would unite rather than divide the factions that constitute the United States—an exploration that might yield rhetorical remedies to this serious problem.

Praising Girls suggests other possibilities. For example, the Gay and Lesbian Archive of Mid-America in Kansas City is a trove of textual and material artifacts including mid-twentieth-century gay and lesbian publications that represent through visual and written epideictic rhetoric the efforts of people to declare and celebrate their collective identities. A longitudinal epideictic study of the student publications of a particular high school with a long history could offer insights on the construction of youth culture during the twentieth and early twenty-first centuries. The constructions of many "cultures" might be illuminated by discerning and examining the way that members use epideictic rhetoric to declare who they are, and I hope that this book encourages further exploration of an issue that is fundamental to collective identity in an increasingly complex and diverse world.

NOTES

WORKS CITED

INDEX

NOTES

1. GIRLS AND RHETORIC: CONTEXTS

1. Various editions of these school publications are located in the following archives. *The Weather-cock* of Miss Barstow's School: State Historical Society of Missouri Research Center–Kansas City and University of Missouri–Kansas City Libraries, Dr. Kenneth J. LaBudde Deptartment of Special Collections. The *Indian Leader* of the Haskell Institute: Kansas Historical Society and Haskell Cultural Center and Museum. *Indian Legends* (1914) of the Haskell Institute: LSC. The *Lincolnian* and *The Lincolnite* of Lincoln High School: Lincoln High School Collection (AC9), Black Archives of Mid-America, Kansas City, Missouri; LSC; and Missouri Valley Special Collections, Kansas City Public Library, Kansas City, Missouri (MVSC). *The Centralian, The Luminary* magazine, and the *Luminary* newspaper of Central High School: LSC and MVSC.

2. Contemporary scholars debate why Isocrates presented his rhetoric through printed rather than spoken means, and they often cite his claim that he lacked the strong voice and self-assurance required to address Athenian audiences. Yun Lee Too challenges the ready acceptance of this explanation. Historicizing Isocrates's remark, Too contends that Isocrates

> deliberately distances himself from a democratic Athens in which civic and political life is above all defined by public and oral performance of discourse. He constructs his identity against the alleged background of the "new politicians" of the fifth century. (112)

Too cites commentary by contemporaries of Isocrates to suggest that "public oratory had become public ranting" (92).

3. Scholars who use epideictic theory to analyze contemporary rhetorical events include J. C. Adams, "Epideictic and Its Cultured Reception"; Agnew, "'Day Belongs to the Students'"; Bostdorff, "George W. Bush's Post–September 11 Rhetoric"; Ervin, "Academics and the Negotiation of Local Knowledge"; Rollins, "Ethics of Epideictic Rhetoric"; and Vivian, "Neoliberal Epideictic."

4. The Barstow catalog does not identify the rhetoric textbooks that girls used, but it describes two courses: "1. Elementary Rhetoric. Correction of faulty English. Outlines and Reproductions. Applications of Principles in Composition and the Study of English Classics. 2. Rhetoric continued. Composition in paraphrasing, description, and narration. Study of illustrative English Classics continued" (9).

151

152
Notes to Pages 14–41

5. Beverly Guy-Sheftall, in her book *Daughters of Sorrow*, quotes Bruce and many other white commentators of the period on their derogatory views of African American women.

6. George M. Frederickson confirms Wilkin's assertions about white attitudes toward African Americans in *The Black Image in the White Mind: The Debate on Afro-American Character and Destiny, 1817–1914*.

2. AMPLIFYING IDENTITY: BARSTOW "NEW GIRLS"

1. After the first two issues of 1901 and 1902, *The Weather-cock* was not published again until 1906, as the only editorial of that volume confirms. The yearbook was not published in 1907 or 1908, according to Brayman (22). Regular annual publication resumed in 1909.

2. The phrase "school paper" suggests that the editors expected *The Weather-cock* to become a periodical issued more frequently than once a year, but it remained an annual publication during the period of this study.

3. Cooper did not name the playwright, but *Bianca* has been attributed to Louisa May Alcott and is one of several dramas published under the title of *Comic Tragedies Written by "Jo" and "Meg" and Acted by the "Little Women"* in 1893. Alcott was author of *Little Women* (1868), one of the best-selling books for girls in the history of U.S. publishing. The novel includes one of the most famous dramatic scenes in American literature as the March sisters perform a melodrama in their attic. It is fitting that Barstow girls would make their dramatic debut in a play by Alcott, but unlike their fictional peers, they played for an audience in a public space.

4. Boys had participated in military drill since the revolutionary era, but the popularity of paramilitary organizations waned after the Civil War, according to Jane H. Hunter. The imperialistic impulses of the 1890s, however, inspired a resurgence of these groups, which allowed boys to imitate real soldiers and prepare to join their ranks. Two decades later, World War I engendered another renaissance of military squads (Hunter 238).

5. I am grateful to Jeffrey Rydberg-Cox of the English Department of the University of Missouri–Kansas City for identifying the source of these quotes and for providing accurate translations.

6. Thompson misspells "Charlie" and does not explain that she refers to Prince Charles Edward Stuart, the eighteenth-century Jacobite claimant to the thrones of England, Ireland, and Scotland. Opponents of the prince called him "the Pretender," and supporters called him "Bonnie Prince Charlie" (S. Hill). Thompson took the middle ground by using both labels. Most likely, Barstow girls were familiar with this historical figure from their studies of British history and literature.

153
Notes to Pages 42–56

7. Earlier editions of *The Weather-cock* included photographs but no student drawings. The 1909 drawing is unsigned, but it may have been produced by Helen Ward, who was the art editor of the yearbook.

8. Girls moved freely through public spaces during the progressive period, but reaction to their movement varied by location and the socioeconomic class of girls. Victoria Bissell Brown contends that girls in turn-of-the-century Los Angeles did not have the same liberty to roam as did boys (215). Hunter charts the public promenades of East Coast middle-class girls who shopped and walked with friends but notes that their parents were concerned about their safety and reputations (280–94). Melissa R. Klapper discusses a Chicago private-school girl who took trams and met her beau in public during World War I (185–86). Mary E. Odem reports that immigrant and working-class families attempted to monitor the activities of daughters who went to amusement parks, dance halls, and movie theaters in Los Angeles and Oakland, California, during the early twentieth century (50–64).

9. There are other possible interpretations to Evans's story: She may, for example, have engaged in romantic racialism that rendered the experience of a slave girl as much less difficult than it was, thereby participating in revisionary historical narratives that David W. Blight discusses in *Race and Reunion: The Civil War in American Memory* (2001). Perhaps, Evans intended to critique the racism of her day in Kansas City through the poignant portrait of a little girl aspiring to an ideal that she could never attain. Or Evans may have used Mirabella Ann to communicate her own anxiety about her adolescent appearance and her inability to meet certain physical standards for white girls. Discussing the evolution of the body consciousness of girls, Joan Jacobs Brumberg observes that girls and their parents began to become concerned, if not obsessed, with the appearance of adolescent skin around the turn of the twentieth century (61). By writing about a lower-class character from a racial minority who wants to alter her appearance, Evans may have projected into fiction her own real-life worries. It also is possible that all of these influences are evident in Evans's story.

10. In her study of British new girls, Mitchell contends that an array of forces and factors vanquished the "luminal fluidity and wide possibilities" of the new girl after World War I: School culture became standardized, and adults assumed control of girls' organizations; the growing popularity of film subjected girls to the adult male gaze; and adolescent girls were sexualized, which increased their interest in men and decreased their "centrality in their own lives" (173).

3. PERSUADING DIVERSE AUDIENCES: HASKELL GIRLS

1. Wright entered Haskell in 1895 as a seventeen-year-old member of the Peoria tribe from Miami, Indian Territory, which would become the state of Oklahoma (Wright, "Student Case Files"). The National Archives at Kansas City is the repository

154
Notes to Page 58

for official records of the Haskell Institute. Unless otherwise noted, all biographical information about Haskell girls comes from these records. Like other student files from the early years of Haskell, Wright's folder contains only one typewritten page with brief biographical information, such as the date that she entered and left Haskell and her age, presumably upon arrival. Wright's age is ambiguous, however, since her birth date is not provided. Her student file also notes that she was one-sixteenth Peoria. The degree of "Indian blood" that students allegedly possessed was an important issue to government authorities who intended that Indian schools serve "real Indians," meaning full-blooded Indians from the 141 reservations listed in the *Annual Report of the Commissioner of Indian Affairs* in 1880. The number of reservations changed in the following decade, with the admission of Oklahoma as a state and other historical developments (Vučković 40).

2. My description of the audience for these two publications is based on textual evidence from the newspaper and anthology, my inferences from closing reading of these publications, and the scant information contained in files held by the National Archives at Kansas City. These files do not include subscription lists, but there are many notes from former students asking for newspaper subscriptions; there are also requests from people without apparent affiliation to Haskell. For example, the *Indian Leader* files contain a letter to Haskell Superintendent H. B. Peairs from Herbert A. Clark of the Department of Physics at Syracuse University, Syracuse, New York. In the letter dated 23 October 1907, Clark requests back copies of the *Indian Leader*, which he had not received since a fire at Haskell in the summer of 1907 destroyed the subscription list of the newspaper. There are subscription renewals from the State Historical Society of Wisconsin in 1917 and the Geological Survey office of Ontario, Canada, in 1919. The Carlisle Indian Industrial School published two newspapers and sent copies to every member of Congress, all of the Indian agencies and military posts, and major newspapers in the country, according to Jessica Enoch ("Resisting" 122). Haskell may have done the same.

3. Late nineteenth-century reformers distinguished between "nonprogressive" and "progressive" Native Americans, according to Francis Paul Prucha, who cites the descriptions of reformer Herbert Welsh as typical for the time (Prucha 644). Writing for *Scribner's Magazine* in 1891, Welsh describes divisions among the Sioux:

> There is the old pagan and non-progressive party. Inspired by sentiments of hostility to the Government and to white civilization, it believes in what is Indian, and hates what belongs to the white man. Its delight is in the past, and its dream is that the past shall come back again—the illimitable prairie, with vast herds of the vanished buffalo, the deer, the antelope, all the excitement of the chase, and the still fiercer thrill of bloody struggle with rival savage men. (443)

155

Notes to Pages 59–63

Welsh continues by discussing leaders of the nonprogressive party and then characterizes progressive Native Americans:

A new, progressive, and what may be properly termed Christian party, whose life was begotten, nourished and trained by missionary enterprise and devotion. . . . In these Christian Indians is to be found abundant food for a study of the germs and first awakening of civilized life rich in variety and suggestion. (443–44)

Prucha contends that reformers such as Welsh wanted to encourage progressive Indians and "stamp out" nonprogressives (645). Hazel W. Hertzberg notes the active role that "red progressives" played in organizing Native Americans into a national group; see her chapter "The Red Progressives" in *The Search for an American Indian Identity*.

4. Quotations from the *Indian Leader* are from the microfilm of the Kansas State Historical Society, reels L2952–58, and from the files of Haskell Cultural Center and Museum. This editorial does not have a headline or a byline, but it may have been written by Helen W. Ball, the white teacher who was identified as editor of the newspaper in the June 1898 issue of the *Indian Leader*. On the same page of the first issue is a note that there was no editor, foreman, proofreader, or "organized force of compositors" in the *Leader* office; therefore, "no one can be blamed or criticized" (2). What these allegedly nonexistent figures might be blamed or criticized for was left unsaid. Despite this disingenuous declaration, there obviously was an editor or editors who compiled excerpts from professional publications, wrote news about Haskell, gathered information about other Indian schools, and solicited Haskell student contributions. I surmise that Ball filled this role from the debut of the *Indian Leader*.

5. I have not found production notes on this anthology, which is held by University of Missouri–Kansas City Libraries, Dr. Kenneth J. LaBudde Special Collections. The Haskell Cultural Center and Museum holds a 1911 edition of *Indian Legends* that has only thirteen narratives that do not identify their authors and, thus, makes it impossible to determine if girls wrote the compositions; it also features illustrations and photographs.

6. Before 1876, the U.S. government relied on private religious organizations to educate Native Americans and provided some financial support to these missionaries (M. C. Coleman 38–41). In the Kansas City area, for instance, Methodist missionaries established the Shawnee Methodist Mission in 1830. The mission was founded to serve the Shawnees, an eastern tribe that the government moved to present-day Kansas in the 1820s and 1830s. In 1839, a central school for different tribes was built at a point where a branch of the Santa Fe Trail crossed through Shawnee lands. The mission eventually owned more than two thousand acres and sixteen buildings, enrolled nearly two hundred Indian boys and girls aged five to twenty-three, and

156
Notes to Pages 63–75

provided basic academic, agricultural, and manual training. The Shawnee Indian Mission closed in 1862. Three of its original buildings still stand at a state historic site in Fairway, Kansas ("Shawnee"). In addition to education, the General Allotment, or Dawes, Act of 1887 was viewed as crucial to Indian assimilation. It authorized the dissolution of reservations through the allotment of tribal lands in specified quantity to individual tribal members. The United States retained the title to allotted lands for twenty-five years or longer. At the end of the trust period, the allottee was to receive title and do as he or she wished with the property. After receiving documentation, he or she became eligible for citizenship. Proponents of the Dawes Act saw it as a solution to bringing Native Americans into American society; opponents saw it as the means of depriving Indians of their land (Hertzberg 4–5).

7. Robert A. Trennert notes that the organizer of the first government-sponsored school for Native Americans had trouble recruiting girls. In 1878 Captain Richard Henry Pratt sought Native girls to enroll in a fledgling program at the Hampton Institute in Hampton, Virginia, but he could locate only nine girls whose families were willing to let them go. Pratt attributed this resistance to his belief that Native Americans valued the labor of their girls more than the possibility of their education ("Educating" 274). In 1879 Pratt went on to found the Carlisle Indian School in Carlisle, Pennsylvania, which was the model for the Haskell Institute ("Educating" 273–74, 277). During the 1880s, the disparity between enrollment of girls and boys in Native American schools began to diminish ("Educating" 277).

8. Some of the items in the *Indian Leader* do not have headlines, so I identify them in the text and works-cited section with the first two words of the article. While the editor does not name the commissioner, signifying, perhaps, his omnipotent stature among the audience of the newspaper, William A. Jones was the Commissioner of Indian Affairs in 1898.

9. Among scholars who use the writing of Native American students and their families as primary sources in histories of Indian education are David Wallace Adams, *Education for Extinction*; Child, *Boarding School Seasons*; Michael C. Coleman, *American Indian Children at School*; Theresa Milk, *Haskell Institute*; Jon Reyder and Jeanne Eder, *American Indian Education*; Trafzer, Keller, and Sisquoc, *Boarding School Blues*; Vučković, *Voices from Haskell*; and Kim Cary Warren, *Quest for Citizenship*.

10. Washee attended Haskell from 1915 to 1920. In an undated autobiographical sketch—the first of its kind that I have found in Haskell student files—Washee reveals some of the complexities of Native American identity, as well as some of the challenges for scholars attempting to reconstruct Native American boarding-school experiences. Washee writes that she is the second child of Mary Moran and James Rouse "and am now known as Emily Washee, although my rightful name is Nellie Rouse. My parents are Cheyenne and French, which makes me Cheyenne and French

157
Notes to Pages 90–94

too" ("Autobiography"). Washee does not explain why she went by a name that was not her own, but it was common for white Indian officials and teachers to rename students. She notes that she was born at Fort Reno, which began as a military camp in 1874 in Oklahoma during the Indian wars ("Fort Reno"). Washee recalls that "at five, I ran away from home and went to an Indian school (Seger) and enrolled there, but mother came after me and took me home thinking that I was too young. At eight I reenrolled at Seger and stayed there six years" ("Autobiography"). Perhaps, Washee did make her way to the school as such a young child or was taken there by agency officials. Washee's application for reenrollment at Haskell in 1918 indicates that she attended the Hampton Institute in Virginia from 1914 to 1915 before transferring to Haskell ("Student Case Files").

4. GLOSSING (OVER) HISTORICAL REALITIES: LINCOLN GIRLS

1. This time span is dictated by the availability of primary sources. The title page of the Lincoln annual of 1926 designates this edition as "Volume XXVI," which suggests that the first annual was issued in 1900, but the two archives that have the largest holdings of these yearbooks do not have such early editions. The University of Missouri–Kansas City Libraries, Dr. Kenneth J. LaBudde Department of Special Collections, has the yearbooks for 1917, 1920, and 1922 to 1928. The Missouri Valley Special Collections of the Kansas City Public Library has volumes for 1915, 1919, 1929, and 1930. The Black Archives of Mid-America, Kansas City, Missouri, holds the 1918 annual. An article by Lucile Bluford in the 1928 Lincoln annual, "The Lincolnite Staff," reports that the school newspaper began as a monthly periodical in the school year of 1925–26 and was produced by students outside of school hours. A year later, a newswriting class was organized and published the *Lincolnite* every two weeks. I have not found copies of the monthly periodical, and the Missouri Valley Special Collections of the Kansas City Public Library has incomplete runs of the newspaper, beginning in 1926.

2. Coulter draws on Darlene Clark Hine's model of African American community development during the first half of the twentieth century. Hine maintains that the African American professional class combated white supremacy by founding parallel organizations, such as the National Medical Association in 1895, the National Association Colored Graduate Nurses in 1908, and the National Bar Association in 1925 (1279).

3. Significantly, a higher percentage of African Americans attended high school in Missouri than any other southern state in 1910. As for whites, 10.9 percent of this age group attended high school in Missouri that year (Anderson 190–91).

4. Anderson's survey of the curricula of African American high schools in sixteen southern states between 1880 and 1920 shows that most schools offered classical or college preparatory training, despite the call for industrial training for students (199).

158

Notes to Pages 96–115

5. Not all young African American women embraced Cooper's call to serve as the foundation of the race. African American novelist Nella Larsen, for example, registers the resistance of young women in two novels. In *Quicksand* (1928), Larsen writes about a young well-educated African American woman who initially rejects her proscribed role as a teacher and mother-to-be of children who would help to lift the race. Larsen's second novel, *Passing* (1929), focuses on a young woman of mixed blood who takes advantage of her light skin tone to pass for white, although the consequences of her masquerade are dire.

6. Three years after Franklin and Williams saluted Love in the Lincoln yearbook, he opened a movie theater in the main African American business district of Kansas City, Missouri. As opposed to Kansas City theaters that catered to white customers and forced patrons of color to enter buildings through back doors and sit in balconies, Love's "Theater Beautiful" cultivated an African American audience. When the theater showed *The Three Musketeers*, the proprietor advertised it as an adaptation of a novel by Alexander Dumas, "the world's greatest Negro writer" (Coulter 241–42).

7. Most of the Lincoln graduates that Franklin and Williams saluted in "Bird's Eye View of the Alumni" had become teachers or were training to become teachers. Edward W. Parrish, a 1908 graduate, is "teaching under Booker T. Washington at Tuskegee, Ala." Three Lincoln graduates had returned to the high school to teach: Edward B. Thompson was an instructor of civics and physiology; Lula Shelby, who graduated from Manhattan College in 1913, was a domestic science teacher; and Neosha E. Venerable, who graduated from the University of Kansas in 1914, taught English and German (28–29). Franklin became a music teacher who offered lessons at her home in Kansas City, Missouri ("Missouri Certificate").

8. The Kansas City Colored Women's League began working in 1913 to found a YWCA for African Americans in Kansas City. The project was led by Kansas City activists, including Jean McCampbell, whose daughter Anna Jean McCampbell attended Lincoln in the late 1920s. Other leaders include Ida M. Becks, Anna Jones, and Myrtle Foster Cook, who was head of the English Department at Lincoln until she married the assistant principal of Lincoln High School, Hugh O. Cook (Coulter 93, 139–41, 146).

9. Bluford worked for the *Kansas City Call* for sixty-nine years as a reporter, managing editor, editor, and publisher (Trout).

5. CREATING CONSUBSTANTIALITY: CENTRAL GIRLS

1. The occupations of the parents and guardians of the 19,189 students enrolled in the public schools of Kansas City for the school year of 1894–95 indicate that the majority of students came from working- and middle-class families. The tabulation

159
Notes to Pages 116–24

did not distinguish between the parents of elementary school pupils and students at Central High School and Lincoln High School, but it provides a useful overview. The largest number of parents (3,218) worked in jobs classified as "miscellaneous," followed by laborers (2,478), mechanics (2,416), merchants (2,343), agents (1,293), clerks (1,226), and "professionals" (1,044). Other occupational categories include railroadmen (1,028), farmers and gardeners (341), laundresses (570), saloon keepers (201), and seamstresses (339) (Kansas City Board of Education, *Twenty-Fourth Annual Report* 57–58). *The Centralian* 1907 lists the names and addresses of seniors, which allowed me to locate some students in the city directory of Kansas City. Among the parents of students were a draftsman, a huckster, several salesmen, a junk dealer, a bank clerk, the controller of a local distillery, the treasurer of a preserving company, and two physicians, one of whom was a woman. Copies of all school district reports cited in this chapter are held by Missouri Valley Special Collections, Kansas City Public Library, Kansas City, Missouri (MVSC).

2. The Central yearbook of 1899 devotes six pages of coverage to the fraternities in a section illustrated by an ominous drawing of hooded halberd-wielding figures that resemble members of the Ku Klux Klan.

3. Henry D. Sheldon reports that Alpha Phi was the first Greek-letter society for secondary schools and began at schools in Delaware, New Jersey, and New York in 1876. Sheldon writes that nine other fraternities existed, and the most prominent were Alpha Zeta, Gamma Eta Kappa, and Omicron Kappa Pi—none of which had chapters at Central. Sheldon also notes that most school authorities disapproved of and often banned fraternities because they created factions (297–99).

4. The Central yearbook of 1907 is the only yearbook from 1899 to 1925 to list the names and addresses of seniors, which allowed me to find some students in the U.S. Census for 1900 and 1910. I have not been able to locate other Central student records from this time period.

5. The first issue of *The Luminary* was produced in December 1885, according to the unnamed author of "History of Central High School" (195). The earliest edition of *The Luminary* that I have been able to locate is dated 1889–90 and is held by MVSC. For my analysis of Central student publications, I reviewed every volume of the yearbook from 1899 to 1925 and the literary magazine, which became a weekly newspaper in 1921, in five-year increments for the school years ending in 1895, 1900, 1905, 1910, 1915, 1920, and 1925. The fragile condition of extant copies of the *Luminary* after 1925 prohibited their perusal; therefore, I ended my survey in 1925.

6. The term "New Woman" was coined in 1894 during a debate between Sarah Grand and Ouida in the *North American Review*. Martha H. Patterson summarizes common views of this model:

160
Notes to Pages 133–37

Within the dominant white press, she was either what her detractors called an unattractive, browbeating usurper of traditionally masculine roles, or she was what her champions proclaimed an independent, college-educated, American girl devoted to suffrage, progressive reform, and sexual freedom. (*Beyond* 2)

The "angel in the house" ideal was inspired by the portrait of the perfect woman in English writer Coventry Patmore's narrative poem "The Angel in the House" (1862; first published 1854 and expanded).

7. For discussions of Jim Crow codes in Kansas City, see Coulter; Martin; Schirmer; and Wilkins. From 1908 to 1919, Kansas City developer J. C. Nichols refused to allow homes in his new subdivisions to be sold to Jews, and while this discrimination diminished in the following decades, his company continued to restrict Jewish property purchases until the 1970s (Worley, *J. C. Nichols* 151–55). The Kansas City Country Club, founded in 1896 and regarded as the most prestigious social club in town, refused to admit Jews until professional golfer Tom Watson resigned his membership in 1990 to protest the exclusion of Jewish businessman Henry Bloch (Garrity). The Kansas City Club was organized in 1882 to allow leading white businessmen and professional men to socialize; from 1887 to 1968, all of the presidents of the Kansas City Chamber of Commerce were white men; and the Woman's City Club, founded in 1917, excluded African American women (Green 206–9, 229, 247).

8. The four schools were Lincoln, Manual, Northeast, and Westport (Kansas City Board of Education, *Fiftieth Annual Report* 63–66).

9. The Board of Education decided to build a separate junior high school in the fall of 1924, but the *Luminary* editorial makes no mention of that fact, and thus its publication must have preceded the announcement ("History" 200–201).

WORKS CITED

Abbott, Allan. "High-School Journalism." *The School Review* 18.10 (1910): 657–66. JSTOR. Web. 13 Aug. 2015.

Abrams, M. H. *A Glossary of Literary Terms.* 8th ed. Boston: Wadsworth, 2005. Print.

Adams, David Wallace. *Education for Extinction: American Indians and the Boarding School Experience, 1875–1928.* Lawrence: UP of Kansas, 1995. Print.

Adams, John C. "Epideictic and Its Cultured Reception: In Memory of the Firefighters." *Rhetorics of Display.* Ed. Lawrence J. Prelli. Columbia: U of South Carolina P, 2006. 293–310. Print.

Agnew, Lois. "'The Day Belongs to the Students': Expanding Epideictic's Civic Function." *Rhetoric Review* 27 (2008): 147–64. Print.

Alcott, Louisa May. *Comic Tragedies Written by "Jo" and "Meg" and Acted by the "Little Women."* Boston: Roberts, 1893. Print.

Anderson, James D. *The Education of Blacks in the South, 1860–1935.* Chapel Hill: U of North Carolina P, 1988. Print.

Appleby, Joyce, Lynn Hunt, and Margaret Jacob. *Telling the Truth about History.* New York: Norton, 1994. Print.

Aristotle. *On Rhetoric: A Theory of Civic Discourse.* Trans. George A. Kennedy. Oxford: Oxford UP, 2007. Print.

———. *"Poetics" I, with the "Tractatus Coislinianus," a Hypothetical Reconstruction of "Poetics" II, and the Fragments of the "On the Poets."* Trans. Richard Janko. Indianapolis: Hackett, 1987. Print.

"As the Wind Blows." *The Weather-cock* 1902: 122. Print.

Bakhtin, Mikhail M. "Discourse in the Novel." *The Dialogic Imagination.* Trans. Caryl Emerson and Michael Holquist. Ed. Holquist. Austin: U of Texas P, 1981. 259–422. Print.

"Be Considerate." *Luminary* 16 Oct. 1924: 2. Print.

Bederman, Gail. *Manliness and Civilization: A Cultural History of Gender and Race, 1880–1917.* Chicago: U of Chicago P, 1995. Print.

"Be Friendly." *Luminary* 2 Oct. 1924: 2. Print.

Berger, Julia. "The Evolution of the Freshman: In Four Chapters." *The Centralian* 1899: 103–4. Print.

Blight, David W. *Race and Reunion: The Civil War in American Memory.* Cambridge: Belknap Press of Harvard UP, 2001. Print.

Blitefield, Jerry. "It's Showtime! Staging Public Demonstrations, Alinsky-Style." *Rhetorics of Display.* Ed. Lawrence J. Prelli. Columbia: U of South Carolina P, 2006. 255–72. Print.

Works Cited

Bluford, Lucile. "New Schools." *Lincolnite* 4 Nov. 1926: 2. Print.

Bongo, Julia. "Indian Burial Rites." *Indian Legends*. Lawrence, KS: Haskell, 1914. 56–57. Print.

Bostdorff, Denise M. "George W. Bush's Post–September 11 Rhetoric of Covenant Renewal: Upholding the Faith of the Greatest Generation." *Quarterly Journal of Speech* 89 (2003): 293–319. Print.

Brayman, Walter W. *Standards High: Barstow's First 100 Years*. Kansas City: Lowell, 1984. Print.

Brinkley, Alan. *The Unfinished Nation: A Concise History of the American People*. 4th ed. Vol. 2. New York: McGraw-Hill, 2004. Print.

Broome, Mary Anne. *Colonial Memories*. London: Smith, Elder, 1904. Print.

Brown, Dovie. "Parting." *The Lincolnian* 1930: 40. Print.

Brown, Victoria Bissell. "Golden Girls: Female Socialization in Los Angeles, 1880–1910." Diss. U of California–San Diego, 1985. Print.

Bruce, Philip A. *The Plantation Negro as a Freeman; Observations on His Character, Condition, and Prospects in Virginia*. 1889. Williamstown, MA: Corner House, 1970. Print.

Brumberg, Joan Jacobs. *The Body Project: An Intimate History of American Girls*. New York: Vintage, 1998. Print.

Buchanan, Lindal. *Regendering Delivery: The Fifth Canon and Antebellum Women Rhetors*. Carbondale: Southern Illinois UP, 2005. Print.

Burke, Kenneth. *A Rhetoric of Motives*. Berkeley: U of California P, 1969. Print.

Burton, Gideon O. "Audience." Silva Rhetoricae. College of Humanities. *Brigham Young University*, 2007. Web. 19 Nov. 2009.

———. "Kairos." Silva Rhetoricae. College of Humanities. *Brigham Young University*, 2007. Web. 19 Nov. 2009.

"The Cadets." *The Centralian* 1917: 154. Print.

Cahn, Susan K. *Coming on Strong: Gender and Sexuality in Twentieth-Century Women's Sport*. New York: Free Press, 1994. Print.

"Catalog c. 1901." Barstow School Records, ca. 1892–1989 (K0277). 35 vols. State Historical Society of Missouri–Research Center, Kansas City. Microfilm.

Cayton, Andrew R. L., and Susan E. Gray. "The Story of the Midwest: An Introduction." *The American Midwest: Essays on Regional History*. Ed. Cayton and Gray. Bloomington: Indiana UP, 2001. 1–26. Print.

"Central Leads Other Schools in Enrollment." *Luminary* 18 Sept. 1924: 1. Print.

"The Central Literary Club." *The Centralian* 1899: 30. Print.

"The Central Spirit." Editorial. *Luminary* 2 Oct. 1924: 2. Print.

Chase, Mary M. "The Medicine Man." *Indian Legends*. Lawrence, KS: Haskell, 1914. 83–84. Print.

Works Cited

Child, Brenda J. *Boarding School Seasons: American Indian Families, 1900–1940*. Lincoln: U of Nebraska P, 1998. Print.

"The Class." *The Weather-Cock* 1901: 21–22. Print.

"The Class of 1917." *The Lincolnian* 1917: N. pag. Print.

"Class of '95." *The Luminary* 1895: 19. Print.

Clements, William M., and Frances M. Malpezzi. *Native American Folklore, 1879–1979: An Annotated Bibliography*. Athens, OH: Swallow, 1984. Print.

Cogan, Frances B. *All-American Girl: The Ideal of Real Womanhood in Mid-Nineteenth-Century America*. Athens: U of Georgia P, 1989. Print.

Coleman, Michael C. *American Indian Children at School, 1850–1930*. Jackson: U of Mississippi P, 1993. Print.

Coleman, Richard P. *The Kansas City Establishment: Leadership through Two Centuries in a Midwestern Metropolis*. Manhattan, KS: Kansas, 2006. Print.

"The Color Line." *Lincolnite* 7 Dec. 1927: 2. Print.

Connelly, Judith. "Our Foreign Cousins." *The Centralian* 1906: N. pag. Print.

Connors, Robert J. *Composition-Rhetoric: Backgrounds, Theory, and Pedagogy*. Pittsburgh: U of Pittsburgh P, 1997. Print.

———. "Dreams and Play: Historical Method and Methodology." *Methods and Methodology in Composition Research*. Ed. Gesa Kirsch and Patricia A. Sullivan. Carbondale: Southern Illinois UP, 1992. 15–36. Print.

Cook, Delia Crutchfield, and Kathleen Thompson. "African American Girls in the Twentieth Century." *Girlhood in America: An Encyclopedia*. Ed. Miriam Forman-Brunell. Vol. 1. Santa Barbara, CA: ABC-CLIO, 2001. 26–34. Print.

Cooper, Anna Julia. *The Voice of Anna Julia Cooper*. Ed. Charles Lemert and Esme Bhan. Lanham, MD: Rowman, 1998. Print.

Cooper, Helen. "Bianca: An Operatic Tragedy Given by the Barstow Dramatic Club." *The Weather-cock* 1901: 12–14. Print.

Coulter, Charles E. *"Take Up the Black Man's Burden": Kansas City's African American Communities, 1865–1939*. Columbia: U of Missouri P, 2006. Print.

"Course of Study." *The Lincolnian* 1915: 10–11. Print.

Craig, Susan V. "Ruth Harris Bohan." *Biographical Dictionary of Kansas Artists Active Before 1945*. 2006. U of Kansas. Web. 29 Dec. 2008. <http://kuscholarworks.ku.edu/dspace/bitstream/1808/1028/1/BDKAversion1.pdf>.

"The Cross-Country Run." *The Weather-cock* 1909: 20. Print.

Dagbovie, Pero Gaglo. *The Early Black History Movement, Carter G. Woodson, and Lorenzo Johnston Greene*. Urbana: U of Illinois P, 2007. Print.

Daniel, Walter C. *Black Journals of the United States*. Westport, CT: Greenwood, 1982. Print.

164
Works Cited

Datnow, Amanda. "Using Gender to Preserve Tracking's Status Hierarchy: The Defensive Strategy of Entrenched Teachers." *Anthropology and Education Quarterly* 28 (1997): 204–28. Print.

de Beauvoir, Simone. *The Second Sex*. 1949. Trans. Constance Borde and Sheila Malovany-Chevallier. New York: Knopf, 2010. Print.

Diner, Steven J. *A Very Different Age: Americans of the Progressive Era*. New York: Hill, 1998. Print.

"The Domestic Science Department." *Indian Leader* 15 Jan. 1899: 2. Print.

Driscoll, Catherine. *Girls: Feminine Adolescence in Popular Culture and Cultural Theory*. New York: Columbia UP, 2002. Print.

Du Bois, W. E. B. *Dusk of Dawn: An Essay toward an Autobiography of a Race Concept*. 1940. Millwood, NY: Kraus-Thomson, 1975. Print.

———. *The Souls of Black Folk*. 1903. Millwood: Kraus-Thomson, 1973. Print.

Dye, Nancy S. Introduction. *Gender, Class, Race, and Reform in the Progressive Era*. Ed. Noralee Frankel and Dye. Lexington: U of Kentucky P, 1991. 1–9. Print.

Editorial. *Indian Leader* Mar. 1897: 2. Print.

Editorial. *The Luminary* Oct. 1899: 22–24. Print.

Editorial. *The Weather-cock* 1902: 112–13. Print.

Editorial. *The Weather-cock* 1910: 18. Print.

Editorials. *The Luminary* Feb. 1900: 6–7. Print.

Editorials. *The Weather-cock* 1901: 19–20. Print.

Editorials. *The Weather-cock* 1909: 18. Print.

Edwards, Gwendolen. "Central High School." *The Centralian* 1899: 68–71. Print.

———. Editorial. *The Luminary* Oct. 1899: 22–24. Print.

Edwards, Marion. "A Match Game between the Manual Training High School and Miss Barstow's Girls." *The Weather-cock* 1901: 15–16. Print.

Enoch, Jessica. *Refiguring Rhetorical Education: Women Teaching African American, Native American, and Chicano/a Students, 1865–1911*. Carbondale: Southern Illinois UP, 2008. Print.

———. "Resisting the Script of Indian Education: Zitkala-Ša and the Carlisle Indian School." *College English* 65.2 (2002): 117–41. Print.

Ervin, Elizabeth. "Academics and the Negotiation of Local Knowledge." *College English* 61.4 (1999): 448–70. Print.

Evans, Christine. "Mirabella Ann's Experiment." *The Weather-cock* 1902: 100–102. Print.

"Faculty." *The Centralian* 1925: 18. Print.

Ferreira-Buckley, Linda. "Serving Time in the Archives." Octalog II: The (Continuing) Politics of Historiography. *Rhetoric Review* 16.1 (1997): 26–28. Print.

165
Works Cited

"The Fighting Spirit." *Luminary* 16 Oct. 1924: 2. Print.

"Fort Reno." *Historic Fort Reno*. Web. 11 Aug. 2015. <http://www.fortreno.org>.

Franklin, Arzethyr, and Stella Williams. "Bird's Eye View of the Alumni." *The Lincolnian* 1915: 28–29. Print.

Franklin, Vincent P. *Black Self-Determination: A Cultural History of African American Resistance*. New York: Hill, 1992. Print.

Frederickson, George M. *The Black Image in the White Mind: The Debate on Afro-American Character and Destiny, 1817–1914*. Middletown, CT: Wesleyan UP, 1971. Print.

"The Freshmen." *The Centralian* 1899: 19. Print.

Fultz, Michael. "'The Morning Cometh': African-American Periodicals, Education, and the Black Middle-Class, 1900–1930." *Print Culture in a Diverse America*. Ed. James P. Danky and Wayne A. Wiegand. Urbana: UP of Illinois, 1998. 129–48. Print.

Gaither, Mollie V. "Education for True Womanhood in Indian Schools." *Report of the Superintendent of Indian Schools to the Secretary of the Interior 1896*. Washington, DC: Government Printing Office, 1896. Google Books. 64–66. Web. 8 Aug. 2015.

Garrity, John. "An Act of Conscience: Tom Watson Takes a Stand against Prejudice." *Sports Illustrated* 10 Dec. 1990. Web. 24 Sept. 2010.

Gates, Henry Louis, Jr. "The Trope of a New Negro and the Reconstruction of the Image of the Black." *Representations* 24 (1988): 129–55. Print.

Gatewood, Willard B. *Aristocrats of Color: The Black Elite, 1880–1920*. Bloomington: Indiana UP, 1990. Print.

Gaylord, Claudia. "Life in a French Boarding School." *The Weather-cock* 1914: 30–31. Print.

"Gems from the Caesar Class." *The Weather-cock* 1901: 14. Print.

Genung, John F. *The Practical Elements of Rhetoric with Illustrative Examples*. 1887. Delmar, NY: Scholars', 1995. Print.

Gilbertson, Cathrene P. *The Barstow School through Eighty Years*. Kansas City, MO: N.p., 1965. Print.

Gilmore, Glenda Elizabeth. *Gender and Jim Crow: Women and the Politics of White Supremacy in North Carolina, 1896–1920*. Chapel Hill: U of North Carolina P, 1996. Print.

Glenn, Cheryl. *Rhetoric Retold: Regendering the Tradition from Antiquity through the Renaissance*. Carbondale: Southern Illinois UP, 1997. Print.

Gold, David. "The Accidental Archivist: Embracing Chance and Confusion in Historical Scholarship." *Beyond the Archives: Research as a Lived Process*. Ed. Gesa E. Kirsch and Liz Rohan. Carbondale: Southern Illinois UP, 2008. 13–19. Print.

166
Works Cited

Goodburn, Amy. "Girls' Literacy in the Progressive Era: Female and American Indian Identity at the Genoa Indian School." *Girls and Literacy in America: Historical Perspectives to the Present.* Ed. Jane Greer. Santa Barbara, CA: ABC-CLIO, 2003. 79–101. Print.

Gordon, Lynn D. *Gender and Higher Education in the Progressive Era.* New Haven: Yale UP, 1990. Print.

———. "The Gibson Girl Goes to College: Popular Culture and Women's Higher Education in the Progressive Era." *American Quarterly* 39 (1987): 211–30. Print.

Gray, Rebecca. Editorials. *The Weather-cock* 1911: 23. Print.

———. "The Legend of the Laboratory." *The Weather-cock* 1911: 21. Print.

Green, George Fuller. *A Condensed History of Kansas City Area: Its Mayors and Some V.I.P.s.* Kansas City: Lowell, 1968. Print.

Greene, Lorenzo J., Gary R. Kremer, and Antonio F. Holland. *Missouri's Black Heritage.* Columbia: U of Missouri P, 1993. Print.

Greer, Jane. Introduction. *Girls and Literacy in America: Historical Perspectives to the Present.* Ed. Greer. Santa Barbara, CA: ABC-CLIO, 2003. xv–xxxi. Print.

Guy-Sheftall, Beverly. *Daughters of Sorrow: Attitudes toward Black Women, 1880–1920.* New York: Carlson, 1990. Print.

Haff, Madeline. Editorials. *The Weather-cock* 1911: 22. Print.

Hahn, Steven. *A Nation under Our Feet: Black Political Struggles in the Rural South from Slavery to the Great Migration.* Cambridge: Belknap Press of Harvard UP, 2005. Print.

Hall, G. Stanley. *Adolescence: Its Psychology and Its Relations to Physiology, Anthropology, Sociology, Sex, Crime, Religion, and Education.* 1904. New York: Appleton, 1916. Print.

Halloran, S. Michael. "The Rhetoric of Picturesque Scenery: A Nineteenth-Century Epideictic." *Oratorical Culture in Nineteenth-Century America: Transformations in the Theory and Practice of Rhetoric.* Ed. Halloran and Gregory Clark. Carbondale: Southern Illinois UP, 1993. 226–46. Print.

Hanley, Margaret. "To Central." *The Centralian* 1910: N. pag. Print.

Harris, Joseph. "The Idea of Community in the Study of Writing." *College Composition and Communication* 40.1 (1989): 11–22. Print.

Harvey, Bernice, and Reginald F. Fisher. "History Club." *The Lincolnian* 1923: 52. Print.

"Haskell Indian Nations University, Cultural Center and Museum." *Haskell Indian Nations University.* 2007. Web. 14 Aug. 2007.

"Haskell Institute." *Indian Leader* Mar. 1897: 2. Print.

"Helen W. Ball." *Indian Leader* 12 Sept. 1924: 2–3. Print.

Hertzberg, Hazel W. *The Search for American Indian Identity: Modern Pan-Indian Movements.* Syracuse: Syracuse UP, 1972. Print.

167
Works Cited

Hickum, Hazel. "Our Future Lies before Us!" *The Lincolnian* 1917: 1. Print.

Hill, Beatrice. "A Tribute to Central." *The Centralian* 1907: 17. Print.

Hill, Simon. "Bonnie Prince Charlie and the Jacobites." *Scottish History Online*. Web. 23 Mar. 2011.

Hinds, Stuart. "From Blackface to Max Factor: The Evolution of Female Impersonation in Kansas City." University of Missouri–Kansas City. 24 Feb. 2014. Lecture.

Hine, Darlene Clark. "Black Professionals and Race Consciousness: Origins of the Civil Rights Movement, 1890–1950." *Journal of American History* 89.4 (2003): 1279–94. Print.

"History of Central High School." *The Centralian* 1925: 193–201. Print.

Hoffman, Lynn M. "Why High Schools Don't Change: What Students and Their Yearbooks Tell Us." *High School Journal* 86.2 (2002–3): 22–37. Print.

Horsechief, Mary. "Superstitions of Indians." *Indian Legends*. Lawrence, KS: Haskell, 1914. 30. Print.

Howes, Doris. "Our Cross-Country Run." *The Weather-cock* 1910: 19. Print.

———. "A Weather-cock Letter from Smith." *The Weather-cock* 1915: 78–80. Print.

———. "The Year." *The Weather-cock* 1914: 11. Print.

Hunter, Jane H. *How Young Ladies Became Girls: The Victorian Origins of American Girlhood*. New Haven: Yale UP, 2002. Print.

Indian Legends. Lawrence, KS: Haskell, 1914. Print.

Isocrates. *Isocrates, with an English Translation by George Norlin*. Vol. 2. Cambridge: Harvard UP, 1966. Print.

"J. H. Bluford." Obituary. *Kansas City Call*. 29 Mar. 1946. J. H. Bluford file, John Ramos Collection, Missouri Valley Special Collections, Kansas City Public Library, Kansas City, Missouri. Print.

Jim, Susie Bearchief. "Letters from Ex-Pupils." *Indian Leader* 14 Oct. 1910: 1, 4. Print.

Johnson, Nan. *Gender and Rhetorical Space in American Life, 1866–1910*. Carbondale: Southern Illinois UP, 2002. Print.

Jones, Jacqueline, Peter H. Wood, Thomas Borstelmann, Elaine Tyler May, and Vicki L. Ruiz. *Created Equal: A Social and Political History of the United States*. 2nd ed. New York: Pearson, 2006. Print.

"The Juniors." *The Centralian* 1899: 16. Print.

Kansas City (MO) Board of Education. *Fiftieth Annual Report of the Secretary and Treasurer of the School District of Kansas City, Missouri, for the Year Ending June 30, 1921*. Kansas City, MO: Cline, [1921]. Print.

———. *Fifty-Fourth Annual Report of the Secretary and Treasurer of the School District of Kansas City, Missouri, for the Year Ending June 30, 1925*. Kansas City, MO: Capitol, 1925. Print.

168
Works Cited

———. *Forty-Sixth Annual Report of the Board of Education of the School District of Kansas City, Mo. for Year Ending June 30, 1917.* N.p.: Smith-Grieves, [1917]. Print.

———. *Report of the Board of Education, Kansas City, Missouri, for the Years 1928–1930.* N.p.: N.p., [1930]. Print.

———. *Report of the Superintendent of Schools of the School District of Kansas City, Missouri, for the Six Years from July 1, 1921, to June 30, 1927.* N.p.: N.p., [1927]. Print.

———. *Twenty-Eighth Annual Report of the Board of Education of the Kansas City Public Schools, Kansas City, Missouri, for the Year Ending June 30, 1899.* Kansas City, MO: Burd and Fletcher, 1900. Print.

———. *Twenty-Fifth Annual Report of the Public Schools of Kansas City, Missouri, 1895-1896.* Kansas City, MO: Lechtman, 1896. Print.

———. *Twenty-Fourth Annual Report of the Board of Education of the Kansas City Public Schools, Kansas City, Missouri, for the Year 1894-1895.* Kansas City, MO: Weber, 1895. Print.

———. *Twenty-Ninth Annual Report of the Board of Education of the Kansas City Public Schools, Kansas City, Missouri, for the Year Ending June 30, 1900.* N.p.: N.p., [1900]. Print.

Kaplan, Amy. *The Anarchy of Empire in the Making of U.S. Culture.* Cambridge: Harvard UP, 2002. Print.

Katanski, Amelia V. *Learning to Write "Indian": The Boarding-School Experience and American Indian Literature.* Norman: U of Oklahoma P, 2005. Print.

Kaufman, Eric P. *The Rise and Fall of Anglo-America.* Cambridge: U of Harvard P, 2004. Print.

Kennedy, George A. *Comparative Rhetoric: An Historical and Cross-Cultural Introduction.* New York: Oxford UP, 1998. Print.

———. *A New History of Classical Rhetoric.* Princeton: Princeton UP, 1994. Print.

Kerber, Linda K. *Women of the Republic: Intellect and Ideology in Revolutionary America.* Chapel Hill: UP of North Carolina, 2006. Print.

Kett, Joseph F. *Rites of Passage: Adolescence in America, 1790 to the Present.* New York: Basic, 1978. Print.

King James Bible. 1611. *King James Bible Online.* Web. 12 Aug. 2015.

Kitch, Carolyn. *The Girl on the Magazine Cover: The Origins of Visual Stereotypes in American Mass Media.* Chapel Hill: U of North Carolina P, 2001. Print.

Klapper, Melissa R. *Jewish Girls Coming of Age in America, 1860–1920.* New York: New York UP, 2005. Print.

Kleine, Glen. "A Brief History of the Student Press in America." *Directory of the College Student Press in America.* Ed. Dario Politella. New York: Oxbridge, 1977. 651–52. Print.

Works Cited

Knollin, Mabel M. "Our New Outdoor Basketball Court." *The Weather-cock* 1918: 53. Print.

Kostelanetz, Richard. "Richard Kostelanetz Interviews Kenneth Burke." *Iowa Review* 17.3 (1987): 1–14. Print.

Kremer, Gary R. "'Just like the Garden of Eden': African American Community Life in Kansas City's Leeds." *Kansas City, America's Crossroads: Essays from the Missouri Historical Review, 1906–2006*. Ed. Diane Mutti Burke and John Herron. Columbia: State Historical Society of Missouri, 2007. 252–76. Print.

La Flesche, Francis. "Who Was the Medicine Man?" *Journal of American Folklore* 18.71 (1905): 269–275. Print.

Laib, Nevin K. "Conciseness and Amplification." *College Composition and Communication* 41.4 (1990): 443–59. Print.

———. *Rhetoric and Style: Strategies for Advanced Writers*. Englewood Cliffs, NJ: Prentice-Hall, 1993. Print.

Lanham, Richard A. *A Handlist of Rhetorical Terms*. 2nd ed. Berkeley: U of California P, 1991. Print.

Larsen, Nella. Quicksand *and* Passing. 1928 and 1929. Ed. Deborah E. McDowell. New Brunswick: Rutgers UP, 1986. Print.

Latimer, John. *What's Happened to Our High Schools?* Washington, DC: Public Affairs, 1958. Print.

Lawrie, Nina R. "Negro History Club." *The Lincolnian* 1924: N. pag. Print.

Leidigh, Paul. "The New Man." *The Luminary* May 1895: 26. Print.

Leitch, Vincent B., ed. "Mikhail M. Bakhtin." *Norton Anthology of Theory and Criticism*. 2nd ed. New York: Norton, 2010. 1072–75. Print.

Lincoln, Abraham. "Address Delivered at the Dedication of the Cemetery at Gettysburg." *The Collected Works of Abraham Lincoln*. Ed. Roy P. Basler. Vol. 7. New Brunswick: Rutgers UP, 1953. 18. Print.

"Lincoln High School Corps of Teachers." *The Lincolnian* 1915: 9. Print.

Lissak, Rivka Shpak. *Pluralism and Progressives: Hull House and the New Immigrants, 1890–1919*. Chicago: U of Chicago P, 1989. Print.

Littlefield, Daniel F., Jr., and James W. Parins. *American Indian and Alaska Native Newspapers and Periodicals, 1826–1924*. Westport: Greenwood, 1984. Print.

Litwack, Leon F. *North of Slavery: The Negro in the Free States, 1790–1860*. Chicago: U of Chicago P, 1961. Print.

Livermore, Mary A. *The Story of My Life*. Hartford: Worthington, 1897. Print.

Logan, Shirley Wilson. *"We Are Coming": The Persuasive Discourse of Nineteenth-Century Black Women*. Carbondale: Southern Illinois UP, 1999. Print.

Lunsford, Andrea, ed. *Reclaiming Rhetorica: Women in the Rhetorical Tradition*. Pittsburgh: U of Pittsburgh P, 1995. Print.

170
Works Cited

Lyons, Scott Richard. "Rhetorical Sovereignty: What Do American Indians Want from Writing?" *College Composition and Communication* 51.3 (2000): 447–68. Print.

"Madeline H. Field." Obituary. *Kansas City Star* 13 Apr. 1989: E-8. Print.

Mallea, Amahia K. "Progressive Kansas City and the Missouri River." MA thesis, U of Missouri–Columbia, 2001. Print.

Marmon, Belle. "A Story of the Pueblo Indians." *Indian Leader* June 1901: N. pag. Print.

Martin, Asa E. *Our Negro Population: A Sociological Study of the Negroes of Kansas City, Missouri.* Kansas City: Hudson, 1913. Print.

Mattingly, Carol. *Well-Tempered Women: Nineteenth-Century Temperance Rhetoric.* Carbondale: Southern Illinois UP, 1998. Print.

McClure, Andrew S. "Sarah Winnemucca: [Post]Indian Princess and Voice of the Paiutes." *MELUS* 24.2 (1999): 29–51. Print.

McGee, Susan De. "Hockey at Last." *The Weather-cock* 1914: 56. Print.

"Military Training." *The Lincolnian* 1919: 16–18. Print.

Milk, Theresa. *Haskell Institute: 19th Century Stories of Sacrifice and Survival.* Lawrence: Mammoth, 2007. Print.

"Missouri Certificate of Death of Arzethyr Louise Franklin Ellis." Death Certificates. *Missouri Digital Heritage Collections.* Web. 26 Sept. 2009.

"Miss Reel." *Indian Leader* 1 Jan. 1899: 2. Print.

Mitchell, Sally. *The New Girl: Girls' Culture in England, 1880–1915.* New York: Columbia UP, 1995. Print.

Morton, Patricia. *Disfigured Images: The Historical Assault on Afro-American Women.* New York: Greenwood, 1991. Print.

Mossell, Gertrude. *The Work of the Afro-American Woman.* 1894. New York: Oxford UP, 1988. Print.

Mott, Frank Luther. *American Journalism: A History, 1690–1960.* Toronto: Macmillan, 1962. Print.

Nathanson, Constance A. *Dangerous Passage: The Social Control of Sexuality in Women's Adolescence.* Philadelphia: Temple UP, 1991. Print.

Odem, Mary E. "Teen-Age Girls, Sexuality, and Working-Class Parents in Early Twentieth Century California." *Generations of Youth: Youth Cultures and History in Twentieth-Century America.* Ed. Joe Austin and Michael Nevin Willard. New York: New York UP, 1998. 50–64. Print.

"The Opening of School." *Indian Leader* 15 Sept. 1899: 2. Print.

O'Sheel, Shaemas. "Kansas City: The Crossroads of the Continent." *New Republic* 16 May 1928: 375–78. Print.

"Our Alumni, 1889–1919." *Indian Leader* 6–27 June 1919: 13–57. Print.

171
Works Cited

"Our History: Pittsburgh Peabody High School." *Pittsburgh Public Schools*. Web. 3 Feb. 2013.

Paryas, Phyllis Margaret. "Double-Voicing/Dialogism." *Encyclopedia of Contemporary Literary Theory: Approaches, Scholars, Terms*. Ed. Irena R. Makaryk. Toronto: U of Toronto P, 1993. 537–39. Print.

Patmore, Coventry. "William Makepeace Thackeray: The Angel in the House." Rev. ed. 1862. Department of English, Brooklyn College. *City University of New York*, 2 Mar. 2011. Web. 22 Mar. 2011. <http://academic.brooklyn.cuny.edu/english/melani/novel_19c/thackeray/angel.html>.

Patterson, Martha H., ed. *The American New Woman Revisited: A Reader, 1894–1930*. New Brunswick: Rutgers UP, 2008. Print.

———. *Beyond the Gibson Girl: Reimagining the American New Woman, 1895–1915*. Urbana: U of Illinois P, 2005. Print.

Peebles, Willa Glenn, and Irene Loretta Smith. "Lincoln High School Crowded to Doors." *Kansas City Sun*. 13 Sept. 1919: 1, 8. Print.

Perelman, Chaim, and Lucie Olbrechts-Tyteca. *The New Rhetoric: A Treatise on Argumentation*. Trans. John Wilkinson and Purcell Weaver. Notre Dame: U of Notre Dame P, 1969. Print.

Petrillo, Lauren. "The Visible Rhetoric and Composition of Invisible Antebellum Female Seminary Students: Clay Seminary, Liberty, Missouri, 1855–1865." *Young Scholars in Writing: Undergraduate Research in Writing and Rhetoric* 4 (2006): 15–24. Print.

Phegley, Jennifer. *Educating the Proper Woman Reader: Victorian Family Literary Magazines and the Cultural Health of the Nation*. Columbus: Ohio State UP, 2004. Print.

"The Philos." *The Centralian* 1899: 25. Print.

"Phi Sigma." *The Centralian* 1899: 61. Print.

"The Platonian Society." *The Centralian* 1899: 27. Print.

Poulakis, Takis. "Towards a Cultural Understanding of Classical Epideictic Oratory." *PRE/TEXT* 9.3–4 (1988): 147–66. Print.

Powell, Barry B. *Classical Myth*. New York: Pearson, 2009. Print.

Prucha, Francis Paul. *The Great Father: The United States Government and the American Indians*. Lincoln: U of Nebraska P, 1984. Print.

"The Red Cross Corps." *The Centralian* 1917: 158. Print.

Revised Standard Version Bible. Cleveland, OH: World, 1962. Print.

Reyhner, Jon, and Jeanne Eder. *American Indian Education: A History*. Norman: U of Oklahoma P, 2004. Print.

Riley, Minnie. "The Returned Student." *Indian Leader* 1 July 1899: N. pag. Print.

Robertson, Emily. "Customs among the Sioux Indians." *Indian Legends*. Lawrence, KS: Haskell, 1914. 81–83. Print.

172
Works Cited

"Robertson-Pugh." Clipping from unidentified newspaper dated Sept. 1915. Emily Robertson, "Student Case Files, 1884–1920." Haskell Institute. RG 75. Bureau of Indian Affairs, National Archives at Kansas City. Print.

Robinson, Edna May. "Class History." *The Lincolnian* 1917: 4–5. Print.

Rollins, Brooke. "The Ethics of Epideictic Rhetoric: Addressing the Problem of Presence through Derrida's Funeral Orations." *Rhetoric Society Quarterly* 35.1 (2005): 5–23. Print.

Rountree, J. Clarke, III. "Kenneth Burke: A Personal Retrospective." *Iowa Review* 17.3 (1987): 15–23. Print.

Royster, Jacqueline Jones. *Traces of a Stream: Literacy and Social Change among African American Women.* Pittsburgh: U of Pittsburgh P, 2000. Print.

Royster, Jacqueline Jones, and Gesa E. Kirsch. *Feminist Rhetorical Practices: New Horizons for Rhetoric, Composition, and Literacy Studies.* Carbondale: Southern Illinois UP, 2012. Print.

Rury, John L. *Education and Women's Work: Female Schooling and the Division of Labor in Urban America, 1870–1930.* Albany: State U of New York P, 1991. Print.

"Ruth Tinsley." *The Centralian* 1925: 26. Print.

Said, Edward W. *Orientalism.* 1978. New York: Random, 1994. Print.

Schirmer, Shirley Lamb. *A City Divided: The Racial Landscape of Kansas City, 1900–1960.* Columbia: U of Missouri, 2002. Print.

"The School Yell." *The Weather-cock* 1901: 20. Print.

Schrum, Kelly. *Some Wore Bobby Sox: The Emergence of Teenage Girls' Culture, 1920–1945.* New York: Palgrave, 2004. Print.

Schultz, Lucille M. *The Young Composers: Composition's Beginnings in Nineteenth-Century Schools.* Carbondale: Southern Illinois UP, 1999. Print.

Seelatsee, Julia. "Christmas Festival among Indians." *Indian Legends.* Lawrence, KS: Haskell, 1914. 87–88. Print.

Shaw, Willa. "Know Thy Race." *The Lincolnian* 1923: 44–45. Print.

"Shawnee Indian Mission, History." *Kansas State Historical Society.* 2009. Web. 30 Nov. 2009.

Sheard, Cynthia Miecznikowski. "The Public Value of Epideictic Rhetoric." *College English* 58.7 (1996): 765–94. Print.

Sheldon, Henry D. *Student Life and Customs.* New York: Appleton, 1901. Print.

Shields, Caroline. "Bloomers." *The Weather-cock* 1919: 19. Print.

Slavens, George Everett. "Missouri." *The Black Press in the South, 1865–1979.* Ed. Henry Lewis Suggs. Westport, CT: Greenwood, 1983. 211–56. Print.

"The S.L.H.'s." *The Centralian* 1899: 33–34. Print.

Smith, Gladys. "A Tribute to Lincoln." *The Lincolnian* 1925: N. pag. Print.

173
Works Cited

Smith, Karen Manners. "New Paths to Power: 1890–1920." *No Small Courage: A History of Women in the United States.* Ed. Nancy F. Cott. New York: Oxford UP, 2000. 353–412. Print.

Snyder, Thomas D., ed. *120 Years of American Education: A Statistical Portrait.* Washington, DC: National Center for Education Statistics, 1993. Web. 12 Aug. 2012.

Spack, Ruth. "Translation Moves: Zitkala-Ša's Bilingual Indian Legends." *Studies in American Indian Literatures* 18.4 (2006): 43–62. Print.

Splitlog, Carrie B. "Our Vocational Course and What It Provides for Girls." *Indian Leader* June 1917: 15, 17–18. Print.

Stanton, Elizabeth Cady. "Our Girls." *The Selected Papers of Elizabeth Cady Stanton and Susan B. Anthony.* Ed. Ann D. Gordon. Vol. 3. New Brunswick: Rutgers UP, 2003. 484–514. Print.

Stanton, Elizabeth Cady, Susan B. Anthony, and Matilda Joslyn Gage, eds. *History of Woman Suffrage (1848–1861).* Vol. 1. New York: Fowler, 1881. Print.

Stebner, Eleanor J. *The Women of Hull House: A Study in Spirituality, Vocation, and Friendship.* Albany: State U of New York P, 1997. Print.

Stromberg, Ernest, ed. *American Indian Rhetorics of Survivance: Word Medicine, Word Magic.* Pittsburgh: U of Pittsburgh P, 2006. Print.

"Student Case Files, 1884–1920." Haskell Institute, RG 75. Bureau of Indian Affairs, National Archives at Kansas City, Missouri. Print.

Sullivan, Dale L. "The Ethos of Epideictic Encounter." *Philosophy and Rhetoric* 26.2 (1993): 113–33. Print.

Tann, Helen J. "Cock-a-Doodle-Do." *The Luminary* Feb. 1915: 6–7. Print.

———. Editorial. *The Luminary* Nov. 1914: 5–6. Print.

Thompson, Agnes. "The Pretenders." *The Weather-cock* 1910: 25. Print.

Tong, Benson. "Native American Girls." *Girlhood in America: An Encyclopedia.* Ed. Miriam Forman-Brunell. Vol. 2. Santa Barbara, CA: ABC-CLIO, 2001. 472–82. Print.

Too, Yun Lee. *The Rhetoric of Identity in Isocrates.* Cambridge: Cambridge UP, 1995. Print.

Trafzer, Clifford E., Jean A. Keller, and Lorene Sisquoc, eds. *Boarding School Blues: Revisiting American Indian Educational Experiences.* Lincoln: U of Nebraska P, 2006. Print.

Trennert, Robert A., Jr. "Educating Indian Girls at Nonreservation Boarding Schools, 1878–1920." *Western Historical Quarterly* 13.3 (1982): 271–90. Print.

———. *The Phoenix Indian School: Forced Assimilation in Arizona, 1891–1935.* Norman: U of Oklahoma P, 1988. Print.

Trout, Carlynn. "Famous Missouri Journalists: Lucile Bluford." *State Historical Society of Missouri.* Web. 15 Nov. 2009.

Works Cited

Turcotte, Rebecca. "The Story of Little Bear." *Indian Legends*. Lawrence, KS: Haskell, 1914. 62–64. Print.

Tyack, David, and Elisabeth Hansot. *Learning Together: A History of Coeducation in American Schools*. New Haven: Yale UP, 1990. Print.

Ueda, Reed. *Avenues to Adulthood: The Origins of the High School and Social Mobility in an American Suburb*. Cambridge: Cambridge UP, 1987. Print.

United States. Census Bureau. "1900 United States Federal Census." *Ancestry.com*. Web. 22 Feb. 2011.

———. ———. "1910 United States Federal Census." *Ancestry.com*. Web. 15 June 2011.

———. ———. "1930 United States Federal Census." *Ancestry.com*. Web. 31 Oct. 2009.

———. Office of Indian Affairs. *Report of the Commissioner of Indian Affairs, Part I for Fiscal Year Ending June 30, 1899*. Washington, DC: Government Printing Office, 1899. Print.

Vecoli, Rudolph J. "The Italian Immigrant Press and the Construction of Social Reality, 1850–1920." *Print Culture in a Diverse America*. Ed. James P. Danky and Wayne A. Wiegand. Urbana: U of Illinois P, 1998. 17–33. Print.

Veix, Katie. "The Munsee Indians." *Indian Leader* June 1901: N. pag. Print.

Vivian, Bradford. "Neoliberal Epideictic: Rhetorical Form and Commemorative Politics on September 11, 2002." *Quarterly Journal of Speech* 92.1 (2006): 1–26. Print.

"Vocational Training." *The Lincolnian* 1918: 35–40. Print.

Vučković, Myriam. *Voices from Haskell: Indian Students between Two Worlds, 1884–1928*. Lawrence: UP of Kansas, 2008. Print.

Walker, Jeffrey. *Rhetoric and Poetics in Antiquity*. New York: Oxford UP, 2000. Print.

Warren, Kim Cary. *The Quest for Citizenship: African American and Native American Education in Kansas, 1880–1935*. Chapel Hill: U of North Carolina P, 2010. Print.

Washee, Emily. "Autobiography." "Student Case Files, 1884–1920." Haskell Institute. RG75. Bureau of Indian Affairs. National Archives at Kansas City. Print.

———. "Briefs by Haskell Debaters." *Indian Leader* 18 June 1920: 13–15. Print.

Washington, Booker T., N. B. Wood, and Fannie Barrier Williams. *A New Negro for a New Century: An Accurate and Up-to-Date Record of the Upward Struggles of the Negro Race*. 1900. New York: Arno, 1969. Print.

Weatherford, Doris. *A History of the American Suffragist Movement*. Santa Barbara, CA: ABC-CLIO, 1998. Print.

Welsh, Herbert. "The Meaning of the Dakota Outbreak." *Scribner's Magazine* 9 (Apr. 1891): 439-452. *Internet Archive*. Web. 10 Aug. 2015. <https://archive.org/details/cihm_18298>.

Welter, Barbara. "The Cult of True Womanhood: 1820–1860." *American Quarterly* 18.2 (1996): 151–74. Print.

"We Quote . . . ." *Indian Leader* June 1898: 4. Print.

175
Works Cited

"What They Are Doing." *Indian Leader* 12 July 1901: 2–3. Print.

Wheeler, Helen. "Young Women's Christian Association." *The Lincolnian* 1917: 32–33. Print.

White, Deborah Gray. *Too Heavy a Load: Black Women in Defense of Themselves, 1894–1944.* New York: Norton, 1999. Print.

White, Walter. *Rope & Faggot: A Biography of Judge Lynch.* New York: Knopf, 1929. Print.

Wilkins, Roy. *Standing Fast: The Autobiography of Roy Wilkins.* With Tom Mathews. New York: Viking, 1982. Print.

Williams, Fannie Barrier. *Invented Lives: Narratives of Black Women 1860–1960.* Ed. Mary Helen Washington. Garden City, NY: Anchor, 1987. 150–56. Print. Rpt. of "The Colored Girl." *Voice of the Negro* 2 (June 1905): 400–403.

Wilson, Thomas D. "Chester A. Franklin and Harry S. Truman: An African American Conservative and the 'Conversion' of the Future President." *Kansas City, America's Crossroads: Essays from the* Missouri Historical Review, *1906–2006.* Ed. Diane Mutti Burke and John Herron. Columbia: State Historical Society of Missouri, 2007. 220–51. Print.

Winnemucca, Sarah. *Life among the Piutes: Their Wrongs and Claims.* 1883. Ann Arbor: UMI, 1976. Print.

Wise, John R. Introduction. *Indian Legends.* Lawrence, KS: Haskell, 1914. N. pag. Print.

Wolin, Ross. *The Rhetorical Imagination of Kenneth Burke.* Columbia: U of South Carolina P, 2001. Print.

Work, Monroe N., ed. *Negro Year Book: An Encyclopedia of the Negro, 1921–1922.* Tuskegee: Tuskegee Institute, 1922. Print.

Worley, William S. "Historic Lincoln [High] School in Kansas City." *KC Tribune* 20 Feb. 2009. Web. 23 July 2009.

———. *J. C. Nichols and the Shaping of Kansas City: Innovation in Planned Residential Communities.* Columbia: U of Missouri P, 1990. Print.

———. *Kansas City: Rise of a Regional Metropolis.* Carlsbad, CA: Heritage, 2002. Print.

Wright, Nellie. "An Aim in Life." *Indian Leader* May 1897: 4. Print.

———. "From South Dakota." *Indian Leader* 1 Oct. 1898: 2. Print.

Yates, Josephine Silone, and Anna H. Jones. "News from the Clubs." *Woman's Era* 1.1 (1894). Women's Advocacy Collection. *Emory University,* 2006. Web. 12 June 2009. <http://bohr.library.emory.edu/ewwrp/advocacy>.

Zitkala-Ša. "Impressions of an Indian Childhood." *American Indian Stories.* Lincoln: U of Nebraska P, 1985. 7–45. Print.

———. "An Indian Teacher among Indians." *American Indian Stories.* Lincoln: U of Nebraska P, 1985. 81–99. Print.

———. *Old Indian Legends.* Boston: Ginn, 1901. Print.

INDEX

Abbott, Allan, 9, 28
academic achievement and intellectual ability: of African Americans, 93, 104; at Barstow, 1, 25, 32–33, 37, 49, 54; at Central, 123, 130, 143, 144; of Native Americans, 77; public opinion of girls', 15, 37, 38, 120
academic class, Central factions by, xx, 125–26, 134–35, 137–38
academic education versus vocational training, 89, 93–94, 157n4
Addams, Jane, 12
Addison, Joseph, 118
Adolescence; Its Psychology and Its Relations to Physiology, Anthropology, Sociology, Sex, Crime, Religion, and Education (Hall), 15
adolescent (term), 15
advertising, in *Weather-cock*, 30
advisers' roles, 28, 39, 133
African American girls, 3, 6, 7, 10, 16; Evans on, 52–53, 54, 153n9; racist stereotyping of, 19, 52–53, 54, 153n9; social class and, 14, 20; treatment of, in own culture, 14–15
African American men, 14
African Americans: Jim Crow laws, xx, 18–19, 51, 132, 145–46, 160n7; in Kansas City, 18, 91, 92, 103–4; whites' opinions of, 14–15, 93, 112–13, 152n6. *See also* race
African American women, 12, 14, 104–5
age, 6, 67
"Aim in Life" (Wright), 56–58
alcohol abuse, 71–72, 77

Alcott, Louisa May, 152n3
Alinksy, Saul, 120
Allen, Barbara, 36
all-girls' school, 20. *See also* Miss Barstow's School
alumni, 9; of Barstow, 27, 41, 55; of Haskell, 58, 62, 64, 74, 77, 86, 87; of Lincoln, 98–99, 103–4, 110, 111, 158n7
Amazons, 51
American Woman Suffrage Association, 10
amplification device, xix, 3, 6, 23, 145; forms of, 25; methods of, 24–26
amplification in *Weather-cock*, 23–26, 28–54, 146, 147; confirmation, 37–42, 49; emphasis, 42–48; enlargement, 50–55; magnification, 31–37, 49; restatement, 48–50. See also *Weather-cock, The* (Barstow yearbook)
Anderson, James D., 157n4
"Angel in the house" ideal, 124, 159n6
annuals. See *Centralian, The* (Central yearbook); *Lincolnian, The* (Lincoln yearbook); *Weather-cock, The* (Barstow yearbook); yearbooks
Anthony, Susan B., 24
apostrophe (rhetorical figure), 100
Appleby, Joyce, 132
archival research, xvi–xvii
Aristotle, 37, 96, 129: amplification, xix, 24; audience, xx, 3, 61; epideictic rhetoric definition, 1, 3, 4
artistic proof and inartistic proof, xix, 37–38

177

178
Index

assimilation, 60, 67, 69, 75, 78; versus acculturation, 72–73; through education, 13–14, 18, 20, 63, 86; promoted by white reformers, 63, 64, 65–66; versus segregation, 63, 89

Association for the Study of Negro Life and History, 108

"As the Wind Blows" (*Weather-cock* column), 38

athletics at Barstow, 25, 27, 33–35, 37, 40–41, 42; emphasis of, 44–46, 47; enlargement of, 50–51

athletics at Central, 35, 139; factions by, xxi, 126, 127–28; gender and, 34, 123, 128; school spirit and, 140, 141–42; team rivals for, 117, 135, 141–42

athletics at Haskell, 35

athletics at Lincoln, 35

Atlantic Monthly (magazine), 64–65

audience, xix–xx, 5, 6, 60–63; Aristotle on, xx, 3, 61; of Barstow publications, xix, 30–31, 38, 54; of Central publications, 134, 144; expectations of, 61–62; factionalized, 60–61; skeptics, 58, 62; support of, 58. *See also* double-voicing (dialogism)

audience of Haskell publications, xix–xx, 61; *Indian Leader*, 58, 59, 62, 69–77, 154n2; *Indian Legends*, 58, 80–81, 154n2; of Wright's speech, 56–58

Bakhtin, Mikhail M., xx, 67–68

Ball, Helen W., 69, 73, 86, 155n4

Barstow. *See* Miss Barstow's School

Barstow, Mary L. C., 26, 27, 35, 51, 55; *Weather-cock* advising by, 28, 38–39

Barstow Dramatic Club, 35

Barton, Helen, 36

Beauvoir, Simone de, 52

Bederman, Gail, 51, 124

"Be Friendly" (Tinsley), 136–37

Berger, L. Julia, 124

"Best Men" paradigm, 101

Bianca (Alcott), 35–36, 49, 152n3

Bible, the, 42–43, 100

Bimmerman, Edna, 122

"Bird's Eye View of the Alumni" (Franklin and Williams), 158n7

blame and praise purposes of epideictic rhetoric, 3, 77, 105–8, 111

Blight, David W., 153n9

Blitefield, Jerry, 120

blue-collar workers, 7. *See also* social class; working class

Bluford, Addie, 93

Bluford, John H., 93

Bluford, Lucile, xi–xii, 93, 157n1; at *Kansas City Call*, 110, 147, 158n9

boarding schools, 63; for Native Americans, 7–8, 18. *See also* Miss Barstow's School

Body Project, The: An Intimate History of American Girls (Brumberg), xvii

Bongo, Julia, 81–82

boosterism, 138

boys, 7, 27, 66: athletics and, 34, 123, 128; Central factions and, 122–23; at Haskell, 63, 64; men, 3, 14, 73–74, 86; military training for, 139, 152n4. *See also* gender; girls *entries*; women

Brann, Ada, 26, 27

Brenninger, Ada, 69

Brinkley, Alan, 12

Broome, Mary Anne, 23

Brown, Dovie, 93, 100–103

Brown, Victoria Bissell, 153n8

Brown, Walter P., 124

Index

Bruce, Philip A., 14–15
Brumberg, Joan Jacobs, xvii, 15, 153n9
Bryn Mawr, 27
Buchanan, Lindal, xi, xiv
Bureau of Ethnology, 78–79
burial rites, 81–82
Burke, Kenneth, xviii, xxi, 118–19, 120, 129, 144
Burns, Lucy, 13
Burton, Gideon O., xx, 61–62
Bush, George W., xiii

Cahn, Susan K., 34–35
Carlisle Indian School, 156n7
Carlisle Institute (Native American boarding school), 7, 64–65
Central High School, 3, 8, 17, 18, 20, 114, 115–44; academic achievement at, 123, 130, 143, 144; audience of publications of, 134, 144; collective identity definition and celebration at, xxi, 116–18, 137, 146; demographics of, 121–22, 123, 158n1; founding and early years of, 93, 115, 117; fraternities at, 116, 117–18, 159nn2, 3; gender factions in, xx, 116, 122–25; immigrants in, 19, 121–22, 129; Lincoln and, 117, 135, 144; literary magazines of, xxi, 9, 120, 123, 138; literary societies of, xxi, 116, 118, 126–27, 133–34; *Luminary* (newspaper), 9, 124; school spirit at, 138–43, 146; size of, 136, 138; social class and, 121, 129; team rivals for, 117, 135, 141–42; venerable institution image of, 129–32, 146. *See also* athletics at Central; *Centralian, The* (Central yearbook); consubstantiality; factionalism at Central; *Luminary, The* (Central magazine)

"Central High School" (Edwards), 115, 116–18
Centralian, The (Central yearbook), xiv, 8, 26, 126, 128, 136; academic class factions in, 126; "Central High School," 115, 116–18; fraternities in, 121, 159n2; gender politics in, 123, 124; literary society factions in, 116, 127; poetry in, 130–32; "Tribute to Central," 130–31
Central Literary Club (Central co-ed literary society), 116, 118, 127
"Central Spirit, The" (anonymous), 142–43
Charles Edward Stuart ("Bonnie Prince Charlie"), 41, 152n6
Chase, Mary M., 82
chauvinism, 53
Child, Brenda J., 62
Chilocco Indian School (Native American boarding school), 7
Chippewa tribe, 81–82
Christianity, 56–57, 108, 154n3, 155n6
"Christmas Festival among Indians" (Seelatsee), 83
Christy, Howard Chandler, 46–47
citizenship for Native Americans, 70, 75–76, 156n6
class. *See* social class
class, academic, Central factions by, xx, 125–26, 134–35, 137–38
"Class, The" (Barstow editorial), 34
Clayton, Andrew R. L., 17
coeducational public high schools, 8, 20, 120. *See also* Central High School; Haskell Institute; Lincoln High School
Cogan, Frances B., 11
Coleman, Bessie, 106

Index

collective identity definition and celebration, xxi, 5, 37, 48–49, 55, 58–59, 80, 148; at Barstow, xiii, 21, 22–24, 34–35, 114, 146; at Central, xxi, 116–18, 137, 146; through exclusion of Other, 51–53; female group, 3–4, 5; at Haskell, 14, 59–60, 70, 86, 114, 146; tribal, 56, 64, 65, 74. *See also* amplification in *Weather-cock;* community construction at Barstow

collective identity definition and celebration at Lincoln, xx, 88–114, 146

collective memory, 132

college, 2, 27, 35, 69, 129; Barstow students, 23, 27, 39, 55; college-preparatory curriculum, 8, 22, 27, 157; gender and, 2, 38–39; Lincoln graduates attending, 98, 110, 111; "New Woman's" attendance of, 23, 124, 147

Colonial Memories (Broome), 23

"colored journalism," 106

color line, 92, 93, 94, 114, 146; Du Bois and, 18, 112

"Color Line, The" (anonymous), 112

Columbia image, 44, 46–47

Columbia University, 9

Commercial Club, 17

communism, 76

community construction at Barstow, 21, 23, 37, 50, 52, 54; through *Weather-cock,* 25–26, 27, 29. *See also* collective identity definition and celebration

Concord High School, 139–40

confirmation, 25, 37–42, 49, 69. *See also* amplification in *Weather-cock*

Connelly, Judith, 122

Connors, Robert J., xvii

Conservatory of Music in Ithaca, 98

consubstantiality, xviii, xxi, 118–20, 128–44; Burke on, 118–19, 120, 144; inclusivity and, 132–38, 146; school spirit countering, 138–43, 146; Tinsley and, 135–38; venerable institution image, 129–32, 146

Cook, Jessie W., 77

Cook, Myrtle Foster, 158n8

Cooper, Anna Julia, 16, 49, 96, 106, 158n5

Cooper, Helen, 35–36

Coulter, Charles E., 90, 91, 95, 157n2

country clubs, 133, 160n7

Cowley, Malcolm, 119

Crews, Nelson C., 93, 95, 111

Crisis: A Record of the Darker Races (NAACP newspaper), 89, 95

critical imagination, xv, xvi

curriculum: at Barstow, 8, 27, 151n4; at Central, 8; college-preparatory, 8, 22, 27, 157; at Haskell, 8, 72–73, 77; at Lincoln, 8, 89, 93–94

"Customs among the Sioux Indians" (Robertson), 84–85

Dakota tribe, 78–79, 80

debate teams, 75, 116, 123

"Declaration of Sentiments and Resolutions" (Stanton et al.), 24

dialogism. *See* double-voicing (dialogism)

"Discourse in the Novel" (Bakhtin), 67

double-voicing (dialogism), xx, 6, 67–68, 77, 87, 147; in Chases' essay, 82; in *Indian Legends,* 79–80; in Marmon and Veix's essays, 71; in Riley's essay, 72; in Splitlog's editorial, 75; in Washee's oratory, 75–76

Douglas, Mary, 132

Index

drama clubs, 22, 41, 49–50. *See also* public performance

Driscoll, Catherine, xvii

Du Bois, W. E. B., 94, 95, 101, 106, 107; color line and, 18, 112

Dye, Nancy S., 11

Eastman, Charles Alexander, 77, 79

editorials. *See under specific publication*

education, 70: assimilation and, 13–14, 18, 20, 63, 86; opinions of girls', 15–16, 66

Edwards, Gwendolen, 115, 116–18, 129, 138; as *Luminary* editor, 133, 139–40; on school spirit, 142, 143

Edwards, Marion, 33–34

Eliot, Charles William, 39

Emerson, Ralph Waldo, 57

emphasis, xix, 25, 42–48; of achievement at Lincoln, 89–90, 103–13. *See also* amplification in *Weather-cock*

English language, 64

enlargement, xix, 25, 50–55. *See also* amplification in *Weather-cock*

Enoch, Jessica, xi, xiv

epideictic rhetoric, definitions and qualities of, 4, 23, 145; male associations of, xv, 2, 3, 20–21; reconceptualizing of, xix, xviii, 1, 3–6, 90–92, 145

epideictic rhetoric, purposes of, 4–5, 20, 58, 70; praise or blame, 3, 77, 105–8, 111. *See also* collective identity definition and celebration; consubstantiality

epideictic rhetoric, stylistic execution of, 4, 146. *See also* amplification device; amplification in *Weather-cock*; double-voicing (dialogism)

Epstein, Philip L., 122

ethnic stereotypes, 19, 51–53. *See also* immigrants and immigration; racism

ethos (speaking credentials), 6; at Barstow, 37–38, 39, 41, 50; at Central, 116; at Haskell, 66; at Lincoln, 96

Evans, Christine, 52–53, 54, 153n9

Evans, Henry W., 17

"Evolution of the Freshman, The: In Four Chapters" (Berger), 124

exclusion, 51–53, 132–33; inclusivity, 132–38, 146. *See also* factionalism at Central

factionalism, 60–61, 121

factionalism at Central, xx–xxi, 115–16, 120–28; by academic class, xx, 125–26, 134–35, 137–38; by athletic organizations, xxi, 126, 127–28; consubstantiality to counter, 120, 130–32; by gender, xx, 116, 122–25; inclusivity to counter, 133–38; by literary societies, xxi, 116, 118, 126–27, 133–34. *See also* Central High School

feminist rhetorical inquiry, xv

Ferreira-Buckley, Linda, 5

Fisher, Reginald F., 108

Fiske, H. H., 73

foreign-born residents, 17, 19, 76, 122, 142; native-born residents, 10

Franklin, Arzethyr, 103–4, 158nn6, 7

fraternities: at Central, 116, 117–18, 159nn2, 3; Ueda's study on, 121

French girls, 53

freshmen, 125–26, 134, 138

Fultz, Michael, 95

Funeral Oration (Pericles), xii, 3, 4, 61

Gage, Matilda Joslyn, 24

Gaither, Mollie V., 66

182
Index

Garvey, Marcus, 107, 113, 146

Gates, Henry Louis, Jr., 94

Gay and Lesbian Archive of Mid-America (Kansas City), 148

Gaylord, Claudia, 53

Gender, 6, 38–39, 63, 64, 95–96, 153n8; athletics and, 34–35, 123, 128, 139; Central factions by, xx, 116, 122–25; *Centralian* and, 123, 124; consubstantiality creation by, 129–30; culture change by mothers' teaching children, 65, 66, 158n5; demographics in high schools, xiv, xvi, 2, 6–7, 8, 95–96, 123; epideictic rhetoric's historically male association, xv, 2, 3, 20–21; *Indian Leader* and, 69, 74–75; national debate about young women, 9–16; patriarchy and, 3, 123; progressivism and, 11–13, 153n8; school spirit and, 139, 143. *See also* mothers and motherhood

Gender and Rhetorical Space in American Life, 1866–1910 (Johnson), xv

Genoa Indian School (Native American boarding school), 7, 67

Genung, John Franklin, 8, 48, 54

German Club (Central), 122

Gettysburg Address (1863), xii, 133–34

Gilman, Charlotte Perkins, 53

Gilmore, Glenda Elizabeth, 101

girls. *See* African American girls; gender; Native American girls; "new girls"; women

girls, public opinions of: academic or intellectual ability, 15, 37, 38, 120; education, 15–16, 66

girls, scholarship on, xvii–xviii

Girls and Literacy in America: Historical Perspectives to the Present (Greer), xv

Girls' Athletic Association (Central), 128

Girls: Feminine Adolescence in Popular Culture and Cultural Theory (Driscoll), xvii

Glenn, Cheryl, xiv–xv, 67, 102, 119

globalization, xv, xvi, xvii

Glover, Janet, 43–44

Gold, David, xiii, xvii

Goldman, Emma, 76

Goodburn, Amy, xi, 67

Gordon, Lynn D., 38–39

Grace Boarding School for Native Americans, 85–86

graduation rates, 98

Grand, Sarah, 159n6

Gravelle, Omar, 86

Gray, Rebecca, 1, 21, 22, 39, 48–49, 50

Gray, Susan E., 17

Great Depression, 102

Greek mythology, 38, 83–84

Greene, Lorraine Richardson, 103–4

Greer, Jane, xi, xv

Guy-Sheftall, Beverly, 104

Haas, Louise, 44–45

Haff, Madeline, 1, 21, 22, 49, 55

Half-Century Magazine, 95

Hall, G. Stanley, 15

Halloran, S. Michael, 5

Hanley, Margaret, 131–32

Hansot, Elisabeth, 7

Harris, Joel, 26

Harris, Ruth, 1–2, 21, 22, 55

Harvey, Bernice, 108, 110

Haskell Institute, xix–xx, 3, 7, 18, 35, 56–86, 145; alumni of, 58, 62, 64, 74, 77, 86, 87; Barstow and, 87; Central and, 144; Christian ideology at, 56–57; collective identity definition

Index

and celebration at, 14, 59–60, 70, 86, 114, 146; curriculum at, 8, 72–73, 77; demographics of, 63–64; ethos of students at, 66; founding and early years of, 63–65; "Indian blood" in students of, 154n1; nursing program at, 74–75; oratory contest at, 56–58; Wise's promotion of image of, 73–74; yearbook of, 69. *See also* assimilation; audience of Haskell publications; *Indian Leader* (Haskell newspaper); *Indian Legends* (Haskell folklore anthology)

Hertzberg, Hazel W., 155n3

Hickum, Hazel, 88, 89–90, 96–99, 101, 102

high school attendance, 2, 15; gender, xvi, 6–7; race, 7, 93, 157n3; social class, 7–8, 158n1

Hill, Beatrice, 130–31

Hine, Darlene Clark, 157n2

historical realities, xviii, xx, 90, 92–94, 145–46, 148; emphasizing achievement, 103–13; glossing over hardship, 96–103

History of Women's Suffrage (Stanton), 24

Hi-Y club conference, 112–13

Hoffman, Lynn M., 25–26

holiday tradition, 83

homonoia ideal (union of hearts and minds), 119

Horsechief, Mary, 81

House, William, 103

Howes, Doris, 35, 40, 51

How Young Ladies Became Girls (Hunter), xvii

Hueston, William C., 91

Hull House, 12

Hunt, Lynn, 132

Hunter, Jane H., xvii, 10, 15, 23, 122–23, 124; on girls' movement through public spaces, 153n8; on military training, 152n4; school spirit and, 138

identity. *See* collective identity definition and celebration

identity, tribal, 56, 64, 65, 74

illustrations: in *Centralian*, 159n2; of female imagery in magazines, 42; in *Indian Legends*, 78, 155n5; in *Weather-cock*, 2, 25, 42–48, 153n7

immigrants and immigration: Barstow girls' othering of, 19, 25, 51–54, 72; at Central, 19, 121–22, 129; discourse about young women and, 10; foreign-born residents, 17, 19, 76, 122, 142; government restrictions on, 76; Italian, 19, 113, 122, 147; suffrage movement and, 12

imperialism, 18

inclusivity, attitude of, 132–38, 146

Indian Citizenship Act (1924), 76

Indian Leader (Haskell newspaper), xiii, 9, 59–60, 69–77, 86–87; as alumni portal, 87; audience of, 58, 59, 62, 69–77, 154n2; Ball as editor of, 69, 73, 155n4; confirmation of assimilation in, 69; content of, 62–63; editorial staff of, 69, 73–74, 86, 154n2, 155n4; epideictic rhetoric in, before and after curriculum change, 72–73, 77; gender and, 69, 74–75; on girls' education, 66; official agenda of, 59; Peairs as editor of, 73; poetry in, 62; suspension of publication of, 76; Wise as editor of, 73–74; Wright's speech in, 56–58

Index

Indian Leader, The (Haskell magazine), 69, 73, 75

Indian Legends (Haskell folklore anthology), xiii, 66, 78–87, 155n5; audience of, 58, 80–81, 154n2; burial rites described in, 81–82; "Customs among the Sioux Indians," 84–85; implied purpose of, 59, 60; "Story of Little Bear," 83–84

Indian schools, 7–8, 18, 64–65, 72–73, 155n6, 156n7

individualism, 57, 63, 64

Industrial Areas Foundation (IAF), 120

insinuatio tactic, 6

intellectual ability. *See* academic achievement and intellectual ability

Isocrates, 3–4, 61, 151n2

Italian immigrants, 19, 113, 122, 147

Jacob, Margaret, 132

Jesus Christ, 56–57

Jewish people, 20, 133, 160n7

Jim, Susie Bearchief, 87

Jim Crow laws. *See* race; racism; segregation or Jim Crow laws

Johnson, Nan, xi, xv, 36

Johnson-Reid Act (1924), 76

Jones, Anna H., 95, 104

Jones, William A., 72–73, 156n8

journalism, 106

juniors, 125–26

kairos (opportune occasion for speech), 61

Kansas City Call (African American newspaper), 18, 89, 106, 110, 147, 158n9

Kansas City Colored Women's League, 95, 104, 158n8

Kansas City Consolidated Smelting and Refining, 17

Kansas City Country Club, 160n7

Kansas City region, xiv, 17–19, 122; African Americans in, 18, 91, 92, 103–4

Kansas City Sun (newspaper), 93, 95, 111

Kansas State Normal School, 98

Kaplan, Amy, 18

Kapy, Ethel, 122

Katanski, Amelia V., 67

Kaufman, Eric P., 117

Keller, Jean A., 65

Kempe, Margery, 67

Kennedy, George A., xviii, xx, 3, 4, 61, 78, 90, 102

Kerber, Linda D., 129

Kett, Joseph, 15

Kirsch, Gesa E., xv–xvi, xvii

Kitch, Carolyn, 30, 42, 46

Klapper, Melissa R., 153n8

Knollin, Mabel M., 36, 47

"Know Thy Race" (Shaw), 88, 105–8

labor, 14, 15, 64, 102; manual, 7, 72–73, 77; by servants, 10, 64; theme of, in *Weather-cock*, 42–43, 49

La Flesche, Francis, 77, 82

Laib, Nevin, xix, 25, 31, 37

Lanham, Richard A., xix, 24–25, 31, 37

Larsen, Nella, 158n5

Latin translations, 38

Lawrie, Nina R., 108, 110

leadership of Barstow girls, 31, 32–33, 37

"Legend of the Laboratory, The" (Gray), 39, 48

Leidigh, Paul J., 124

Life among the Piutes (Winnemucca), 68

Lincoln, Abraham, xii, 133–34

Index

Lincoln High School, xx, 3, 17, 18, 19, 35, 87, 88–114; alumni of, 98, 103–4, 110, 111, 158n7; Bluford at, xi–xii, 93, 110, 147, 157n1, 158n9; campaign for new building for, 103, 110–11; Central and, 117, 135, 144; college attendance and, 98, 110; curriculum at, 8, 89, 93–94; gender demographics at, 95–96; girls' YWCA at, 104–5; Hickum's ode to, 96–99; historical realities surrounding, xx, 92–94, 145–46, 148; location of, 110–11; NAACP junior branch at, 108; "New Negro" principles espoused at, 94–96; odes to, 96–99, 99–100, 132; overcrowding in, 93, 101, 110; race representation and, 91–92; Smith's ode to, 99–100; social class and, 20, 92–93. *See also* collective identity definition and celebration at Lincoln; *Lincolnian, The* (Lincoln yearbook); *Lincolnite* (Lincoln newspaper)

Lincolnian, The (Lincoln yearbook), xiii–xiv, 8, 26, 89, 90, 94; alumni achievements in, 103–4; "Know Thy Race," 88, 105–8; missing editions of, xvi–xvii, 157n1; poetry in, 96–103

Lincolnite (Lincoln newspaper), xiii–xiv, 9, 89, 90, 110–11, 112, 157n1

"Lincolnite Staff, The" (Bluford), 157n1

literary magazines (Central), xxi, 9, 120, 123, 138

literary societies (Central), xxi, 116, 118, 126–27, 133–34

Livermore, Mary, 10

Locke, Alain, 99, 106

Logan, Shirley Wilson, xi, xv, 67, 100

logos (logical appeal), 37–38, 39, 41

London, Jack, 51

Love, G. W. K., 103, 158n6

Luminary (Central newspaper), 9, 124

Luminary, The (Central magazine), 123–25, 160n9; audience of, 134; editions of, 159n5; Edwards as editor of, 133, 139–40; "Girls" section of, 124–25; inclusivity in, 133–35; school spirit in, 139–40; Tinsley as editor of, 135–38

Lunsford, Andrea, xv

lynchings, 105

Lyons, Scott Richard, 60

magnification, xix, 25, 31–37, 49. *See also* amplification in *Weather-cock*

manual labor, 7, 72–73, 77

Manual Training High School, 33–34, 35, 117, 141

Marmon, Belle, 70–71, 76, 86

marriage ideal, 10, 11

Martin, Asa E., 92, 97

masculinity, 124; girls' athletics and, 34–35

Mattingly, Carol, xi, xv, 72

McCahon, Ione, 122

McCampbell, E. J., 103

McCampbell, Jean, 158n8

McCampbell, T. T., 103

McClure, Andrew S., 68

McGee, Susan De, 41

McLaughlin, Marie, 79

Meade, Hortense, 44–47

medical care or medicine men, 82

medical opinion of adolescence, 15

"Medicine Man, The" (Chase), 82

men: African American, 14; as editors of *Indian Leader*, 73–74, 86; epideictic rhetoric's historically male association, xv, 2, 3, 20–21; masculinity, 124. *See also* boys; gender; women

Meyer, August R., 17

middle class, 3, 11–12, 103–4, 129, 146; high school attendance by, 7, 158n1; Lincoln girls, 93, 104–5; "New Negro" ideals of, 95, 103. *See also* social class

military training, 36–37, 47, 139, 152n4, 152n4

minorities. *See* African Americans; immigrants and immigration; Native Americans; race

"Mirabella Ann's Experiment" (Evans), 52–53, 54, 153n9

Miss Barstow's School, xix, 17, 22–55, 87, 89; academic achievement in, 1, 25, 32–33, 37, 49, 54; alumni of, 27, 41, 55; audience of publications of, xix, 30–31, 38, 54; Central and, 123, 144; cock as mascot of, 29, 42–43; collective identity definition and celebration in, xiii, 22–24, 34–35, 114, 146; college acceptance from, 27, 39; curriculum at, 8, 27, 151n4; ethos of students at, 37–38, 39, 41, 50; family of students of, 17, 29, 30; founding and early years of, 26–29; girls' othering at, 19, 25, 51–54, 72; military training at, 36–37, 47, 152n4; social class in, 20, 28, 29, 34, 40, 51–53, 55. *See also* amplification in *Weather-cock;* athletics at Barstow; community construction at Barstow; *Weather-cock, The* (Barstow yearbook)

Mitchell, Sally, 23, 153n10

Momaday, N. Scott, 80

Montezuma, Carlos, 77

moralism, 129

Morton, Patricia, 15

Mosher, Ruth, 134–35, 138

Mossell, Gertrude, 94–95

mothers and motherhood: of African American girls, 14–15; assumptions about, 22, 89; cultural change through teaching children, 65, 66, 158n5; New Woman ideal, 11; preparation for, 7, 10. *See also* gender; women

Munger, Ruth, 47

Munsee tribe, 70

"My First Experience in Housekeeping" (Brenninger), 69

Myths and Legends of the Sioux (Mc-Laughlin), 79

National American Woman Suffrage Association, 12

National Association for the Advancement of Colored People (NAACP), 12, 95, 107, 108

National Association of Colored Women (NACW), 12

nationalism, 80, 142

Native American girls, 2–3; discourse about young women and, 10; gendered labor at Haskell, 64; number of, at Haskell, 63; support for education of, 16; treatment of, in own culture, 13; whites and, 13–14, 20, 64, 65

Native Americans, xix–xx; alcohol use by, 71–72, 77; Bureau of Ethnology project, 78–79; disparaging own culture, 8, 13–14, 60; federal boarding schools for, 7–8, 18, 155n6; intellectual ability of, 77; progressiveness of, 154n3; solidarity among, 56. *See also* pan-Indian movement; *specific tribe*

Native American women, 57; temperance movement and, 72; whites' opinions of, 13–14, 65

187
Index

native-born residents, 10; foreign-born residents, 17, 19, 76, 122, 142

Negro History Club (Lincoln), 108–9

"Negro within Our Gates, The" (Woodson), 106–7

Nelson, Alice Dunbar, 106

"new girls," xix, 87; after WWI, 153n10; Barstow girls' identification as, 23, 25, 26, 28, 29, 31, 146; definition of, 23. *See also* amplification in *Weather-cock*

"New Man, The" (Leidigh), 124

New Negro, The (Locke), 99

New Negro for a New Century, A: An Accurate and Up-to-Date Record of the Upward Struggles of the Negro Race (Washington, Wood, and Williams), 95

"New Negro" ideals, 3, 6, 103; Lincoln girls' espousing of, 94–96

New Republic (newspaper), 17

"New Schools" (Bluford), 110–11

newspapers: of Central High School (*Luminary*), 9, 124. See also *Indian Leader* (Haskell newspaper); *Lincolnite* (Lincoln newspaper); *specific newspaper*

New Woman ideal, 10, 11, 23, 146–47, 159n6; athletics and, 35; "New Man" essay mocking, 124

Nichols, J. C., 160n7

Nineteenth Amendment (U.S. Constitution), 13, 74

normal-school curriculum, 72–73

Northeast High School, 141

nursing education at Haskell, 74–75

O'Connell, Daniel, 141

Odem, Mary E., 153n8

Olbrechts-Tyteca, Lucie, 119

Old Indian Legends (Zitkala-Ša), 79–80

On Rhetoric (Aristotle), 24

originality of thought, 32–33

O'Sheel, Shaemas, 17, 19

Ouida (Maria Louise Ramé), 159n6

"Our Foreign Cousins" (Connelly), 122

"Our Future Lies before Us!" (Hickum), 88

"Our Vocational Course and What It Provides for Girls" (Splitlog), 74–75

outing system, 64

overcrowding: at Central, 137; at Lincoln, 93, 101, 110

Owen, Robert Dale, 57

paenismus (expression of joy for blessings obtained), 96

Paiute tribe, 68

Panathenaicus (Isocrates), 4

Panhellenism, 4, 61

pan-Indian movement, 3, 6, 81, 85, 146; double-voicing and, 87; Wright's speech and, 57

Parrish, Edward W., 158n7

"Parting" (Brown), 100–103

Paryas, Phillis Margaret, 67–68

pathos (appeal to emotions), 37–38, 39, 41, 137

patience, 107, 111–12

patriarchy, 3, 123

Patterson, Martha H., 159n6

Paul, Alice, 13

Peabody High School (Pittsburgh), 119

Peairs, H. B., 72, 73

Perelman, Chaim, 119

Pericles, xii, 3, 4, 61

Petrillo, Lauren, xi

Phi Lambda Epsilon, 116

Philomathean Society (Central all-girl literary society), 116, 118, 127

Phi Sigma, 116, 121

Pindar, 99, 132

Pindaric ode form, 99

plantation fiction, 52–53

Plato, 61

Platonian Society (Central all-male literary society), 116, 118, 127

Plessy v. Ferguson (1896), 18, 93

Poetics (Aristotle), 96

poetry: in *Centralian*, 130–32; in *Indian Leader*, 62; in *Lincolnian*, 96–103; in *Weather-cock*, 39, 48

Ponca tribe, 81

Poulakis, Takis, 4–5

praise and blame purposes of epideictic rhetoric, 3, 77, 105–8, 111

Pratt, Richard Henry, 78, 156n7

"Pretenders, The" (Barstow drama club), 41, 49, 50

privilege, 20, 28, 29, 34, 40, 51–53, 55

progressivism, 11–13, 153n8

proof, inartistic and artistic, xix, 37–38

Prucha, Francis Paul, 154n3

publications, 52, 94–96; racial discrimination in, 105–6, 107. *See also under individual publication*

public opinions of girls: academic or intellectual ability, 15, 37, 38, 120; education, 15–16, 66

public performance, 35–36, 37, 41–42, 49, 50

public or private schools: class and, 7–8; coeducational, 8, 20, 120; college attendance and, 129; demographics in, xiv, xvi, 2, 6–7, 8, 95–96, 123; establishment of public, 15

Pueblo tribe, 70

Pythagoras, 119

Quicksand (Larsen), 158n5

race, 2–3, 145–46; citizenship and, 70, 75–76, 156n6; discrimination in publications, 105–6, 107; girls' education seen as support for, 16, 20; at Haskell, 56–57, 74, 87, 89; "human race," 56–57; poetry and, 96–103; progressivism and, 12; race representation, 91–92; race riots, 105; "race suicide," 39. *See also* African Americans; Native Americans; segregation or Jim Crow laws

Race and Reunion: The Civil War in American Memory (Blight), 153n9

racial uplift, 89, 90, 92, 95, 105

racism, xx, 19, 89; community construction at Barstow and, 51–52; as independent of social class, 14; indicated through Lincoln's underfunding, 93; "Mirabella Ann's Experiment," 52–53, 54, 153n9; "representative Indians," 77. *See also* segregation or Jim Crow laws

Radcliffe College, 27

Real Woman ideal, 10–11, 146–47

Reclaiming Rhetorica: Women in the Rhetorical Tradition (Lunsford), xv

Red Hunters and the Animal People (Eastman), 79

Red Lake Agency, 82

"red penny" custom, 85

Red Scare, 75–76

Reel, Estelle, 72

Refiguring Rhetorical Education: Women Teaching African American,

Index

Native American, and Chicano/a Students, 1865–1911 (Enoch), xiv
Regendering Delivery: The Fifth Canon and Antebellum Women Rhetors (Buchanan), xi, xiv
religion, 56–57, 100; Christianity, 56–57, 108, 154n3, 155n6
"representative Indians," 77
"Republican Mother," 66
research methods, xii–xviii
reservations, regulations on, 84–85
restatement, xix, 25, 48–50. See also amplification in Weather-cock
"Returned Student, The" (Riley), 71–72
rhetoric, instruction in, 8, 48
Rhetorica ad Herennium, 37
Rhetoric Retold: Regendering the Tradition from Antiquity through the Renaissance (Glenn), xiv–xv
Richardson, Lorraine (Mrs. Wendell Greene), 103–4
Riley, Minnie, 71–72, 73, 77
Robertson, Emily, 84–85
Roosevelt, Theodore, 39
roosters, 42–44
Ross, David N., 124
Rossington, Alice, 36
Royster, Jacqueline Jones, xv–xvi, xvii
Rury, John L., 7
Russian immigrants, 122

Said, Edward, 52
Sappho, 61
scholarship on girls, xvii–xviii
school publications, xiii–xiv, 9, 26. See also Centralian, The (Central yearbook); Indian Leader (Haskell newspaper); Indian Legends (Haskell folklore anthology); Lincolnian,

The (Lincoln yearbook); Lincolnite (Lincoln newspaper); Luminary (Central newspaper); Weather-cock, The (Barstow yearbook)
school spirit, 49, 50; at Central, 138–43, 146
Schrum, Kelly, 54
Schultz, Lucille M., 8
Scott, Fred Newton, 8
Seelatsee, Julia, 83
segregation or Jim Crow laws, xx, 18–19, 51, 132, 145–46, 160n7; versus assimilation of Native Americans, 63, 89; in Missouri, 92; "separate but equal" legislation, 18, 93; subversion of, 91. See also race; racism
self-help, 95, 96–103
seniors, 49–50, 98, 116, 125–26
"separate but equal" legislation, 18, 93
September 11, 2001, xiii
servant work, 10, 64
settlement house movement, 12
sexualized stereotypes: of African American women, 14; of Native American women, 65
Shaw, Willa, 88, 90, 105–8, 111
Shawnee tribe, 155n6
Sheard, Cynthia Miecznikowski, 4
Shelby, Lula, 158n7
Sheldon, Henry D., 159n3
Shields, Caroline, 41
significiatio (emphasis), 47. See also emphasis
silence, as intentional rhetorical device, 102–3
single women, 10
Sioux tribe, 83–85, 154n3
Sisquoc, Lorene, 65
slaves, 52–53

Index

Smith, Gladys, 99–100, 102
Smith, Karen Manners, 12
Smith College, 27, 35
Smithsonian Institute, 78
social circulation, xv, xvi, xvii
social class, 3, 10, 15; of African American girls, 14, 20, 92–93; athletics and, 34; Barstow and, 20, 28, 29, 34, 40, 51–53, 55; Central and, 121, 129; freedom of movement based on, 153n8; high school attendance and, 7–8, 158n1. *See also* middle class; upper class; working class
social evolutionism, 72
Society of American Indians (SAI), 57
Society of Literature and History (SLH, Central co-ed literary society), 127
Socrates, 61
sophomores, 125–26
sororities, 121
Souls of Black Folk, The (Du Bois), 18
Spack, Ruth, 79–80
Splitlog, Carrie B., 74–75, 77
Stanford University, 27
Stanton, Elizabeth Cady, 15–16, 24
Stein, Arthur, 122
Stewart, Maria W., 100
"Story of Little Bear, The" (Sioux myth recounted by Turcotte), 83–84
strategic contemplation, xv, xvi, xvii
strikes, 76
student government, 123
suffrage movement, 12–13, 74
Sullivan, Dale L., xx, 5, 58, 119, 140
sun dance ritual, 85
swastikas, 78

tableaux (dramatic genre), 36
"Talented Tenth," 101, 103, 106

Tann, Helen J., 124, 125, 140–42, 143
teachers, 16, 28, 64–65, 85, 129, 158n7; as audience, 31, 58, 144; at Central, 123, 143; at Haskell, 60, 69, 155n4; at Lincoln, 93, 94, 95; "Republican Mother," 66
teacher training program (Haskell), 58, 59, 73, 146
temperance movement, 72
Terrell, Mary Church, 106
Thompson, Agnes, 41, 49, 152n6
Thompson, Edward B., 158n7
Tinsley, Ruth, 135–38, 142–43
tobacco, 82
"To Central" (Hanley), 131–32
Tong, Benson, 13
Too, Yun Lee, 151n2
Traces of a Stream: Literacy and Social Change among African American Women (Royster), xv
Trafzer, Clifford E., 65
Trennert, Robert A., 63, 156n7
tribal affiliations of Haskell students, 63–64
"Tribute to Central, A" (Hill), 130–31
"Tribute to Lincoln, A" (Smith), 99–100
True Woman ideal, 10, 68, 146
Turcotte, Rebecca, 83–84
Turner, Frederick Jackson, xiii
Tyack, David, 7

Ueda, Reed, 7, 121, 138
unions, 76
U.S. Census (1890), xiv, 10, 19, 76
U.S. Census (1920), 19
U.S. government, 63
U.S. Supreme Court, 18, 93
Universal Negro Improvement Association (UNIA), 107

Index

University of Chicago, 27
University of Kansas, 27, 98, 110
University of Missouri, 147
upper class: at Barstow, 20, 28, 29, 34, 40, 51–53, 55; at Central, 129
urbanization, 11

Vassar, 27, 55
Vecoli, Rudolph J., 147
Veix, Katie, 70–71, 76, 86
Venerable, Neosha E., 158n7
venerable institution image, 129–32, 146
visual rhetoric, 42–48. *See also* illustrations
vocational training: versus academic education, 89, 93–94, 157n4; in Lincoln curriculum, 89, 93–94; manual labor, 7, 72–73, 77
Vučković, Myriam, 16, 65, 72–73, 80

Walker, Jeffrey, xx, 61
Wasco tribe, 83
Washee, Emily, 75–76, 77, 156n10
Washington, Booker T., 94, 95
Watson, Tom, 160n7
wealth, distribution of, 11
"We Are Coming": The Persuasive Discourse of Nineteenth-Century Black Women (Logan), xv
Weather-cock, The (Barstow yearbook), xii–xiii, 1–2, 21, 22, 31–32, 34; advertising in, 30; alumni department of, 27; Barstow, Mary and, 28, 38–39; debut of, 8, 27–28; features in, 29; frequency of publication of, 152nn1, 2; illustrations in, 2, 25, 42–48, 153n7; labor theme in, 42–43, 49; as marketing tool, 28; poetry in, 39, 48; staff photo of, 1901, 30. *See also*

amplification in *Weather-cock;* Miss Barstow's School
Webster, Daniel, 141
Wellesley College, 27
Wells, Ida B., 12
Well-Tempered Women: Nineteenth-Century Temperance Rhetoric (Mattingly), xv
Welsh, Herbert, 154n3
Welter, Barbara, 10
Westport High School, 141
Wheeler, Helen, 104–5
Wheelock, Dennison, 77
White, Deborah Gray, 104
White, Walter, 108
white-collar jobs, 7
white girls, 15; privilege of, 20; support for education of, 16
white men: alcohol use by, 72
white people, 1–2, 10; assimilation and, 63, 64, 65–66; "Best Men" paradigm and, 101; as brothers and sisters of Native Americans, 68; community construction at Barstow and, 51–52; Haskell students' indictment of, 71–72; high school attendance and gender and, 7; high school construction for, 111; Native Americans as joining the culture of, 56–58; opinion of African Americans of, 14–15, 93, 112–13, 152n6; opinion of Native Americans of, 13–14, 65; "race suicide" of, 39
white women: clubs of, 104
Wilkins, Roy, 18
Williams, Fannie Barrier, 14, 95, 106, 158n6, 158n7
Williams, Kathryn E., 95
Williams, Stella, 103–4
Wilson, Thomas D., 106

Winnemucca, Sarah, 68
Wise, John R., 60, 73–74, 78
Wollin, Ross, 119
Woman's Era (periodical owned and published by African American women), 95
Woman's Journal (American Woman Suffrage Association periodical), 10
women: depictions of, 42; group identity of, 3–4; progressivism and, 11–2; Real Woman ideal, 10–11, 146–47; single, 10; suffrage movement, 12–13, 74; in World War I posters, 46. *See also* mothers and motherhood; New Woman ideal
women's rights movement, 6, 23–24, 147
Wood, N. B., 95
Woodson, Carter G., 106–7
workers' movements, 76
working class, 3, 7, 158n1; Central and, 120, 129; Lincoln and, 93–94; women and progressivism and, 12

Work of the Afro-American Woman, The (Mossell), 89, 94–95
World War I, 36; African American soldiers in, 105, 108; Central students and, 122, 141, 142; military training and, 152n4; posters advocating good sentiment, 46–47
Wright, Nellie, 56–58, 68, 69, 73, 76, 153n1; after graduation, 85–86

Yates, Josephine Silone, 95, 104
yearbooks, 8–9, 25–26; of Haskell, 69. See also *Centralian, The* (Central yearbook); *Lincolnian, The* (Lincoln yearbook); *Weather-cock, The* (Barstow yearbook)
Young Women's Christian Association (YWCA), 64, 103, 104–5, 113, 158n8

Zitkala-Ša, xi, 13, 57, 64–65, 77, 78–80; *Old Indian Legends*, 79–80; public prominence of, 85

HENRIETTA RIX WOOD is an assistant teaching professor in the Honors College at the University of Missouri–Kansas City, where she teaches courses in composition and rhetoric, literature, and women's and gender studies. Her work has appeared in *American Periodicals*, *Rhetoric Review*, and edited collections, including *In the Archives of Composition: Writing and Rhetoric in High Schools and Normal Schools*, which she coedited. She won the Rhetoric Society of America's 2012 Dissertation Award.

Studies in Rhetorics and Feminisms

Studies in Rhetorics and Feminisms seeks to address the interdisciplinarity that rhetorics and feminisms represent. Rhetorical and feminist scholars want to connect rhetorical inquiry with contemporary academic and social concerns, exploring rhetoric's relevance to current issues of opportunity and diversity. This interdisciplinarity has already begun to transform the rhetorical tradition as we have known it (upper-class, agonistic, public, and male) into regendered, inclusionary rhetorics (democratic, dialogic, collaborative, cultural, and private). Our intellectual advancements depend on such ongoing transformation.

Rhetoric, whether ancient, contemporary, or futuristic, always inscribes the relation of language and power at a particular moment, indicating who may speak, who may listen, and what can be said. The only way we can displace the traditional rhetoric of masculine-only, public performance is to replace it with rhetorics that are recognized as being better suited to our present needs. We must understand more fully the rhetorics of the non-Western tradition, of women, of a variety of cultural and ethnic groups. Therefore, Studies in Rhetorics and Feminisms espouses a theoretical position of openness and expansion, a place for rhetorics to grow and thrive in a symbiotic relationship with all that feminisms have to offer, particularly when these two fields intersect with philosophical, sociological, religious, psychological, pedagogical, and literary issues.

The series seeks scholarly works that both examine and extend rhetoric, works that span the sexes, disciplines, cultures, ethnicities, and sociocultural practices as they intersect with the rhetorical tradition. After all, the recent resurgence of rhetorical studies has been not so much a discovery of new rhetorics as a recognition of existing rhetorical activities and practices, of our newfound ability and willingness to listen to previously untold stories.

The series editors seek both high-quality traditional and cutting-edge scholarly work that extends the significant relationship between rhetoric and feminism within various genres, cultural contexts, historical periods, methodologies, theoretical positions, and methods of delivery (e.g., film and hypertext to elocution and preaching).

Queries and submissions:	Studies in Rhetorics and Feminisms
Professor Cheryl Glenn, Editor	Department of English
E-mail: cjg6@psu.edu	142 South Burrowes Bldg.
Professor Shirley Wilson Logan, Editor	Penn State University
E-mail: slogan@umd.edu	University Park, PA 16802-6200

Other Books in the Studies in Rhetorics and Feminisms Series

A Feminist Legacy:
The Rhetoric and Pedagogy
of Gertrude Buck
Suzanne Bordelon

Regendering Delivery:
The Fifth Canon and
Antebellum Women Rhetors
Lindal Buchanan

Rhetorics of Motherhood
Lindal Buchanan

Conversational Rhetoric:
The Rise and Fall of a Women's
Tradition, 1600–1900
Jane Donawerth

Feminism beyond Modernism
Elizabeth A. Flynn

Women and Rhetoric
between the Wars
Edited by Ann George, M. Elizabeth
Weiser, and Janet Zepernick

Educating the New
Southern Woman:
Speech, Writing, and Race at the
Public Women's Colleges, 1884–1945
David Gold and Catherine L. Hobbs

Women's Irony:
Rewriting Feminist
Rhetorical Histories
Tarez Samra Graban

Claiming the Bicycle:
Women, Rhetoric, and Technology
in Nineteenth-Century America
Sarah Hallenbeck

The Rhetoric of Rebel Women:
Civil War Diaries and
Confederate Persuasion
Kimberly Harrison

Evolutionary Rhetoric:
Sex, Science, and Free Love in
Nineteenth-Century Feminism
Wendy Hayden

Liberating Voices:
Writing at the Bryn Mawr Summer
School for Women Workers
Karyn L. Hollis

Gender and Rhetorical Space
in American Life, 1866–1910
Nan Johnson

Appropriate[ing] Dress:
Women's Rhetorical Style in
Nineteenth-Century America
Carol Mattingly

The Gendered Pulpit:
Preaching in American
Protestant Spaces
Roxanne Mountford

Writing Childbirth:
Women's Rhetorical Agency
in Labor and Online
Kim Hensley Owens

Rhetorical Listening:
Identification, Gender, Whiteness
Krista Ratcliffe

Feminist Rhetorical Practices:
New Horizons for Rhetoric,
Composition, and Literacy Studies
Jacqueline J. Royster and Gesa E. Kirsch

Vote and Voice:
Women's Organizations and Political
Literacy, 1915–1930
Wendy B. Sharer

Women Physicians and
Professional Ethos in
Nineteenth-Century America
Carolyn Skinner